THE ARAB W

For my wife, Mina

who has helped me to listen out for the many and various
voices of the postcolonial world.

The Arab Writer in English

Arab Themes in a Metropolitan Language, 1908–1958

Geoffrey P. Nash

Foreword by
Miles L. Bradbury
University of Maryland

sussex
ACADEMIC
PRESS
Brighton • Chicago • Toronto

2 4 6 8 10 9 7 5 3

First published in hardcover 1998, reprinted in paperback 2015, by
SUSSEX ACADEMIC PRESS
PO Box 139
Eastbourne BN24 9BP

Distributed in North America by
SUSSEX ACADEMIC PRESS
Independent Publishers Group
814 N Franklin St, Chicago, IL 60610, USA

British Library Cataloguing in Publication Data
A CIP catalogue record for this book is available from the British Library.

Library of Congress Cataloging-in-Publication Data
Nash, Geoffrey
The Arab writer in English: Arab themes in a metropolitan language,
1908–1958 / Geoffrey Nash.
p. cm.
Includes bibliographical references (p.   ) and index.
ISBN 978-184519-193-1 (h/c : alk. paper)
    1. Civilization, Arab—Western influences. 2. Discourse analysis—
Political aspects. 3. Language and languages—Political aspects.
4. Discourse analysis, Literary. 5. Arabs—Cultural assimilation. I. Title.
DS36.82.N37   1998   97-39709
909'.0974924—dc21

Typeset and designed by Sussex Academic Press, Brighton & Eastbourne.
Printed by Independent Publishers Group, Chicago.

Contents

Foreword by
Miles L. Bradbury

This incisive book focuses on four Lebanese writers – Ameen Rihani, Kahlil Gibran, George Antonius, and Edward Atiyah – whose English-language writings have never before been linked in the way that Geoffrey Nash attempts. By making such a connection through the use of discourse analysis Dr Nash has opened up a new field. He discusses the way these writers, who were also fluent in Arabic, used English to mediate between East and West in the period from 1908 to 1958. As is the case with any pioneering endeavor, the book leaves ample room for further research. In fact, its conclusions demand discussion and debate. One can only hope that such a challenging and stimulating introduction to these writers, who have been much too neglected in the West, will succeed in reviving interest in them.

Western readers, of course, will likely be most familiar with Kahlil Gibran, who has long dominated American ideas of what an Arab writer is. Dr Nash's chapter on this most enigmatic of figures in the history of Arab-American cultural relations is likely to be controversial. Suffice it to say that it is also one that any serious student of Gibran will have to consider.

At the center of the book is the Arab-American traveler, journalist, philosopher, poet, and translator, Ameen Rihani. To a large extent Dr Nash concentrates on subjects Rihani wrote about in English in the first third of the twentieth century. These included Arab emigration to America, the reform of Arab societies, and relations between East and West. Dr Nash views Rihani as a figure of outstanding significance in the delineation of Arab identity to the West.

Assimilation and the persistence of ethnic identity are, of course, matters of almost obsessive interest to many who study American literature. Dr Nash offers a provocative assessment of how these issues play out in *The Book of Khalid*, the experimental and consciously Arab-American novel that Rihani published in 1911. The perspective that Dr

Nash offers may not turn out to be the last word on Rihani's larger status as an Arab-American writer. He would be the first to confirm that much work in this area remains to be done. However, the questions that Dr Nash poses ought to succeed in rescuing many of Rihani's writings from the undeserved obscurity into which they have fallen in the West.

George Antonius and Edward Atiyah were also greatly exercised by questions of the reform of Arab societies and relations between East and West. These two writers, however, fell firmly within the orbit of Great Britain. Their formal university training lay there, and both worked for British authorities in the Arab world. Dr Nash fascinates in his analysis of the traumas both endured in trying to hold onto the Anglo-Arab relationship. His discussion is detailed, challenging, and filled with insight.

Dr Nash's book is a most welcome delineation of a new, or at least previously underexplored, field. All who are interested in the varieties and complexities of the relationship between the Arab world and the West in the twentieth century should consult it and ponder the issues that it so provocatively raises.

Miles L. Bradbury
University of Maryland

Acknowledgments

This book is the outcome of research undertaken during my period as lecturer in The Department of English and Modern European Languages, Qatar University. I would like to thank the President, Dean of the Faculty of Humanities and Social Sciences, and the Chairman of the English Department at Qatar University, for allowing me time off to attend conferences where I delivered the papers out of which this present book has grown.

I would also like to thank Professor Miles L. Bradbury for generously supplying me with documentation from the American archive which has enabled me to get a clearer picture of Ameen Rihani's American links. I also owe a debt of kindness to Mr Ameen A. Rihani and Mr Ramzi Rihani for their help and encouragement, and to Sir Michael Atiyah for graciously allowing me an interview. I am grateful to the librarian of The American University of Beirut Library for kindly allowing me to quote from the Ameen Rihani documents there. Finally, since it was *Orientalism* and *Culture and Imperialism* that opened my eyes to entirely new horizons, I must declare my thanks and appreciation for the work of Professor Edward Said.

I take complete responsibility for the views expressed in this work. Some readers may feel that its thesis is a harsh one. On the other hand, Fouad Ajami was even less indulgent when he wrote: "Arab liberalism turned out to be a fragile plant. The ground under the feet of the self-styled Arab liberals cracked over and over again." If, however, the text I have written might be considered unduly critical of the pro-western stances adopted in particular by Antonius and Atiyah, I must record my personal appreciation of the undoubted integrity and commitment of both these men.

Geoffrey P. Nash

To humankind, O Brother consecrate
Thy heart, and shun the hundred Sects that prate
About the things they little know about –
Let all receive thy pity, none thy hate.

The Luzumiyat of Abu'l-Ala,
translated by Ameen Rihani

Introduction

The Case of the Arab Writer in English

In the latter half of the twentieth century, it has become accepted that the English language has overreached its Anglo-Saxon heartland, becoming the property of the many disparate races who shared in the legacy of British imperialism. The currency of English as the international language of our epoch, with the widespread audience it can command, has lured writers from outside the Anglo-Saxon inner circle to hazard the dangers of cultural dependency and write in it. No eyebrows are raised today at the spectacle of Africans, Indians, Bangladeshis, Malaysians and West Indians publishing poetry, novels, and any other genre of writing for that matter, in English. The case of the Arab writer in English, however, remains anomalous and largely unexplored. Although a trickle of novels by Arabs writing in English is beginning to appear, it can hardly be placed on a par with the established English writings of Africa or India.[1] With the exception of Khalil Jibran, whose books are widely circulated, if perhaps not so widely read, in the West, an ignorance of writings by Arabs in English is almost total. The reason for this is probably that the Arab world, richly served by its own Arabic literary heritage, still remains set apart in terms of the mediation of its culture to the outside world, or at least to the West. Unlike the Latin American literatures, which in its literary-cultural self-sufficiency it could be said to resemble, modern Arabic literature, with the notable exception of its one and only Nobel Prize winner for Literature, Naguib Mahfouz, seems to have made few inroads into the contemporary western literary consciousness.

What then is Anglo-Arab writing, and does it deserve its title? From the point of view of this study, it has to be said at the outset that Anglo-Arab discourse does not represent a settled or emerging tradition. The handful of new novels being published in English today in London and New York by writers of Arab extraction, mostly living in the West, are not our concern here. This book examines the English writings of four twentieth-century Arab writers all of whom were Lebanese Christians, but, with one exception, opted to live outside of Lebanon. They can be said to have inherited the mantle of cultural mediation taken up by the Arab Christians of the Levant from many generations back. The difference in their case was that instead of "serv[ing] as mediators of Western civilization to Arab Asia", as their predecessors had done, they engaged in mediating Arab culture and political concerns to the West.[2] Three of them used English to address the issues of the colonization of Arab lands and the emergence of the Arab national movement and its anti-colonial struggles with the western powers, Great Britain and France. In part products of the late nineteenth and early twentieth-century-penetration of British imperialism into Egypt and the Near East, in part molded by the migratory pull the New World exercised on the poor Lebanese masses, they were, if it seems useful to use such terms, pioneer cultural mediators. But their mediatory stances demonstrate certain salient dangers attending such an enterprise.

I have called the discourse they developed in the process Anglo-Arab, in order to encapsulate the hybrid character of their cross-cultural project, balanced as it is by a mixing of Anglo-Saxon and Arab cultural constituents. If Anglo-Arab discourse is to be considered as an entity rather than as a set of haphazardly-conceived, disparate texts, a coherence has to be demonstrated for the field. This may be attempted either in terms of the texts alone, or, in the approach adopted here, in consideration of both texts and authors. As the period during which this discourse was operative was a relatively short one, a strictly genealogical study would be limited. By using a synchronic approach, however, it should be possible to interrogate a set of conditions, mainly political and cultural, but also more strictly literary, which stimulated a small group of writers, whose first language was Arabic but who had been exposed to sufficiently large doses of English, to want to use it to encode meanings that refracted their Arab interests and concerns. This is not to suggest that our field of study remained constant, or that changes did not take place in response to external transformations occurring within the period, for this is, in fact, exactly what did happen, as was to be expected given the high political content of this discourse. A discourse analysis methodology, such as adopted here, starts with the assumption that texts are social constructs, for "language is not psychologically self-contained, but is culture-dependent and situation dependent [. . .] The social system, not the mind, motivates the language code."[3] The writer is not a lonely genius working within a literary vacuum. "Far from being autonomous, self-contained, self-motivating, context-free objects which exist independently from the 'pragmatic' concerns of 'everyday' discourse, literary works take place in a context, and like any other utterance they cannot be described apart from that context."[4] Analysis of a text can therefore be fruitful only when the context within which the writer writes, and to which he addresses himself, is taken fully into account. Such contexts are interwoven with the national, political, and social conditions that obtain when the writer is active. Discourse is also about interaction and exchange; about people, institutions, power, and status; about relationships and differences. In such circumstances analysis of the text becomes more than just an attempt to recover meanings: "it is always interpretation always criticism, always, as with Heidegger, a process of understanding 'discourse as projecting a world.'"[5]

The writers discussed here were each highly conscious of the context out of which their writings were constructed, of the "world" which their discourse was projecting, more so, perhaps, than the author working within a monocultural space. They were also well aware of relationships and difference, though, as we shall see, they developed variant strategies to cope with these. The Anglo-Arab writer could not escape a consciousness of himself as operating at the margins of two discrete cultures, which were, however, not engaged with one another on conditions of equality. For discourse analysis itself, decoding ideological processes by means of standard intertextual analyses of other texts and readings, must also take on extra complexity when conducted across national-cultural spaces. In describing a literary geography for Anglo-Arab discourse, considerations of both authors and texts demand a division into two groups. These are: the Arab-American, and the British-Arab. The former consists of two founder writers of the *mahjar* (or emigrant) school of Arabic literature, Ameen Faris Rihani (often written, Amin al-Rihani) (1876–1940), and Jibran Khalil Jibran (1883–1931), known to the West as Kahlil Gibran. Writing both in Arabic and English, and domiciled for long periods in the United States, their education in western culture was desultory and largely informal, while the texts they produced in English were experimental. The members of the other group, the British-Arab, were George Antonius (1891–1942) and Edward Selim Atiyah (1903–64). Like Rihani and Jibran, they were born in Lebanon, but subsequently spent much of their lives interfacing with Great Britain, an involvement that included in both cases an Oxbridge education and substantial periods in the service of the British administration in the Arab world. As might be expected, their writings, refracting their acquired British education and their movement within a largely Anglo-Arab milieu, are less experimental than those of the Arab-American group, and marked to a high degree by adherence to standard British registers. Nevertheless, it is the exposure of both sets of writers to western, metropolitan codes, and their use of them to enunciate a common concern with Arab cultural and political meanings, that enables us both to address such a category as Anglo-Arab discourse, and to expatiate on its distinctiveness from other discourses either in Arabic, or in English.

Diachronically, the boundaries of Anglo-Arab discourse can be defined in cultural, and political terms. The fifty years that separate its inception from its closure constitute an epoch in Arab affairs, bounded at the first extremity by the Young Turk Revolution of 1908–9, and at the other by the destabilizing reverberations of the Suez débâcle, culminating in 1958 with the end of the Hashimite monarchy in Iraq, and the inauguration of the United Arab Republic of Egypt and Syria. Culturally speaking, the beginnings of Arab modernism, a broad movement in which, arguably, the legacy bequeathed by Christian Arabs through their contribution to the nineteenth-century Arab literary revival, *al-nahda*, was maintained and strengthened, can be said to coincide with the earlier of these dates. In Arab literary circles, the predominantly Christian New World Arab exiles, or *mahjar* were one group among others agitating for an end to traditionalism and neo-classicism. At the same time, Arabism, the precursor to Arab nationalism, demonstrated the earliest viable political demands for autonomy in the Arab *mashreq* a key date being 1913 when the first Arab Conference was held in Paris, and negotiations (albeit unfruitful ones) were opened with the Young Turk Committee of Union and Progress. While the input of Christians into Arab nationalism may have been marginalized in recent studies, the role of Christian intellectuals as mediators of Arab political ideas and movements East–West has yet to be interrogated in detail.[6] If Arab nationalism, Arab politics and its leaders, acquired any profile at all in the West in the first half of the period under consideration – and this itself is debatable – then some little credit for this is due to the three writers mentioned above. Their input, however, which was facilitated by a capacity to master the major western language, has gone mostly unrecognized, with the one exception of Antonius's *The Arab Awakening*. This can be accounted for relatively easily: the West preferred to listen to its own writers on the topic of Arabia. The public's taste for the author of *The Seven Pillars of Wisdom* far exceeded their interest in the author of *Around the Coasts of Arabia*. Added to this, western scholars of Arab culture and politics have not unnaturally concentrated on Arabic texts. Neither Rihani nor Antonius appear in Albert Hourani's *Arabic Thought in the Liberal Age*. While it may be true that neither had any constituency in the Middle East as Arab nationalists or Arab thinkers, the criteria for their omission from this study is partly due to their cultural hybridity, and in Antonius's case the fact that he did not publish at all in Arabic.

Why did Anglo-Arab discourse come to a sudden end? In a certain sense it may be said to have run itself out. The issues with which it was concerned had undergone radical transformations, which these writers partly envisaged. But given the borders of their own politico-cultural formation, they would have been able to take little part in the new developments, even had their careers not been cut short prematurely, as was the case with Rihani and Antonius. The widening fault line between the Arabs and the West made their own investment in metropolitan discourse suspect. They were of a generation for whom dialogue with the West was axiomatic. The anti-imperialist politics of the post-World War I era meant the invocation of nativist strategies and slogans with which they would have had little sympathy. And yet in spite of this, and in spite of the passing of the colonial world with which they were in dialogue, the cross-cultural positions which they adopted may once again repay interrogation. This at a time when increasingly criticism is concerned with interlocking cultural spaces, with larger blocs of study that refract the closing twentieth-century's concern with a shrinking world.

Working with Metropolitan Codes

Theo D'haen has attempted to ascribe these definitions for colonial literature:

> The centre then is the place from which power is exerted, politically, economically, and socially, but also in terms of culture and literature. The margin is where that power is felt to be exerted. The advantage of this definition is that it also allows for post-colonial literature to be discussed within the same framework. In both colonial and post-colonial literature the confrontation between "centre" and "margin" or "periphery" is a major operative criterion. The difference is whether one looks from the centre to the margin or from the margin to the centre. In the first instance we are dealing with a colonial literature; in the second instance with a post-colonial literature.[7]

The mere fact of the impacting of the West, the expansive hegemonic force of the last two centuries, on other cultures, does not necessarily make the literatures written in the native languages of those cultures colonial or postcolonial. If one of the key strategies of the margins in postcolonial literature is, as D'haen posits, confrontation with the center, it is certainly the case that highly significant writing done in Arabic must be classed in the category of postcolonial literature.[8] The case of Anglo-Arab writing is however variant in two important respects. In opting to encode Arab meanings within the alien, metropolitan language, the Arab writers in English set themselves apart from their compatriots who chose to write in Arabic. By adopting the language of the colonizer, the writer from the colonized peripheries comes to occupy an even more intimately shared terrain with the writers of the metropolitan, colonizing center. But his aim in so doing was to use the colonizer's language less to confront, than to inform, petition, debate, and impress. As I shall argue later, Anglo-Arab discourse situated itself in a sort of half-way house, from which it hoped to defuse confrontation, convincing the metropolitan audience instead of the benefits of understanding and cooperation with the periphery.

Given that Anglo-Arab discourse developed narratives that were highly reactive to the ideological environment and political structures of the period in which it was operative, it follows that the meanings these narratives inscribed should be linked to audience(s) and the negotiation of specific cultural codes. The identification of audiences for whom the texts of this discourse were produced, and to whom they were addressed, might show in the case of each author, a specific audience awareness that was instrumental in the process of constructing the texts themselves. Composing texts in a second, acquired language for the purpose of encoding meanings to do with the author's own native culture connotes engagement in highly conscious speech acts. The precise encoding of meanings will depend not merely on the meanings to be encoded, but on the audience addressed. As these audiences ranged from the cultic to the political and diplomatic, reader expectation comprehended highly disparate codes, which had to be understood and negotiated before the author could be sure his work had a chance of being received. All four writers shared a strategy of formulating a discourse that aspired to give a perlocutionary force to their otherwise locutionary speech acts. That is to say, their discourse embodied transformational intentions towards their readers: in informing they aimed to enlighten, and in arguing to convince. More specifically, within the specific terms of the messages each intended to deliver was to be found a shared mission of cultural mediation. In theory this was to operate both ways, from Arab culture to the West, and vice versa. But so far as their English writings were concerned, disclosure of Arab culture and politics to the West was the prime strategy. Here problems arose, but not just those relating to the matter of finding an appropriate discourse in which to transmit messages across cultures that would, by their very nature, involve the encoding of cultural difference. Rather, these problems centered on the fact of a lack of parity between the two communicating cultures. The world dominance enjoyed by the receiver culture (the West) ensured that the producer culture (the Arab) could only be perceived as operating from a position of inequality. A situation would therefore need to be faced by which cultural difference was sacrificed to the temptation to translate indigenous or native codes into the codes and norms of the hegemonic metropolitan culture. Where the metropolitan code went unchallenged, any cultural difference would be elided, smoothed out, or submerged: native concerns would be almost entirely assimilated to the alien code, or dropped altogether.

With respect, for example, to the medium of translation, crossing the cultural continuum connecting the poles of metropolitan and native codes required making allowance for the fact that translation from oriental languages into western ones had become a genre in itself. In English, an acculturated "Oriental" genre had existed for some while, in which eastern norms had been assimilated into a code that could be accessed and understood to be "Oriental" by the reader. The dangers of working within such a code were obvious: it placed severe impositions on the encoding of genuine messages from the producer culture. Equally hazardous was the adoption of the mainstream language of the dominant speech community, in whose norms the educated colonial subject could be said to have been thoroughly inducted, but still remained a partial practitioner. The problem here was that identification with the dominant speech community implied total adherence to the rules of discourse of a linguistic community with a unified social world which, as such, cut out the world from which the colonial subject had come. The parallel here could be with working class or women participants within a discourse operated by the dominant group (white, male, and middle-class), where "dominated groups [...] are forced into [...] a split subjectivity, because they are required simultaneously to identify with the dominant group and to dissociate themselves from it."[9]

Either as a result of the temptation to assimilate being strong, or out of a simple reading of the mediating mission mentioned above, Anglo-Arab discourse devolved two main strategies with regard to genres and codes. In the case of the two Arab-American writers who worked within the *mahjar* ideology of reconciling East to West, an attempt was made to create a hybrid discourse, in which an intertextuality that seemed to mix both western and eastern writings was the operative feature. But this project had little chance of lasting success, given the cultural imbalance outlined above. The play with different cultural codes and genres resulted not so much in the creation of a new discourse, as in the production of a handful of exotic texts that gravitated towards usage of the acculturated oriental code, albeit with some key exceptions. These texts have certainly failed to "break through horizons of literary expectations so completely that an audience can only gradually develop for them."[10] An audience of sorts was already waiting to receive the more phenomenally popular of them, but the very fact of their "universal" reader intelligibility points less to the production of a new genre, than to the reworking of old seams for a specific western audience. The other group of Arab writers, the British-Arab, for whom the pull of European culture was much stronger, adopted a more conservative orientation and opted to work solely within metropolitan codes. Consciously avoiding experimentation that might involve mixing writings, they adhered to accepted European genres – such as grand narrative but with similar mediatiory intentions to the Arab-Americans. They hoped that Arab meanings could still be disclosed through use of these forms, with the embedded inference that the Arab messages they meant to convey would actually be better received for having been embodied in the civilized discourse of the West. But in maintaining a strict separation of the codes of the two discrete cultures, they effectively demoted those of their own native culture, and ended up producing writings that severely strained the mediatory position that was one of their key raisons d'être.

By working within codes that were, by definition, largely alien to native Arab codes, a tension was set up that can be considered symptomatic of the postcolonial text. The Arab writer in English was no different in this respect to the West Indian, African, or Australian writer in English. Each must decide whether and how far the alien metropolitan code is to be confirmed, or re-appropriated, subverted, or replaced. For example, one way of challenging the total dominance of metropolitan codes is for the writer to carry over words and expressions from his native language and embody these within the text written in the metropolitan language. The western reader is thereby forced to decode their situational if not their denotative meanings. In this way, the reader has to work at decoding cultural difference, and multicultural readings are made possible.[11] This practice, however, largely had to wait for the emergence of the new postcolonial literatures (i.e. those dating from the 1950s and after). African writers employed it, as have second generation immigrant American writers; the intention to challenge metropolitan dominance is a prerequisite. The choice of writing in English does not of itself secure the work of the non-metropolitan writer a place within the category of postcolonial literature, with its implicit oppositional orientation. In the case of Anglo-Arab discourse, working with metropolitan codes often meant foregrounding meanings affirmative of western norms – but invariably at a cost. This was offset not so much by the conscious decision to encode embedded meanings that were at variance with the superficial messages supplied by the text, as by the opening up of omissions, fractures or disjunctions that needed to be submerged.

The Politics of Anglo-Arab Discourse

"The 'last wave' of nationalisms most of them in the colonial territories of Asia and Africa, was in its origins a response to the new-style global imperialism made possible by the achievements of industrial capitalism." The Arab *mashreq* within the epoch in question can be said to have thrown off an outmoded imperialism – that of the Ottomans – only to be absorbed within a newer one of the type described by Benedict Anderson.[12] Formulations of a response to western global imperialism, exercising early on both Turks and Arabs within the Ottoman empire, centered, as Hourani showed, on the questions of reform, modernization, and the development of political strategies to replace the imploding structures of the Ottoman polity. Nationalism was an available riposte to the insidious denuding of indigenous power in the face of the expansion of western technological know-how, economic muscle, and political pressure. "The disintegration of their [the non-industrial nations] political regimes, the occupation of their lands, the humiliation of their cultures – these were the fruits of internal factors abetted by the corrosive influence of European power."[13] For the majority of Arab intellectuals – Muslim or Christian – the prospect of this advancing cultural ascendancy activated reactions that ranged from initial admiration to a deepening hostility towards the West.[14] But the post-World War I colonization of Arab lands by the British and the French under cover of League of Nations mandates, enacted a dual deception upon the Arabs: on the one hand it proffered liberation from a hated oppressor, on the other it essayed to strangle – in Egypt in 1919, Iraq in 1920, and in Syria in 1920 and 1925, incipient nationalisms that, in retrospect as well as at the time, appeared symptomatic of a wider rejection of large power hegemonism. "If there was a moment when the nineteenth-century 'principle of nationality' triumphed it was at the end of World War I."[15]

The reaction of Arab Christians like Ameen Rihani and George Antonius to the western colonization of Arab lands differed perhaps only in detail to that of their Muslim fellow Arabs. As westernized Arabs they welcomed and fully understood the challenge for modernization the westernizing impact on the East was having; as nationalists, they would have wished for the Arab world the chance for modernization to proceed in partnership with the West – as the agent of that modernization. Knowing, or learning by experience, that this was impossible on a level of parity, or at least in conditions honorable to the Arabs, they developed discourses emphasizing the need for Arab solidarity, in the absence of appropriate western responses to rational exposition of the Arab cause. In short, they became involved in the process of decolonization, initially as advocates of Arab self-determination to the West, and later, as the threat of Zionism was translated into reality, as warners of the inevitable break between the Arabs and the West over Palestine. In the process, each moved from a position of friendship towards the West to producers, in their last phase, of a proto-liberationist discourse that presaged further anti-imperialist struggles to come.

The politics of Anglo-Arab discourse, given the period in which it developed, must necessarily have been a discourse concerned with an emerging Arab nationalism. But it differed in one vital respect from the nationalist discourse of the pioneer Arab nationalist, Sati' al-Husri. By virtue of its encoding in English it was aimed at a western audience. Ameen Rihani, it is true, addressed many of his public speeches, books and articles to the Arabs in Arabic. The political discourse of George Antonius and Edward Atiyah, however, is almost entirely written for a western readership. Jibran's outlook may be characterized as apolitical, but his involvement with a specific western audience, and his self-exclusion from nationalist politics, is not devoid of political implications. A response to a set of conditions located within the Arab world, but operative mainly from outside its native constituency, Anglo-Arab discourse transmits sets of messages beyond the borders of the contemporary Arab discourse to the heart of the occidental terrain; the terrain in which is to be found the seat of the metropolitan, colonizing power. The margins address the center, having first become acculturated to the metropolitan landscape. This is not yet what Edward Said, writing of the delivery of messages of resistance from the colonized periphery to the metropolitan center, has termed "the voyage in" – that series of "incursions" that result in postcolonial writers like James Ngugi, Chinua Achebe, and Tayeb Salih operating within "the same areas of experience, culture, history, and tradition hitherto commanded unilaterally by the metropolitan centre." Except in the more strident of Rihani's anti-colonial statements, as compared with the liberationist discourse of the writers Said names, the position occupied by the Anglo-Arab writers is a half-way house, a hybrid space in which the great endeavor is to make the opposing territories hold together against the continual threat of secession.

In terms of the politics of Anglo-Arab discourse, the issue is that of filiation. Edward Said has argued for a period in which "Third World" nationalist discourse, while capable of making strongly anti-western, anti-colonial statements, still operated within the structures of discourse laid down in western culture.[16] But while three of the writers concerned, Rihani, Antonius, and Atiyah, started out from broadly similar standpoints, basically filiastic towards western culture, each reached a destination that was variant in terms of its precise articulation of Arab nationalism and its emerging conflict with the West. The ideological positions their writings inscribe, and the routes they took, will, as we shall see, entitle us to utilize both the terms employed by D'haen (colonial and postcolonial). In the case of Jibran, avoidance of nationalist politics was part of a calculated effort to smooth over or exclude difference altogether, and represented an escape from reality that could in practice be considered a capitulation.

The nationalist writings of Anglo-Arab discourse mostly appeared in an age when Arab nationalism had yet to be codified and its boundaries delimited. The genealogy of Arab nationalism has mainly been discussed with reference to its Ottoman origins, while its theoretical formation has been studied and critiqued by specialists in Middle East politics through the writings of Sati' al-Husri, Michel Aflaq and the subsequent Nasserite and Ba'athist divisions.[17] In contrast, Edward Said has been almost alone in adopting a discourse analysis approach to Antonius's contribution to nationalist thought, viewing his work in the context of liberationist narrative. Rihani's nationalist discourse has been explored little beyond the support it may or may not give to the sectarian formation of early Arab nationalism. This study emphasizes how crucial is the actual encoding of a nationalist discourse. That is to say, considerations of audience, genre and the precise employment of codes determines to a considerable degree the enunciation of such a discourse, in addition to the political landscape of the period in which it operates. Anglo-Arab discourse remains affiliated to western discourse (as perhaps must any nationalist discourse) in that it works with western categories of nationhood.[18] Both Rihani and Antonius essayed to create or imagine an Arab nation, to delimit its borders, inscribe its narrative, and nominate its heroes. They valorized these narratives and heroes in western terms, for the sake of an audience that at best could only register a specialized or ephemeral interest. At the same time, their nationalist discourse embodied the impact of western hegemonism within Arab lands and inscribed a growing Arab opposition to it. This in turn nurtured their sense of a separate Arab identity, as contrasted with the West's. This identity is foregrounded in their narratives, and may account for Antonius's highlighting of the Arab literary antecedents to the Arab Revolt, and Rihani's interest in Wahhabism and Ibn Saud. Without becoming anti-western, they strove to underwrite Arab independence and national unity, endeavored to build up Arab political integrity and, specifically in the case of Rihani, to promote Arab efforts towards modernization. These separate writings of an Arab national narrative were in part meant as representations of Arab identity to the West; they also satisfied a need for self-representation and self-definition, for Arab writers whose identity had become submerged either by nurture in western cultural norms, or by long absence from the Arabic-speaking homeland.

Writers and Texts

Ameen Rihani

Rihani's career covers a number of key areas within Anglo-Arab discourse, and this accounts for the amount of space given over to him in this study. Rihani divided his life between literature and politics. His active years coincided with the earlier stages of the Arab response to the challenge of the West. As a founder member of the *mahjar* group he had a major input into Arab-American poetics. *The Book of Khalid*, begun around 1908, and published in 1911, is the pioneer text of Anglo-Arab discourse. Its significance as a constitutive statement of Rihani's early attempts at producing a hybrid discourse, a point of departure which must have encouraged Jibran to experiment along similar lines, is discussed in chapter 1. Juxtaposition of their early writings would show that Jibran and Rihani started out on a similar project. Both began as anti-clerical visionaries, intent on wakening their countrymen back home to the evils of a superstitious and stagnant society. But the skeptical, humanist strain in Rihani's thought, already evident in his translation of *The Quatrains of Abu'l-Ala* (1903), revised edition entitled *The Luzumiyat* (1918), undercut the mystical utterances of the *Book of Khalid*, which is both knowing and satirical about the American cultic milieu. Rihani himself seemed unsure about the direction in which he wished to take Khalid's mix of Sufi mysticism and *mahjar* universalism. His interest in eastern transcendentalism culminated in his poems, *A Chant of Mystics*, and the small volume of essays, *The Path of Vision*, both published in America in 1921, at a time when his concern had already turned to political matters.

Rihani's engagement in Arab affairs, which can be said to have started with his early satirical writings in Arabic, directed specifically at the Maronite Church, took off after the 1913 Arab Conference in Paris which he attended as a representative of the Syro-Lebanese émigrés of America. His wartime anti-Ottoman propagandist activities started him on a writing career in which he mediated Arab issues for an American audience. Out of this came his three travel books on Arabia at first conceived as newspaper and magazine articles. The development, through these English writings, of Rihani's nationalist discourse, is viewed, in chapters 3 and 4, in the context of his journeys in the Arabian peninsular, and his involvement in the politics of the mandated Arab lands, particularly Palestine. Rihani's writings can thus be linked with those of George Antonius and Edward Atiyah, for whom Syria, and especially Palestine, also became central issues. As an Arab-American, Rihani was more detached from European colonialism than the other two; his statements inscribe both satirical and condemnatory positions on the question of decolonization. Rihani promoted the Arab cause in two key respects. His attempt to forge a Pan-Arab narrative suited to the emergence of the Arab nation in the 1920s led him to sponsor accord between the Arab kings and amirs of the Arabian peninsular. At the same time, he was engaged in representing Arab culture and politics to the West.

He created for himself the role of roving ambassador for the Pan-Arab cause, and in his writings originated a discourse in which the boundaries of the Arab nation incorporate the ambivalent narratives of the Islamic Arabian center, and the Christian Lebanese "Phoenician" periphery. This hybridity called into being a new cultural space in which Christians and Muslims might live as one. The main texts in this Pan-Arab discourse are the trilogy of Arabian travel books, and *The Book of Khalid*. Rihani's nationalist writings exemplify Nehru's axiom "for any subject country national freedom must be the first and dominant urge"; further along the line, however, after the accomplishment of national liberation, they presage a new international order.[19] But Rihani could see no genuine reciprocity between the western powers and the emerging nations of the East, until the latter had succeeded in re-appropriating their cultural and national identities. A counter-narrative to that of imperialism is therefore built, which often reads like a prophecy of the tortured liberation struggles to come.

Khalil Jibran

An attempt is made to situate the writings of Jibran, which begin within the *mahjar* and finish somewhere on the peripheries of Anglo-Arab discourse, in chapter 2. Enveloped in myth and counter myth, they are still recoverable,if, instead of being viewed as existing in a category of their own, they are seen as a response of sorts to the dilemmas facing Arab writers in both Arabic and English. In answer to such anxieties, Jibran's narratives developed egocentrically, working within a space opened up by the demands of a cultic audience, as yet by no means satiated by the oracles of an already ample stream of gurus and savants from "the East", explored by Rihani in *The Book of Khalid*. In the hands of less sophisticated writers like Jibran and Mikhail Naimy, the delivery of quasi-inspired messages lacks authorial remove, but in fact seems intentionally to fuse writer and text with the aim of convincing an audience of the former's messianic pose. Jibran was more successful in this than Naimy: his bestselling oracle, *The Prophet* (1923), has far exceeded Naimy's *The Book of Mirdad* in popularity. Jibran's writings answer to workings and re-workings of various genres and codes, until an optimum mix was arrived at. They move from articulation of difference in the early Arabic *mahjar* texts, to the controlled discourse of the later English writings, in which difference has been smoothed out, and particularist Arab problems exchanged for universal messages tailored to the taste of a western cultic readership. In choosing to submerge his more specific identity as a *mahjar* writer in Arabic within the acculturated "Oriental" genre of his English writings, Jibran seems to have given up on the dilemmas confronting other Arab writers. Even his interest in his native Lebanon is sublimated into a too-often expressed and effete longing, that bided the full length of his stay in New York. The phenomenal success of Jibran's writings, specifically *The Prophet*, achieved by sacrificing native concerns to an acculturated version of "the Orient", raise once again questions of cultural hegemonism, with all their political implications.

George Antonius

The bifurcation between Antonius's acquired British discourse and his role in promoting Arab rights is addressed in chapter 5. Antonius may be said to have traveled in the opposite direction to Khalil Jibran. Formed by his British education, he traversed the gulf separating metropolis and periphery and in the process re-appropriated his Arab identity. For this he had, in part, to thank the British themselves: they made him a victim of the sort of discrimination that "lost the empire" – the syndrome whereby, "people would come to Oxford and Cambridge from dependencies, and then found they were second class when they got back to their own country."[20]

Ambitious and gifted, Antonius found himself demoted in the Palestine Government service, but though he left it eventually, he could not give up his conviction that the British could be made to see the justice of the Arab position in Palestine. *The Arab Awakening* (1938) was thus written as a grand narrative concerning an aspect of "the liberation of humanity", with the dual aim of inscribing the emergence of an Arab nation, and valorizing this to the chief metropolitan power in the Middle East. (Antonius's narrative could be placed in J-F. Lyotard's category of narrative in which the state/the nation/the people are heroes in a totalizing metadiscourse.)[21] Disjunctions are opened up as a result of Antonius's adoption of grand narrative for his account of the Arab national movement. Unwilling to break with British standard codes, he has at the same time to struggle with and attempt to submerge dissonant feelings of betrayal at the hands of his British patrons. Yet the text still stands as an effective, if complex account of the urge to Arab liberation.

Edward Atiyah

With Edward Atiyah, the genealogy of Arab writers in English comes to a close. More unequivocally pro-western than either Rihani or Antonius, he published a range of writings in English some of which were commercially viable once but now have a definite period feel about them. A contrapuntal reading of his novels, *Black Vanguard* (1952), *Lebanon Paradise* (1953), and his autobiography, *An Arab Tells His Story – A Study in Loyalties* (1946), alongside postcolonial Arabic writings in chapter 7, decodes a slippage back to colonialism in Atiyah's discourse. The loyalties which exercised Atiyah for his entire writing career were his acquired British culture and his native Arab identity. These coexisted in a precarious balance which he termed his "Anglo-Arab synthesis", until it appeared to be overturned by the events of 1956. By this period, the final breakdown of Anglo-Arab politics brought about by Suez ensured the anachronism of Atiyah's brand of Arab nationalism, which is anti-colonial only in its rejection of Zionist expansion into Palestine. Taking up the issue of Palestine where Antonius had left it on his death in 1942, Atiyah published his popular overview of Arab history, *The Arabs* (1955 and 1958), in which he struggled to account for the take over of an Arab country by a western-sponsored colonialism (see chapter 8).

Genre

The media in which Anglo-Arab discourse embodies its literary-cultural and political statements and assertions, ranges from lectures, speeches, newspaper and magazine articles and books, to letters, official drafts, polemical pamphlets on behalf of partisan organizations, and translations. An almost equally large range of genres of writing were chosen in which to encode these messages. Rihani adopted those of travel writing and foreign political reportage, as well as poetry and novel-writing (although in these areas he was largely unsuccessful, several draft novels remaining in unpublished manuscript form.) Jibran composed fragments and longer narratives in prose-poetry. Antonius wrote a history in grand narrative style, as did Atiyah, alongside an autobiography, novels and pamphlets.

Given the fact that it is written in English, Anglo-Arab discourse has suffered a predictable fate. The nationalist writings of both Rihani and Antonius addressed a public that cared little for their aims and strategies. *The Arab Awakening* was read mainly by diplomats and academics; Rihani's books have long been consigned to travel writing's forgotten margins, accessed mainly by new biographers of the House of Saud or writers on Middle East oil. Edward Atiyah's one successful foray into fiction was not on Arab themes at all, but his autobiography has been periodically reprinted. Even allowing for the usual fragility of shelf lives, the facts speak for themselves: only the writings of Jibran have passed through many subsequent editions – in itself a sure indictor of the destinations implied by the discourse as a whole.

"Rewriting into the Postmodern Text"

The fate of Anglo-Arab discourse, and the naming and recoverability of its canon, must be discussed from the point of view of rewriting its authors into the postmodern text. For Rihani this is relatively easy to do: his Third World, anti-imperialist credentials, his mimicry of the individualism and "charisma" of the prophet-genius, his celebration of hybridity, all fit him into a recoverable postmodernist text. At the same time, though, Rihani is clearly identifiable – alongside Antonius and Atiyah – as a proponent of Arab modernism. This is evident in his enthusiasm for the modernized nation-state, his espousal of technological innovation, and his qualified advocacy that the East follow the West from the point of view of development and political liberty. But while the westernizing rationale of the *nahda* or Arab awakening is embraced in its entirety by Antonius and Atiyah, Rihani retains an ambivalent posture towards Arab traditionalism, in his advocacy of Abdul-Aziz Ibn Saud seeming to synthesize both modernist and traditionalist versions of Arab nationalism. (Rihani's advocated the founder of the Saudi state as a unifier with a traditionalist pedigree. However, his assessment of Wahhabism was that it was a potential reform movement in Islam analogous to Protestantism in Christianity.) As for Jibran, the persistence of the "canonicity" of *The Prophet* as an anti-modernist cultic text belies the modernism of Jibran's adoption of a prophet/seer pose, or career, as Jameson puts it, of the ambitious early twentieth-century artist.[22]

1

Ameen Rihani: Cross-Cultural Disclosures

The West for me means ambition, the East, contentment: my heart is ever in the one, my soul, in the other.

Ameen Rihani[1]

"The first Arab writer in English", imitator of Carlyle, admirer of Emerson and Renan, translator of one of the chief poets from the classical age of Arabic literature, innovator as a writer of prose-poetry in Arabic: still Ameen Rihani's significance as a pioneer figure in early twentieth-century Arab-American letters remains to be fully evaluated. Together with colleagues in the *mahjar* Arab-American group, such as Khalil Jibran and Mikhail Naimy, Rihani's most radical departure, even allowing for the innovations he incorporated into his Arabic writings, was perhaps to write in English as well as Arabic, so setting into play issues of biculturality, hybridity and ethnicity.

One outcome of Carlyle's, and the orientalist travellers, Burton, Palgrave and Doughty's contact with the East, was that Rihani, the Christian Arab emigrant to the United States, was able to decode from their writings meanings appropriate to his invention of an Arab identity, which subsequently had an input into his making of an Arab national narrative. Rihani's initial aim was to join Arabic and Anglo-American culture in an interpenetrative space within which individual writers from both traditions might operate. Such a space would build on a cross-cultural intersection that, it could be said, was already in place on the margins of the two respective cultures. Rihani's interest in Carlyle and the American transcendentalists is explicable in the terms of this space; especially the Carlyle of *Heroes and Hero-Worship*, whose advocacy of the Prophet of Islam lay outside the West's standard cultural hegemonism. In addition, Rihani's readings into British and American literature led him to experiment with a cross-cultural intertextuality in both his Arabic and English writings.[2]

Specifically, Rihani created a small body of writings in which the English language can be said to be enabling in the disclosure of one culture (Arab) to another (Anglo-American). The texts in which this operated were: his trilogy of Arabian travel books, and the experimental novel, *The Book of Khalid*. In addition, Rihani translated the classical Arabic poet, al-Ma'arri, wrote reviews on literary and philosophical themes, a collection each of poems and essays, and left unpublished a number of manuscripts both fictional and non-fictional.[3] In terms of their disclosure of both Arab and American meanings, these texts need to be problematized by reference to such categories as hybridity, ethnicity, and "Oriental" codes of writing. At times, the English is framed in a discourse clearly borrowed from the western Romantics, and at others in an idiom that reads like a literal translation from Arabic. What can be said for most of these writings is that in foregrounding the Arab and oriental constituency, they make little accommodation for a western readership in the sense of diluting or acculturating oriental idioms to suit occidental pre-dispositions and expectations. I shall argue below that in spite of the American framing of *The Book of Khalid*, Rihani's biculturality is not of the kind that can be considered ethnic American.

Out of Lebanon

Hisham Sharabi's identikit of the Christian Arab intellectual of the years 1875–1914 shows a deracinated outcast eager to discover and re-create the world. Self-motivated, resourceful, energetic, and enterprising, with a rationalist, revolutionary tendency leading to "rebellion against all forms of absolutist, other-worldly thought," he was among the "natural vanguard of change" in the Arab world. Generally speaking, Sharabi argues, the Christian intellectuals as a group were the most strongly oriented toward European culture and tended to see themselves in terms of the ideals and values of the western bourgeoisie. They were "interpreters of the West and purveyors of its values", being at the same time deeply engaged in Arabic literature and politics. Outsiders in Muslim society, they had also fallen foul of the narrow obscurantism of their own sectarian communities. Physically and psychologically uprooted, they moved from village to large cities, and across seas to Egypt, Europe and America. Without a stake in any particular community or political grouping, they embraced intellectual and cultural hybridity with some ease, developing stances on politics and literature that were radical and innovatory.[4]

In 1888, as a boy of twelve, accompanied by his uncle and tutor,

Rihani emigrated to the United States. Although Rihani's father owned a silk factory in Freike, where the family resided, the motive to leave Lebanon was probably economic.[5] In New York, the émigrés found basement accommodation of a type described in *The Book of Khalid* "as deep and dark and damp as could be found."[6] Rihani began his public school education, only to interrupt it at fourteen to become chief clerk, salesman and interpreter in the family's merchandise business. Soon finding this work tedious, he embarked on a voracious diet of reading, his favorite authors being Shakespeare, Victor Hugo, Rousseau, Washington Irving, and Thomas Carlyle. Joining a theater troupe, he traveled America for a few months before returning to New York to resume studies in 1896. These were interrupted by a lung complaint, and there followed a brief two year sojourn in Lebanon which helped Rihani convalesce and brush up on his Arabic at the same time. In 1899, back in New York, he started out on his writing career, producing articles in Arabic for newspapers serving the Syrian emigrant community[7]

For a natural intellectual like Rihani, the restrictions of the Syro-American community, founded on those self-same sectarian divisions to be found in the homeland, were stifling and absurd. These divisions were marked in Arab-American publications; *al-Huda* (The Guidance) was the newspaper read by the Maronite community, while *al-Miraat al-Gharb* (Mirror of the West) was the voice of the Greek Orthodox. However, in 1903, Ameen Goryeb began publication of *al-Muhajir* (The Emigrant), a paper with a more liberal outlook that was both literary and informative in nature. It was in this paper that Khalil Jibran published his first piece, "al-Musiqa", and some of Rihani's early Arabic writings appeared.[8] Already, his speeches and articles had earned him the disfavor of the Maronite Church, but at the same time Rihani had also acquired for himself a literary reputation: 1903 was the year in which he published his first work in English, *The Quatrains of Abu'l-Ala*, his translation of the blind poet from the classical age of Arabic literature, Abu'l-Ala al-Ma'arri. Also that year, a dinner attended by around one hundred from the literary world was held in his honor at the Pleiades Club in New York. Although a complete and accurate bibliography of Rihani's early publications is still wanting, it seems his translation of *The Quatrains* was followed by individual poems and an early volume of poetry, *Myrtle and Myrrh*. Rihani returned to the Arab world between 1905 and 1910. In his Arabic writings he was engaged in the project of challenging the sterility into which Arabic poetry had fallen. The innovations he introduced into the structure and register of his own poetry had some impact on other Arab poets, especially those of the *mahjar* Arab-American school. In the meantime, Rihani had established himself as a figure in American literary circles, counting among his friends the poet Edwin Markham (who anthologized several of Rihani's poems and translations from Abu'l-Ala) , the socialist and editor-proprietor of *Papyrus* magazine, Michael Monahan, and later, the bohemian radical, Max Eastman. While in Egypt and Syria, Rihani sent several pieces on Arab subjects to Monahan for publication. On his return to America in 1910, through the pages of *The Bookman*, Rihani used the success he had achieved through his translation of al-Ma'arri as a base to widen his reputation as a writer. His literary journalism concentrated on topics with an Arab tie-in, such as the introduction of *The Arabian Nights* to the West, and the tragic visit of Ernest and Henriette Renan to Syria.[9] In the same period appeared *The Book of Khalid*, the only novel he was to publish.

Rihani's Early English Writings (1903–1912)

If "style in any kind of discourse can be represented as the context-dependent phenomenon it is", the task of creating such a context may well be too daunting for hybrid writing to surmount.[10] A readership for such writings is usually limited to a tiny bilingual audience from the writer's own native culture, as is the case with Tagore's poetry. Speaking of American writing, Werner Sollors writes: "Ethnic writers in general confront an actual or imagined double audience, composed of 'insiders' and of readers, listeners, or spectators who are not familiar with the writer's ethnic group." He goes on to suggest that "impercep-tibly and sometimes involuntarily, writers begin to function as translators of ethnicity to ignorant, and sometimes hostile outsiders and, at the same time, as mediators between 'America' and green-horns."[11] The potential "insider" readership of Rihani's English writings – Arabs who could read English – was extremely limited. It has been estimated that 90 percent of Arab-speaking immigrants to America were urbanized, the overwhelming majority worked as laborers or derived support from others who were laborers. Only a tiny percentage occu-pied what could be called the middle class professions.[12] In addition, the Arab-American community as an entity had an identity problem stem-ming in part from the sectarian divisions brought by the predominantly Christian Syrian Arabs of the first wave of immigration before World War I.

When Rihani wrote in Arabic, it was to address these same sectarian divisions, but he must soon have found this space too circumscribed for his literary ambitions. In fact, while his early literary journalism addressed two discrete cultures, there is no question but that these were articulated within an Anglo-American discourse, and that he was writing for none other than a cultured, avant-garde American audience. His aim of disclosing Arab culture to this readership was eclectic and transcultural in the sense that he was concerned to mark out precisely where the artifact of Arab culture remained untranslatable to the West, and, at the same time, where it might be possible for its spirit to be made to undergo a "transmigration" into the other. It is this agenda that perhaps distinguishes his article, "The Coming of The Arabian Nights", from so much that has subsequently been written on that topic. Rihani is remarkably alive, given the date when he was writing, to the processes of acculturation the Arabic stories had gone through in order to end up "distorted into Family Editions, Drawing Room Editions, and such like." By tracing a genealogy for translations of *The Nights* into French, German and English, Rihani foregrounds the multiple transcriptions of the stories into western codes. In Galland's translation the "Jinn talk like *boulevardiers*; his women chatter like courtesans; and the absolutely French manner of the ending is quite amusing." But in the hands of the Orientalist Edward Lane an "insipid, [. . .] jejune, [. . .] hideous and hag-like [. . .] literal translation, [. . .] lacks the imaginative quality and the Oriental poetic fervour." The issue was whether a medium could be found for "the picturesqueness, the simplicity, the naivete, the terseness, the plain childish directness of Arabic." A western audience could not appreciate the songs which interspersed the prose stories because, to them "these interruptions are irritating [. . .] the illusion [. . .] is not alive, not real." Finding all existing translations wanting, Rihani stops short at the point of declaring *The Nights* untranslatable. Conveying the spirit of the original was possible, but "not in translation, [. . .] only in what might be called a transmigration," which in the case of *The Nights*, waited accomplishment "in the hands of a true literary genius."[13]

Rihani had already made his own attempt at producing a transmigration of Arab meanings into English. A free translation aimed at capturing the spirit rather than the letter of the Arab poet, *The Quatrains of Abu'l-Ala* were properly his first extended exercise in cross-cultural disclosure. In his preface to the Abu'l-Ala poems, Rihani theorized his translation of the blind poet in a new way. First of all, it was necessary to face up to the dominant position Fitzgerald's translation of Omar Khayyam held in the western canon. The introduction is a clear adumbration of Rihani's cultural nationalism in its attack on Fitzgerald's work as a canonical "Oriental" text. Rihani's project was not to purvey some essentialist version of "the Orient" to the West; he was not one of those who felt Fitzgerald had constructed a distorted image of "the East" by marking Khayyam's apparent nihilism. On the contrary, Rihani had no desire to claim al-Ma'arri as a true representative of any eastern orthodoxy, be it strictly Islamic, Sufi, or an abstract distillation of eastern "spirituality." Nor did he wish to rehabilitate the blind poet as a universal figure, stripped of his race and time, capable of assimilation into some westernized pantheon of great men. Yes, al-Ma'arri was "the Lucretius of Al-Islam, the Diogenes of Arabia and the Voltaire of the East [. . .] a liberal thinker, a trenchant writer, – free, candid," – but above all, by means of an insouciant iconoclasm that escaped the red-necked reviewers, Abu'l-Ala is inscribed as an Arab hero.[14] Rihani derives a phyrric pleasure in demoting Khayyam to the rank of mere imitator of al-Ma'arri. The "skepticism and pessimism of Omar" were "to a great extent imported from Marrah"; "the Arabian philosopher" was "in his religious opinions [. . .] far more outspoken than the Persian poet" (or "tent-maker" in later editions). The relationship is further underscored in the notes by selective quotations from Fitzgerald's and Heron-Allen's translations of *The Rubiyyat:* not a case of plagiarism, Rihani admits, rather direct transmission of a point of view that resulted in a "similarity of though." But since the English readership had long ago made up its mind about Khayyam, Rihani knew he could scarcely hope to shift his reputation as one of the West's chief icons of an acculturated East. His desire was to "expand and not to contract the Oriental influence on Occidental minds." A good many reviewers of the *Quatrains* easily picked up on the echoes of Fitzgerald's Khayyam, and naturally enough, Rihani could only be commended as a follower in the tradition of translation set by the westerner, but few saw that, with his customary insouciance, he was subverting the primacy of Fitzgerald's poet.[15] The radical accent is further sharpened in the revised preface to the later version of the Abu'l-Ala poems, *The Luzumiyat.* Al-Ma'aari was now an iconoclastic Arab hero, who could be enlisted in Rihani's own counter-narrative to eastern obscurantism and western manipulation of the Orient. To foreground this message it was necessary to deconstruct the sententious patrician tones of the British Orientalists, whom Rihani found guilty of marginalizing al-Ma'arri's iconoclastic views on religion by giving credence to the dubious rationalizations of the *ulama*: " I am surprised to find a European scholar like Professor Margoliouth giving countenance to such views; even repeating, to support his own argument, such drivel." Rihani dismisses as cant Arab and Orientalist apologias for al-Ma'arri's heterodoxy. In their place he produces a reading of the poet that might serve as a text for the re-appropriation of a rebellious, albeit submerged eastern identity:

> The Europeans, though they shook off their fetters of moral and spiritual slavery, would keep us in ours to facilitate the conquests of European commerce. Thus the terrible Dragon, which is fed by the foreign

missionary and the native priest, by the theologians and the ulama, and which still prays on the heart and mind of Orient nations, is as active today as it was ten centuries ago. Let those consider this, who think Von Kremer exaggerated when he said, "Abu'l-Ala is a poet many centuries ahead of his time."[16]

In his translation of classical Arabic poetry into English, Rihani was working an already opened seam, even if his notes and commentary were highly original. But in his own poetry he was breaking new ground in an even less compromising manner. Here he made little or no attempt to mediate the "ethnic" content to an "outsider" audience, instead, the hybrid idiom of these writings undercut itself. He deliberately attempted "to introduce Arabic words into his writings" and made few concessions (unlike Jibran who was "simple and direct") to facilitate the creation of a new readership.

The problem with the poems is probably that they "are Arabic in thought and in temperament. To put it simply, [they are] literature in English rather than English literature." Use of only two rhymes over more than one stanza is rarely attempted in English poetry, but repetition of just a single rhyme is a common feature of Arabic poetry, and Rihani adopts both schemes.[17] Even if these writings had outstanding merit, only by successfully adopting the standard codes of metropolitan literary discourse could they have stood a chance of acceptance. But they make no attempt to penetrate the American literary canon. (Perhaps that task would have been impossible to accomplish anyway: American literary critics up till the present have tended to concentrate their attention on "mainstream" American writers, largely white and male, ignoring women and ethnic writers.[18]) The difficulty Rihani had establishing a common terrain between East and West can be seen from the reception of his poetry. The contemporary American reviewers for their part were clearly bewildered by the linguistic exoticism both of his poems and essays: the hacks who took it on themselves to protect the purity of, hegemonically speaking, one of the world's foremost literatures, failed entirely to be seduced by Rihani's esoteric cross-cultural aims:

> Down the hill back of Trinity Church in New York, just a step or two from Wall Street, is the Syrian quarter. There are many exotic looking gentlemen there, with bright eyes and red lips, and among them one may occasionally meet a writer named Ameen Rihani.[19]

Here were "picturesque" and "exotic" texts, written by a denizen of a New York ghetto no less (so close yet so far from the metropolitan center of things). As with Johnson's similitude of the woman preacher, the reviewers were not a little surprised that the dog had attempted to stand on its hind legs in the first place.

A similar problem attends the essays collected in *The Path of Vision*. These have a curiously dated feel about them; their prolixity betrays not only the Arab origins of their author, but his immersion in a transcendentalist idiom that was already archaic by the beginning of the twentieth century. "From Concord to Syria", published in 1913 in *Atlantic Monthly* is a representative essay from the point of view of Rihani's early eclecticism. Discountenancing (at this period) any political or economic motive, he claims he is back in his native Syria on private business, "only, perhaps, to see the cyclamens of the season again." In fact, he has brought with him nothing more revolutionary than three American Transcendentalist authors: "Whitman and Emerson and Thoreau are come to pay you a visit, my beloved Syria." But in spite of his admiration for the Americans, Rihani's project is to appropriate them into the oriental setting. He does this by associating them with plants and bushes from his native landscape, arguing in transcendentalist fashion that the Americans could claim spiritual kinship with Lebanon even though they never visited.[20]

Tempting as it is to categorize Rihani as an ethnic American writer for the sake of claiming for him a niche in a revised contemporary American canon, it is clear that this fails on several important counts. First and foremost, in the tension between descent and consent, there is no contest as far as Rihani's Arab identity is concerned. His adoption of the consensual American principles of democracy, tolerance, and individualism are grafted on to the oriental spiritual birthright that went with an Arab descent: "my American walking shoes are new, and my Oriental eyes are old."[21] Second, Rihani's writings do not fully register the "cultural doubleness" of those writers who chose to address themselves to the ethnic situation in America. Explicating this doubleness, the Jewish writer, Thorstein Veblen, wrote in 1919: "It is by loss of allegiance, or at best by force of a divided allegiance to the people of his origin, that [the ethnic writer] finds himself in the vanguard of modern inquiry."[22] Although Rihani played with cultural doubleness in his early writings in English, they carry no sense of a divided allegiance cognate to what Veblen describes. Rihani was not significantly interested in the assimilation of Arabs into America; what mattered to him was the disclosure of Arab culture to Americans, and beyond that, of western values to oriental Arabs. In a crucial sense, for Rihani the focus never moved for long from a Middle Eastern location.

The Book of Khalid and Arab-American Hybridity

In its September 1911 issue, the American magazine, *The Bookman* , ran a notice on a forthcoming publication from Dodd, Mead and Company of "a book of a very unusual character by a writer who has had remarkable experiences [. . .] His book is one of a peculiar nature, displaying as it does the strange phases of Oriental life, and also of the unusual experiences Mr Rihani has met with, both in the East and in portions of our own country which are little known to us, though they are so near to us."[23] *The Book of Khalid* thus approached life very much as it has continued up till now: as a cultural oddity. Rihani began composing a novel that would encode "possibly the most complete account in English of the modern liberated Arab" in 1907.[24] That he should have chosen the novel form to encode his ideas about the meeting of East and West on a common terrain was certainly avant-garde from an eastern perspective. Muhammad Husain Haykal's *Zaynab*, usually listed as the first novel in Arabic, was written at almost exactly the same time, though published two years after Rihani's novel appeared. Haykal wrote it while studying Law in Paris. Rihani passed through the city in 1910, when he met his compatriot Jibran for probably the first time, and may conceivably have come across the Egyptian writer too. A parallel reading of the two texts discloses familiar twentieth-century Arab concerns: tradition versus modernity, the oppressive impact of society on the alienated individual, and the task of narrating the nation.[25] The eponymous hero of Rihani's novel leaves his native Baalbek because the place is too small to contain his rebellious instincts. But Khalid's experiences in the New World can hardly be considered typical of the ordinary Lebanese immigrant, except in matters relating to material circumstances and the means of earning of a livelihood. Alienated by the materialism of American society, he returns to Lebanon to become embroiled in political and religious controversies of the day.

In the first Arabic novel, the West features only at a superficial level: English interference in Egyptian affairs gets a mention on several occasions, but has no bearing on the events transacted. Otherwise, the topoi of cruel and unjust tradition, in this case arranged marriage, and the traditional round of village life, are monotonously handled. In addition to a heavy-handed moralism, *Zaynab* abounds in descriptive passages which are repetitive and formulaic. Haykal had clearly absorbed a Rousseaurian romanticism with regard to the relationship between the sexes similar to that found in Jibran's early Arabic short stories. The novel ends with the death of the heroine, brought on by grief for her absent lover, in a melodramatic mode that recalls the endings of several of Jibran's writings. [26] It is not merely its dual perspective – looking from the East westwards and vice versa – that distinguishes Rihani's text from Haykal's; or its literary hybridity, joining a rich Arabic intertextuality to an already eclectic re-writing of western texts. *The Book of Khalid* is at its most experimental when it comes to form – in fact the chief problem raised by the text up to now has been one of categorization: in basic terms, how to catalogue it. In this sense, the text joins its author with the ranks of ethnic artists who "in an amazing number of instances [. . .] have embraced innovation and modernity in form."²⁷ If *Zaynab* has its significance in the development of a national literature and a "national longing for form", *The Book of Khalid* embraces the interface of America and the ethnic ghetto, and the confrontation of Middle Eastern traditionalism with a modernizing nationalist awakening, within the boundaries of a literary form that parodies the European *bildungsroman* at the same time as it mimics the most prized oracular literature of the East. The published "work" lives up to the promise of the *Bookman* advertisement in its penetration of the margins of American urban life, its representations both of the Lebanese experience of emigration and exile in the New World and the Arab intellectual's rebellion against obscurantism at home, as well as in its juxtaposition of these alongside a satirical parody of the cultic milieu in America and the Holy Land in the first decade of the twentieth century.

The interface of East and West is enacted not only at a thematic level: Rihani essays to explode the linguistic register with the employment of exotic and recondite signifiers from the English lexicon, and the importation into the English text of a plethora of Arabic idioms and references. He also experiments with a mix of writings that not only transposes, in English, "material from different texts, different kinds of text, 'various signifying systems', both literary and non-literary," but joins to this the further dimensions of an Arabic intertextuality.²⁸ Re-writings of Carlyle, Thoreau and Emerson, are jostled by quotations from the Arab mystics, Rabi'a and al-Farid, and denigrations of al-Mutanabbi, the prime canonical poet of Classical Arabic literature. The mix is of a variety of Arab and western, predominantly American, registers. The importation of Arabic expressions ranges through Lebanese idioms concerning such mundane matters as the staple diet of the Syrian American immigrant, terms relating to peasant labor in Mount Lebanon, and renditions into English of the Maronite priest's "miserable Arabic." Allusions to Arab grammarians, popular and classical Arabic literature, and Sufi poetry, alongside mainstream Islamic vocabulary, liberally pepper the text, and room is even found for the occasional expression in Turkish relating to Ottoman administration. On the western side, Rihani flits through a phalanx of different American language games in such discrete areas as district level city politics, the law registry, popular lectures on atheism, spiritualism, transcendentalism, and occult formulae adopted by the latest oriental cult's American neophytes. Quotations from the literary discourse of the likes of Voltaire and Renan, Emerson and Carlyle abound. The experiences of Khalid, the rebellious young hero from Baalbek, are inscribed in a baroque prose-style within the framework of a dubiously edited narrative. Here, Carlyle's *Sartor Resartus* was of use to Rihani for the space it allowed for the subversion of *langue*. Carlyle took liberties by importing into his text teutonic syntax and neologisms, thereby upsetting predictable syntagmatic relationships and marking deviant meanings.

This provided a particularly appropriate model for the cross-cultural disclosures Rihani had in mind. He was able to re-enact the emigrant's experience of displacement by foregrounding a sense of difference in terms of the unusual and the bizarre at the level of rich linguistic variation.

Clearly devised as a means of inscribing difference, Khalid embodies many of the characteristics listed by Sharabi; his bitter crossing of swords with the Maronite clergy on his return to Lebanon recalls specific instances of rancor between the Church and Lebanese intellectuals. One significant point at issue between Khalid and the Church is its charge that he translated Carlyle's Latter-Day Pamphlet, "On Jesuitism", so linking Rihani's hero with the Protestant mask that provided a cover for promoting western-backed freedom of thought in Lebanon. But Khalid is not a westernizing rationalist in the manner of the Lebanese materialist, Shibli Shumayyil. As much Rihani's own mouthpiece as Teufelsdrokh is Carlyle's, he is given the opportunity by the transcribed form of *Sartor Resartus* to deliver quasi-oracular messages phrased in the mixed registers of American transcendentalism and Sufism. An outsider, he has the self-conceit to claim for his dicta a larger constituency than Carlyle's German professor's handful of transcendentalist acolytes; he is himself not so much the Romantic hero and law-giver, as the bridge between the cultural and political phases of Arab nationalism, the messiah for his nation "awaking, lisping, beginning to speak, waiting for him, the chosen Voice!"[29] Half-hero, half object of farce, Khalid represents the possibilities of a revived East, able to draw from the energy of the New World, and work on it the Orient's deeper spiritual resources. As such, he accesses a potential cultural hybridity, which, although unrealized in the novel, remains on the margins, waiting on Khalid's more pressing project of creating a new Arab nation.

It is fair to say that none of the other *mahjari* authors had as wide an interest in their adopted country as Ameen Rihani. Confident enough of his own biculturality, he set out to make an inventory of the impact upon himself, an Arab, of western codes, exploring in the process the wider implications of being a pioneer Arab-American. He started with the abject experience of the emigrants' arrival in New York – "Here, the unhappy children of the steerage are dumped into the Bureau of Emigration – as such stuff!" Jumping quarantine, Khalid and his friend "smuggle" themselves into America as they had been "smuggled out of their own country by the boatmen of Beirut."[30] America is seen through the eyes of the unworldly immigrant, happy to live in a damp basement, earn his living at peddling, eat his native dish of lentils, and own a bank account. The threat to his oriental innocence comes from occidental blandishments of money and sex. "And these lusty Syrians could not repel the magnetic attraction of the polypiosis of what Shakib [Khalid's friend] likens to the *aliat* (fattail) of our Asiatic sheep." But difference is not limited to "the convex curve beneath the [female] waist" being "hindward" in America, "frontward" in Lebanon. It is inscribed by the flooded cellar the immigrants inhabit, no less than a trope for America itself, the "cellar of the soul", where materialistic pre-occupations stifle the higher aspirations.

> "Think you [. . .] that the inhabitants of this New World are better off than those of the Old? [. . .] The soul I tell you, still occupies the basement, even the sub-cellar. [. . .] The soul, Shakib, is kept below, although the high places are vacant."[31]

Khalid's raillery at American materialism may be standard eastern fare, but it had the merit of being composed at first hand. "After arriving in America [Rihani wrote nearly two decades after *The Book of Khalid*] I became an admirer of the vitality of the American people, of the freedom they enjoyed in their thought, speech and deeds, but at the same time grew to fear their intense materialistic activity, their acquisitiveness."[32] The flooded cellar image may not be Rihani's final word on his adopted land: Khalid pens a letter from prison in which he expatiates on "these United States" as the future enlightened political, artistic and spiritual center for the world.[33] Nevertheless, back in Lebanon, he is disgusted to find the infection of America's materialism brought back by the returning emigrant. The adulteration of cheese and the importation of gramophone "ragtime horrors" are both symptoms of the impact of the New World on Lebanese society. America is Khalid's "Spiritual Mother", the place where he received his call to prophethood, but she is a mother who devours her own children. And the enactment, Rihani seems to be saying, is not confined to the borders of America.

A further inscription of difference is to be seen in Khalid's encounter with the American, largely female, cultic milieu. This has an added intertextual dimension if read alongside Khalil Jibran's career in America. Acting out the role of oriental messiah seems to have been unnecessary for Rihani who, once he had invented a fictive messiah, and produced an appropriate prophetic discourse for him, left the field open for Jibran's later adoption of the cultic charisma. It may have been close personal contact of his own with the ready American neophyte, that, enlivening his always keen awareness of occidental difference, led him to find a trope for the "unity of East and West" in the outlandish liaison of Khalid with an American medium:

> Now, this fair-spoken dame, who dotes on the occult and exotic, delights in the aroma of Khalid's cigarettes and Khalid's fancy. And that he might feel at ease, she begins by assuring him that they have met and communed many times ere now, that they have been friends under a preceding and long vanished embodiment. Which vagary Khalid seems to countenance by referring to the infinite power of Allah, in the compass of which nothing is impossible. And with these mystical circumlocutions of cere-mony, they plunge into an intimacy which is bordered by the metaphysical on the one side, and the physical on the other.[34]

Khalid's relationship with the American woman in search of spiritual (and sexual) fulfilment from the Orient resurfaces again at the end of the novel, this time in the East. Although more serious than his earlier dalliances, Khalid's association with Mrs Gotfry, who is beautiful but physically handicapped, and "a votary of Ebbas Effendi, the Pope of Babism at Heifa," is no less abortive.[35] She saves Khalid, who has embarked on a messianic career to his fellow Arabs, from martyrdom at the hands of angry mobs, but is unable to convert him to her new reli-gion. Eventually, unwilling to consummate their relationship physically, she leaves Khalid in the desert. Their disagreement is more than a failure to unite the Orient and the Occident, as Khalid wishes. It represents both a refusal on Rihani's part to sublimate the national struggle in a universal religion, and "a rebellion against all other-worldly, absolutist authority" typical of the radical Arab Christian intellectual of the period.

The Book of Khalid looks forward to Rihani's later writings in a number of important areas. Written before the epoch of postcolonial struggles got fully underway (though it is in part formed around the Young Turk Revolution of 1908–9) the novel is precocious for its fictional exposition of a Pan-Arab narrative (see chapter 3). It calls for a political and spiri-tual revolution in the East, drawing on western material and political advances, at the same time defending Arab self-determination. This is in line with Khalid's project "to graft the strenuosity of Europe and

America upon the ease of the Orient, the materialism of the West upon the spirituality of the East."[36] For Khalid's mission is not to America, but to his fellow brethren in the East. At the very moment when the ship of emigrants is in sight of New York, he has a dream in which he is traveling through the desert dressed as an Arab amir, and is received on the way by ecstatic welcoming crowds, reaching at last a citadel where its princess crowns him "King of ———." His mix of mystical and political messianism is not without its western supports though: later in the novel, Khalid tries to convince his American friend, Mrs Gotfry, to join with him in a crusade to create an Arab Empire, backed by American technological know-how and "an up-to-date Koran."[37]

At this stage, hybridism was a mechanism whereby lift-off into a higher stage of universal civilization might be begun. The unification of East and West was ideal, theoretical, and above all, potential, involving contributions from both sides, and aimed at achieving a synthesis beyond anything that was on offer in either cultural space. The author was in the grips of a teaming, *mahjar* optimism. Apart from its remarks on the infiltration into Mount Lebanon of modern capitalism, *The Book of Khalid* is silent on a theme that would later exercise Rihani a great deal: colonialism, or the political subjection of the Orient by the West. Rihani also carried intercultural, intertextual perspectives over into his Arabic writings. As his nephew points out: "Rihani's adoption of *Sartor's* format [in *The Book of Khalid*] becomes one episode in a series of borrowed masks from one culture to another: a western mask to eastern literature and an eastern mask to western literature. After all, Rihani never felt that he was an alien to one of the two. On the contrary, he belonged to both, experienced both, and had both as his audience."[38] But whereas biculturality implies simultaneous inhabitance of two separate cultures, involving the subject, either as protagonist or author, in mediation of one culture to another, the sort of hybridity Rihani builds into his novel means that two cultures actually interpenetrate (quite literally in the case of Khalid and his American mistresses.) In its studied literary and cultural hybridism, *The Book of Khalid* is distinct from Rihani's other English writings, which are exercises more in bicultural mediation. Although his later publications and manuscripts revisited a number of the topoi embodied in his experimental novel, he never again utilized the same hybrid format. (A fully-blown postcolonial author like Tayeb Salih also revisits key areas opened up by Rihani, notably the relations between western women and Arab men, using this as a metonym for the penetration of the East by western imperialism.) Rihani's wish to balance and even marry the western and oriental codes, rather than sacrifice one code for the other, makes for the formation of a discourse that is rich, overlaid, and ultimately overwrought. By experimenting with cross-culturality in this manner, a path had been laid which other *mahjar* writers like Khalil Jibran and Mikhail Naimy would later try to follow. At the same time the style of Rihani's English writings discloses something of the *déraciné* quality of *mahjar* writing in English; mannered and sometimes grotesque in the prose of *The Book of Khalid*, fined out to an ultimate rootlessness in Jibran's later offerings.

Conclusion

Khalid's return to the East in the second half of the novel underscored where Rihani's priorities lay for most of his later life. Far from giving up residence there himself, he spent long periods in his native Freike. Between these, he fitted in his travels through the Arab world, and periods of propagandist activity in the United States where he lectured and wrote articles on Arab issues, such as the emergence of Abdul-Aziz Ibn Saud, and the Palestine question. Ten years separated the publication of *The Book of Khalid* and Rihani's first journey to the Arabian peninsular. During that time he balanced the idealism of the *mahjar*, with its theoretical universalism and belief in the writer's function as a prophet, with a deepening commitment to Arab unity politics. The themes which he, Jibran and Mikhail Naimy articulated in their *mahjar* period – reconciling East and West, reviving Arab culture, impregnating literature with a radical reforming zeal – continued to exercise the later Rihani, but in a refracted form. "He paid more attention than the others to the problems of the larger Arab fatherland by personal visits, study and writing. Perhaps because of this he was the most nationalistic among the Christian writers in America, and he among them came nearest to identifying himself with the sentiments and aspirations of the Muslim majority."[39] Biculturality remained important, but Rihani was disposed to utilize his mastery of Arab and American culture towards wider political ends. His universal dreams were sublimated in the struggle against colonialism, and in this struggle he was eager to enlist on the Arab side an American public who, he believed, should be better informed of Arab cultural achievements, changing political allegiances, and future aspirations.

2

Khalil Jibran: From Arab mahjar *to Consumerist Prophet*

Although [Jibran] addressed his writings to the West and to the Arab world at different periods of his life, the question which remains to be asked is how far he could retain his individuality and integrity while changing his attitude and thought to suit different audiences.

Khalil Hawi[1]

Although Jibran Khalil Jibran was not the first *mahjar* writer to choose to write in English as well as his native Arabic, that act of switching languages encodes a truly polysemic string of meanings, not least of which is its impact on Jibran's literary reputation. It is not merely that this has been compartmentalized, that his Arabic works are discussed by Arabic scholars and his English ones by almost no scholars at all. The popular success of *The Prophet*, specifically, transposes Jibran's status as most prominent member of the *mahjar* school into the sphere of consumerist writer whose contemporary American readers would, overwhelmingly, fail to have any conversance with what a *mahjar* writer was. Where Jibran once attracted "a big crop of would-be Gibrans, quasi-Gibrans, and Gibran imitators [. . .] all over the Arabic speaking world," his standing as an Arab author today, not unnaturally, has waned as other more culturally relevant literary trends have replaced Arab Romanticism.[2] However, in America, where Khalil is Kahlil, and *The Prophet* has outsold every other book except the Bible, Jibran's utterances continue to be reconstructed by late twentieth-century capitalism to embellish fine art posters and inscribe the wonders of love and friendship on countless all-the-year-round valentine cards. As a contemporary publishing phenomenon, Jibran's popular English writings seem to demand that their author be de-centered in order for the synchronic significations within the texts to be decoded. But neither the author nor the historicity of the text will be sacrificed here, even though effective separations of text from author, and text from historicity have been brought about by the writings' continuing cultic success.

Some voices have argued that Jibran has been the victim of his innovative genius, that is, that he inaugurated a new, eclectic international tradition for the judgment of which the appropriate critical tools have not yet been produced. Critically, Jibran is a victim of the Jibran phenomenon, that is to say, any claims made for his uniqueness work against him, not only because in the postmodern age such claims are brushed aside (no author is unique; genius has no meaning; writing writes, not authors) but because they are rightly taken to be self-validating. A more informed criticism might indeed interrogate how far Jibran's discourse discloses the "traumatic clash of traditional society with the western world, its agonizing search for its own identity, its struggle to attain modernity with all the contradictions that attend such a struggle" which M. M. Badawi identifies as the master code behind "the perennial themes of Modern Arabic literature," and which is a feature of such disparate Anglo-Arab narratives as *The Book of Khalid* and *The Arab Awakening*.[3] Such critical approaches would, however, tend to draw a negative in the sense that, as I shall argue, discussing Jibran's English writings in terms of Anglo-Arab discourse or as extensions of his early Arabic writings, raises the question of difference, not in the sense of its existence as a construct within the text, but as an absence managed by what Fredric Jameson has called a strategy of containment "which allows what can be thought to seem internally coherent in its own terms, while repressing the unthinkable [. . .] which lies beyond its boundaries."[4] We will find that Jibran has sublimated the agonizing search for identity of the modern Arab writer into a construction of a transcendental subject at once "idealistic, essentialist, anti-historical" which may accord with the "static, eternal truths of [. . .] the Western metaphysical tradition" (and of the "Wisdom of the East" no doubt) but appears to stand in binary opposition to the thrust of modernity.[5] In his English writings Jibran succeeds in collapsing the differences that attend his function as an Arab writer in a western metropolis into a homogenizing universality that has captured a huge popular readership in the West while its reception in the East is ambivalent. (Muslim Arabs might find the title of his most celebrated work offensive from the beginning.)

Jibran and Modernism

I would like to pick up on Fredric Jameson's "notes towards a theory of the modern" and apply them to the case of Jibran, or more properly, "Kahlil Gibran." In discussing the "death of the subject" thesis postmodernism proposes, Jameson has argued that a postmodern view of the "great" modernist creators ought not to argue away the "social and historical specificity of those now doubtful 'centered subjects,' but rather provide new ways of understanding their conditions of possibilty."[6] In Jibran's case the epithets "great" and "modernist" would seem highly problematic, but the investigation of the Jibran-phenomenon that follows can be said to operate within the modernist space articulated by Jameson, by arguing that Jibran deliberately set out to produce himself as the charismatic spiritual genius, similar to the way the "Great Moderns" constructed their careers as great artists and writers. It may not be possible according to the postmodern perspective, to take the modernist artist-heroes at their self-validation, still for Jameson "their conditions of possibility" need to be examined. Positing the "uneven moment of social development" with which modernism synchronizes, and instancing the survival of pre-modern archaisms into the new world of Henry Ford mass production, he underscores how the "Great Artist" drew on pre-modern survivals for his aesthetic production, in order to oppose and at the same time build them into a Utopian vision of the transformation of human life made possible by the new conditions of production.

> It is because that object world, in the throes of industrialization and modernization, seems to tremble at the brink of an equally momentous and even Utopian transformation that the "self" can also be felt to be on the point of change.[7]

This insight can be transferred to the Arab-American writers of the *mahjar*, whose position at the heart of the greatest industrialized nation on earth privileged them to form a transformational critique of their native Arabic culture which they denounced for its backwardness and obscurantism. While Rihani and Jibran articulate this message openly in their early Arabic writings, Naimy was its most pointed theorist arguing, "the human psyche, not dictionaries and lexicons, is the right way to literature. We have enough linguistic miracles. It is high time to pay attention to this modern animal who was and still is the greatest of secrets and enigmas."[8] Rihani's awareness of the trends of social radicalism evidenced by his piece *The Descent of Bolshevism*, allies him with modernism's "Utopian sense of the transfiguration of the self and the world [which] are, in ways that remain to be explored, very much to be seen as echoes and resonances of the hopes and optimism of that great period dominated by the Second International."[9] Jibran's Rousseaurian primitivism and nature worship would seem, in contrast, to place him in a condition of alienation from the modern world, although in his incorporation of Symbolist practices into both his paintings and writings he is not radically different from Anglo-Saxon modernists like D. H. Lawrence and Katherine Mansfield. To claim Jibran as an Arab modernist is not far-fetched, given his opposition to authority and traditionalism in Lebanon, and his pioneer role in Arab romanticism. Also, in the context of his English writings, it is scarcely conceivable that the transformational message of *The Prophet*, let alone its framing, in which Orphalese is obviously America, and Mustapha, Jibran himself, could have been produced without the author's positioning in the New World. This is to do with the object world of modern production in a very specific sense: with an audience who, fully placed within the new order of production, had an appetite for messages of an archaic pre-industrial world (the imaginary Orient) which Jibran was well positioned to oblige, "especially in Bohemia, where many of its daughters set their caps for him."[10] In Jibran's case we see an intentional construction by the author (and his collaborator) of apparently decontextualized, universal texts, into which subsequent generations of interpreters have continued to read their own meanings and pre-occupations.

Beyond the *Mahjar*

A decade before *The Prophet* was published, Max Reinhardt transferred his successful mime theater from Europe to North America, bringing with him *Sumurum*, a pantomime lifted out of *The Arabian Nights* that capitalized on an earlier invasion of the New York stage by productions with an oriental setting such as *Kismet* – "Audiences gasped, critics thrilled when the curious, murderous and sensuous fancy passed before their eyes." The hypnotic art of Reinhardt was soon upstaged by the celluloid fantasies of the Arabian desert and the Arab sheik, about whom Rihani wrote:

> The "sheik", the harem of the "sheik", the luxury and glamour of the desert dwelling of the "sheik", and the little army of fierce-looking knights, on the swiftest dromedaries or the most fiery Arab steeds, in quest of the European girl for the harem [. . .] – nothing is more thrilling, more bewitching in the pages of fiction or on the screen; nothing is more poignantly pathetic in reality.[11]

Jibran's mature English writings should be seen in the context of this western taste for an exotic Orient. In an important sense they are to be categorized as products of a history of acculturation of the Oriental

Other that goes back to Galland's translation of *The Arabian Nights* in the second decade of the eighteenth century, arriving at Valentino's *The Sheik* at around the same time as *The Prophet* in 1923. That is not to say that Jibran did not bring to the western construct something of his own. His achievement was to fuse the rebellion of the Arab Christian radicals of his generation, founded upon their experience of deracination and sense of separation from their indigenous Middle Eastern communities, with existing libertarian and romantic elements in western thought.[12] That the writings produced out of this rebelliousness were clothed in the garb of oriental mysticism can be accounted for in part by Jibran's desire for assimilation in America, hence his tapping into the taste for the oriental and the exotic which Rihani had already exposed in his satirical depiction of the young Syrian prophet Khalid's encounters with female American devotees of the occult (see below on the oriental savant visitors to America in the first decade or so of the twentieth century).

In the process of acculturating his writings in this way, Jibran sacrificed virtually all that, initially, articulated difference in his earlier Arabic writings. It was these, after all, which had gained him his reputation as the leading *mahjar* figure: works like *al-Arwah al-Mutamarridah* (Nymphs of the Valley (1906)) and *'Ara'is al-Muruj* (Spirits Rebellious (1908)) which like Rihani's *al-Makari wa'l Kahin* (The Muleteer and the Monk) radically attacked traditional social customs and the Church. Written in Boston before his removal to Paris in 1908, Jibran's early stories hardly get beyond the stage of romantic denunciation: their politics is unsophisticated to say the least, and the social relations against which he directs his criticism lack specificity and differentiation. Rather than disclosing a concrete critique of the social problems with which he is concerned, Jibran mystifies them.

The story "Martha", for example, adopts a melodramatic narrative to juxtapose an idealized Lebanese village life against the corruption of the city. A girl yields to her warm natural instincts but is deceived and left to live the life of a fallen woman in the slums of Beirut. The theme of the "destructive war between the corrupt laws of men and the sacred emotions of the heart" is taken up again in "Wardah al-Hani", which explains why an eighteen year old bride has deserted her older husband. The girl prefers to live in poverty with her lover, seeing all around her the results of falsely contracted marriages: couples living in deceit and misery even as they dwell in palaces. The people, however, ignore her story "for they fear the revolt of their spirits and [. . .] are afraid lest the foundations of their society be shaken and fall about their heads." In "Yuhanna al-majnun" (Yuhanna the mad), the Church is the specific object of Jibran's attack. A young shepherd boy accidentally allows his sheep to stray and damage the monastery's land. The superior refuses to show mercy and invokes "Elisha's wrath" against the lad unless he pays reparation. The boy, who against the priests' injunction has taught himself to read the Gospels, later delivers a passionate impromptu sermon to the churchgoers of the local village in which he inveighs against the corruption of the Church. Yuhanna only escapes punishment because his father convinces the superior that the boy is mad. Yuhanna is a prototype of the prophet and madman with a mission against social evil and hypocrisy who appears in Jibran's later work. The more developed character of Khalil, in "Khalil al-Kafir" (Khalil the Heretic), is even more clearly the voice of Jibran himself, who was now casting his heroes in the mold of rebel and outcast.[13]

The limitations of this rebellious position could however be seen in Jibran's impractical schemes for realizing his ideals in actual social terms. Soon after his return to America from Paris, Jibran founded a political society, *al-Halqat al-Dhahabiyih* (The Golden Circle), aimed, like similar efforts by other Arab exiles in America, at expressing anti-Ottoman propaganda. But the society's program of social reform was "too impractical to appeal to the emigrants, [and] the society was dissolved after one meeting."[14] In the Great War, Jibran helped organize a League of Liberation, and a Relief Committee which raised funds to fight starvation caused by the conflict in the Middle East. But activities like these seemed to delimit his restricted political geography:

> He told Mary [Haskell] that he was a Syrian and would always remain so; but although Rihani and the other Syrian immigrants understood one another, he did not understand them nor they him [. . .] This helped him to realize that "Syria is not the purpose of my life [. . .] perhaps I shall find myself as much an alien there as anywhere else."[15]

Around the beginning of the war Jibran began to cultivate the skill of writing in English: so alienating him still further from his Arab background. Rihani, who had mastered the metropolitan language much earlier and remained a far more subtle practitioner of it than Jibran ever became, was also developing his early *mahjar* positions along new lines. Together they had once sketched plans for a new opera house in Beirut. It was to be a symbol of the *mahjar* dream of uniting East and West, but was, of course, never realized. By the start of the 1920s, each man had reached a watershed in his career. *The Path of Vision* recapitulated the liberal, mystical themes of Rihani's earlier writings, but by then he had already proceeded on a highly significant modification of *mahjar* universalism in his attempt to formulate an Arab nationalist discourse. Jibran was by now set on his own project of etherizing this universalism in his new English writings. The disagreement between the two writers crystallized over *al-Rabitah Qalamiyah* (The Pen-bond Society): Jibran became its president on its foundation in 1920, and Mikhail Naimy its secretary. But Rihani chose not to join, increasingly dedicating himself to political concerns instead of strictly literary ones. Each in their different ways channeled the romantic rebellion of their earlier work into new courses. Rihani went looking for living Arab heroes in his project of re-inventing the Arab nation. Jibran stayed in America and adopted for himself the prophetic role for the artist that Rihani had already toyed with in *The Book of Khalid* and Mikhail Naimy was theorizing in his attempt to produce a *mahjar* ideology.[16]

The Prophet and the Encoding of Cultic Meanings

In spite of his apolitical primitivism, his Rousseau-like preachings on the need "to return to nature and seek lost innocence and pure love," Jibran was developing his own ideological narrative, centered on himself as deliverer of inspired, messianic messages.[17] The key to this was Mary Haskell, with whom he had first come into contact in 1904. She was largely responsible for transforming him from a limited, if influential poet in Arabic, into "The Prophet of Lebanon", to be figured by later acolytes in almost divine terms: "sometimes, a few times, a Light [. . .] showed above and about him as he walked [. . .] and I said [. . .] 'Kahlil! the Light.'"[18] By re-casting Jibran's Arabic preachings in an orientalized English mold, Mary helped "universalize" his message, suppressing in the process the local differences that pertained to Arab identity and concerns.

No doubt this was an astute move in the long term, for in 1908, a year after his friendship with Mary began in earnest, Jibran was already having doubts about his impact on the Arab world:

> The people in Syria are calling me heretic, and the intelligentsia in Egypt vilifies me, saying, "He is the enemy of just laws, of family ties, and of old traditions" [. . .] Will my teaching ever be received by the Arab world, or will it die away and disappear like a shadow?[19]

However, as an Arab-American, cut off willingly or not from his Arab roots, Jibran may have been easier to convince of the limitations of his mission to the Arabs. In his New York apartment, Jibran secluded himself away from the actual living inchoate world that would otherwise continue to impact in ways that might not be easily managed, and replaced it by a transcendent image of impassioned longing. An absence of both a lived and a textual kind was opened up, either of which was capable of being played off against the other. The feelings of exile and nostalgia for his native land that permeated Jibran's writings substituted the need to address the clash of tradition and modern values even in the mystified terms of his early Arabic writings. Jibran went home to Lebanon only once in the last thirty years of his life – this long before the success of *The Prophet* "brought him great fame and a considerable income within two years," money enough to buy the ticket many times over.[20] "Aloofness from the local scene [. . .] was a partial key to his personal expression."[21]

Although he continued to write in Arabic, his English writings were constitutive of the new orientation. In his Arabic writings beginning with *Dama'ah wa Ibtisamah* (A Tear and a Smile) (1914), Jibran had taken up the prose-poem form pioneered by Rihani in his "poems in prose", *al-Rihaniyat*. According to Rihani himself, this new genre was imitative in part of Walt Whitman, while some have argued it derived from the Qur'an, which might explain one critic's assertion that "la perfection achevée [in the best of these prose-poems] peut à peine être rendue dans une autre langue." But where Rihani's use of the prose-poem was innovatory, and did not entirely sacrifice rhyme, Jibran appropriated the form to position himself closer to a specific register:

> le style biblique représente, depuis saint Jérôme, pour la majorité des chrétiens, un style de traduction, dont la langue anglaise posséde même une "version autorisée."[22]

It was as an *ersatz* biblical style that the prose-poem form appeared in *The Madman* and *The Forerunner* (1920), writings which prepared the way for the style's most polished use in *The Prophet*. Jibran continued to utilize fabular and parable forms as vehicles for moral messages in both his Arabic and English writings. The English texts assemble intertextual fragments whose Arabic or eastern anteriors are, at this stage, presented in a way that make few concessions to the sophisticated westerner:

> Representative of this category is the story of the three frogs [from *The Forerunner*], each of whom has an explanation for the movement of the log upon which they are floating downstream. One says the log itself is moving; a second says it is being borne along by the river; a third says that the sensation of movement is purely subjective. When a fourth asserts that all of them are right, they become angry and push him into the river. Hence the wisest who sees further is punished by his less gifted peers.[23]

As it stands, this mode of writing, even allowing for their familiarity with the biblical style, is hardly tailored for a western audience, and is not the stuff of bestsellers. Clearly, further alterations had to made on the original, heavily orientalized prototype. How far Mary Haskell helped in this may be still unclear; Jibran's English was still weak enough for Mary to ghost to an unspecified degree the writing of *The Madman* (1918), his first published English work – "He gave always every idea and I simply found the phrase sometimes."[24] In addition to the crude homiletic of the fabular and parable forms used up to now, the rebellious isolation of the early Arabic writings remained to be smoothed over. In *The Madman* there is repetition of the earlier masks of the madman and gravedigger who look down from the tower, and continue to rage at men and wage war with society, although some critics have probably made too much of Jibran's pose as the "rootless outsider" in America. Going back to well before the Great War, his friendships with other artists, and particularly American bohemian and society women, provided comfort and solace enough to suggest that the polar opposition between the madman as the ultimately sane, and the ordinary people as the actual deranged, represented a space that could now be closed.[25]

By playing with different writings and achieving a mix that suited perfectly the cultic tastes of the affluent American society women whose penchant for eastern masters had already been satirized by Rihani, Jibran achieved the transition from Arab *mahjar* to consumerist prophet. What is sure is that the switch to English had multiple audience implications. To begin with, where an Arab readership had had to be awakened to the twin evils of *jumud* (stagnation) and *taqlid* (imitation) within traditional Arab societies, a western one would have far other concerns. Khalil Hawi pointed out how in sacrificing the rebelliousness of his early Arabic phase for his later "mystic" stage, Jibran modeled himself on a line of oriental savants and sages who visited America around the turn of the century, including Tagore, Krishnamurti, Swami Vivekananda (whom Hawi does not mention) and the Baha'i leader, Abbas Effendi (Abdul-Baha), whose portrait Jibran painted, and who, along with his western acolytes, Rihani had earlier built into *The Book of Khalid*.[26] In adopting for himself the role of prophet-messiah, and dramatizing it within in his English writings, Jibran exemplifies the axiom: "Literature is always written with a certain reading public in mind, or at least with an intention to develop one."[27] If Mary Haskell provided the language back up, Jibran certainly had the gift to align his product with that ongoing project, in place on the margins of western thought since the early nineteenth century, whereby "Europe [and America] will be regenerated by Asia" – not an actual Asia but *"our Asia"*, sufficiently derived from the Bible and the world of eighteenth century and Romantic oriental exoticism for a western audience to recognize and assimilate.[28]

Both *The Madman* and *The Forerunner* promote the Indian doctrine of reincarnation and a prophet-figure who is not yet as emollient as Almustafa:

> From the housetop I proclaimed you hypocrites, pharisees,
> tricksters, false and empty earth-bubbles.

Nevertheless:

> It was love lashed by its own self that spoke [. . .]
> It was my hunger for your love that raged from the housetop,
> while my own love, kneeling in silence, prayed your forgiveness.[29]

By the time he had finished writing *The Forerunner*, Jibran had developed confidence enough to omit the denuciatory excesses of his outsider-poet pose and cultivate instead a love for his readership that soon reaped results in terms both of sales and acolytes. A new accommodating tone, as compared with the preceding pieces in English, is the chief outcome, one that effects a closure on his relatively protracted search for the right vehicle by which to dramatize his need for acceptance and acclaim. In May 1920, Jibran wrote to Mary Haskell "an overall scenario" for *The Prophet* that shows a barely masked fantasy of himself:

> In a city between the plains and the sea, where ships come in and where flocks graze in the fields behind the city, there wanders about the fields and somewhat among the people, a man – poet, seer, prophet – who loves them and whom they love – but there is an aloneness after all, about him. They are glad to hear him talk; they feel in him a beauty and a sweetness; . . . young women who are attracted by his gentleness do not quite venture to fall in love with him.[30]

In the text Jibran (and Mary) eventually produced, Almustafa, "the chosen and the beloved, who was a dawn unto his own day," has long embraced a Nietzschean "aloneness", and wishes to embark on his final journey, but is held back in the name of the "People of Orphalese" by Almitra, the "seeress." He must articulate "that which even now is moving within [their] souls" before he can gain his release.[31] The soul-message thus encoded is a rewriting of a disparate set of de-theologized, non-judgmental propositions that smooth over the strict New Testament code, transpose the selected Sufi adage, and rework the odd

Blakean aphorism, each in such a manner that it is "transformed by its new uses, its new position in a new time and place."[32] In addition, there is an avoidance of encoding any kind of cultural difference at a lexical level that might induce the reader to work at decoding actual meanings. On the contrary, the reader intelligibility that comes of the process of universalizing depends, in practice, on translation of any foreign idiom into an idiom (in this case the biblical one) acceptable to the western readership. The very accessibility of Jibran's English writings to a western readership prevents them from being considered as multicultural literature, for it is clear that they intentionally eschew multicultural meanings in their effort to conform to the West's idea of an acculturated East.

Almustafa's pronouncements are dialogic not only in the sense that they supposedly articulate the innermost thoughts of the imaginary people of Orphalese, but in their interface with the sensibilities of a western cultic readership. Throughout *The Prophet* the disclosure of truths either operates within a privatized mode, directed at the pre-articulated responses of the individual reader, or, if concrete social processes are dealt with, such as the production and exchange of goods, these are mystified through the adoption of strings of nebulous signifiers:

> And before you leave the market-place, see that no one
> has gone his way with empty hands.
> For the master spirit of the earth shall not sleep
> peacefully upon the wind till the needs of the least of
> you are satisfied. [33]

Overall, the text is an assemblage of quotable and not so quotable fragments that strain toward universality while, at the deeper structural level, maintaining "a relationship of tension between presence and absence, [...] demanding the reader to reconstruct the forces or contradictions which the text seeks in vain wholly to control or master."[34] Present is the anaesthetizing voice of Almustafa, the new messiah; absent is the world of unrepresentable signifieds, of benumbing complexities – of diverse and competing ideologies, classes, races, nationalities and religions – which the text omits elides or smoothes out, "appearing to provide answers to questions which in reality it evades."[35]

> Vague and nebulous is the beginning of all things,
> but not their end,
> And I fain would have you remember me as a
> beginning.

> Life, and all that lives, is conceived in the mist and
> not in the crystal
> And who knows but a crystal is mist in decay?[36]

The use of the signifiers "mist" and "crystal" raises the symbolist aspect to Jibran. Bushrui says mist symbolizes mystery and eternity; Hawi, that the two terms together "represent the two states of one and the same thing – definite, particular existence, and its dissolution into universal life." [37] In an article on the influence of the Symbolists on Jibran's paintings, his nephew has argued: "For Gibran, the Symbolists' disenchantment with the materialist age and their interest in Eastern thought must have been magnetic." He goes on to propose the key to Jibran's continuing vogue is in his affiliation to Symbolist art and his dual cultural and linguistic background which attracts dissidents from western materialism, such as "those youths who reject the materialistic era and share concern with those same mysteries and exotic hallucinogenic fantasies [as the Symbolists]."[38] One reason for the popular success of *The Prophet* in the West must certainly be that new readers have continued to decode cultic significations from it long after the author's death. Jibran's reworking of the Sufi adage "Truth is one, paths are many" – "Say not 'I have found the truth', but rather, 'I have found a truth [. . .] For the soul walks upon all paths [. . .] unfolds itself, like a lotus of countless petals'" could be accessed to confirm and celebrate the psychedelic tolerance of the acid-taking sixties.[39] Another example of Jibran's creed of "freedom in all things" is Almustafa's sermon "On Pleasure":

> Some of your youth seek pleasure as if it were all, and
> they are judged and rebuked.
>   I would not judge nor rebuke them. I would have
> them seek. For they shall find pleasure , but not her alone;
>   Seven are her sisters, and the least of them is more
> beautiful than pleasure.
> Have you not heard of the man who was digging in
> the earth for roots and found a treasure?[40]

Libertarianism in matters spiritual was the hallmark of American transcendentalism, and Emerson's influence continued to be felt within cultic circles in the early decades of the twentieth century (even in a brothel, man was moving up towards higher things). Rihani too imitates Emerson in his essay "The Mysticism of Reality": "Why, even the most degenerate of beings is a vital link in the chain of social and spiritual possibilities."[41]

Certainly, "the unprecedented success of *The Prophet* is not an unexplainable mystery or an accident." But it is doubtful that it is satisfactorily accounted for by Jibran's Symbolist interests or his dubious "duality of cultural and linguistic background" – his Arab origins having become submerged by the time *The Prophet* was written.[42] The material and cultural conditions which helped produce the text, especially the vogue for the oriental among bohemian cultic circles in America in the early 1900s, and the new social and economic possibilities opened by an age of rapid modernization, are absent or sublimated in a way that they are present and specifically foregrounded in *The Book of Khalid*. By mixing an anti-materialist transcendentalism with a gratifying individualism and wrapping it in an "oriental" biblical idiom, Jibran managed to produce the twentieth-century's most successful piece of consumerist "spiritual" writing.

Conclusion

Absent from Khalil Jibran's later discourse are not merely concrete social situations and categorizable psychological processes, but the Arab identity which was at least to be found in his early Arabic writings. Even in those, Jibran's criticism of humanity stops at the general level of "a kind of metaphysical melancholy",[43] and avoids such questions of difference as the tension between East and West, Arab and Occidental, to be found in the writings of other contemporary Arab authors. Of Badawi's list of themes treated by modern Arabic writers, "polarities [of] [. . .] town and country, tradition and modernity, East and West, or Arab and European, freedom and authority, society and the alienated individual", some are touched upon in Jibran's early writings only to be submerged by the time he comes to write *The Prophet*, and have disappeared almost completely from the writings that come after.[44] This dissolution of his Arab identity to accommodate his speech acts to untroubling "universal" norms suitable to be received by a western audience, accounts for the unrooted, almost neutered language of Jibran's English writings. By suppressing all traces of difference which we might expect to find in an Arab writer living in the West, in answering to an acculturated version of the Orient, Jibran, in his nephew's telling phrasing, completed his

> growth from a provincial Arabic writer, speaking of problems limited to
> a particular geographical area, to an American writer of commanding
> English, expressing universal ideas and concerns.[45]

Such a judgment forms part of the case of those who believe that Jibran's literary destination can hardly be considered void of political implications. Jibran is a key figure in the Arab Romanticism of the inter-war period of which Jacques Berque has written "whether submissive or not to those in power, it accommodated itself to a vassalage with respect to the West, under the name of universalism."[46] Or as Eagleton has put it:

> Discourses, sign-systems and signifying practices of all kinds [. . .] produce effects, shape forms of consciousness and unconsciousness, which are closely related to the maintenance or transformation of our existing systems of power.[47]

Jibran's decision to turn his back on the concerns that preoccupied his Arab contemporaries writing in both Arabic and in English, can therefore hardly be accounted for in aesthetic or mystic terms, but has to be seen as a conscious decision to accommodate his discourse to the requirements of an audience that was proximate, and by whom he might be received as a modern "living master."[48]

3

Ameen Rihani: Pan-Arab Imaginings

A land of infinite possibilities, of abundant resources and extensive mineral wealth, commanding from the four points of the compass the Oriental highways of civilization, it will always be, in one way or the other, a field of exploitation for many rival nations, a prey too to political aggression, if the Arabs do not succeed in establishing a strong government based upon justice and reason and the broader principles of humanity.

Ameen Rihani

Our task as Arabs and Palestinians is to pay closer attention to our own national narrative, which is neither an idle aesthetic pursuit nor something that can be continually postponed.

Edward Said [1]

In an era when Britain was the dominant power in the Middle East, it would have been difficult for a fluent English-speaking Arab to travel in the Arabian peninsular without arousing some suspicion. The year of Ameen Rihani's journey to Arabia, 1922–3, followed a watershed in Anglo-Arab relations. The events of the immediate post-war period – "this dreadful story of broken promises and friends abandoned" as Elizabeth Monroe characterized it – left the British fulfilling a cherished ambition of holding (with the exception of French Syria), in the imperialist, Leopold Amery's words, "continuity of territory or of control between Egypt and India."[2]

In Rihani's writings about his travels, the hegemony of the imperial powers over Arab lands is taken as given, but rarely taken for granted. It is sometimes openly contested, as when he writes of the recent history of the McMahon-Sharif Husain agreement and its ramifications up to the "betrayal" of the San Remo Conference, or attacks the British policy of fostering division among the nine petty dependent states around Aden. Equally often, it remains embedded within what an early reviewer dismissed as "a flippant superficiality", as well as in disjunctive statements made under the cover of an oriental mask of self-deprecating naivete or prolixity.[3] The accounts themselves take on a variety of forms and formats, from the Arabic *Muluk al-'Arab*, published in 1926, to the English versions appearing at about the same time in article form in *Asia*, the journal of the New York Asiatic Society, and culminating in three successive volumes, beginning in 1928 with *Ibn Sa'oud of Arabia: His People and His Land*, then *Around The Coasts of Arabia*, and finally *Arabian Peak and Desert: Travels in al-Yaman*.[4]

The choice of English as well as Arabic for the language of these narratives is a natural consequence of Rihani's biculturality. The English versions, particularly the portrait of Ibn Saud, are in part re-renderings of an Arabic original, but the result is an articulation and merging of two discrete Arab narratives – the minority Christian and mainstream Islamic – by the language of the metropolitan colonial power. To the colonial ironies implicit in Rihani's text are joined, in the case of the *Asia* articles, the added ambiguity of the journal's format. The magazine, for which Rihani wrote articles on the Arab scene for well over a decade, is a bland mixture of western cultural hegemonism and popular travelogue, with its juxtaposition of cool cigarette advertisements alongside "anthropological" photographs from the Africa bush or steppes of Asia. Even Rihani in his later articles could not escape occasional lapses into the vacuous journalese of the kind adopted in American film documentary, such as the 1940s and 50s "March of Time" newsreels.

The ambiguity of the texts replicates Rihani's complex intellectual identity: an individual amalgam of Pan-Arab ideals, Christian Lebanese origins, adopted American nationality, and western liberal nostrums, comparable, if by no means identical with, the dual western orientation and Arab nationalism of George Antonius. Both Rihani and Antonius advance a nationalist discourse which, like the thought of the pioneer theorist of Arab nationalism , Sati' al-Husri, remains filiated to western notions. "There is no sense in their work," writes Edward Said of Antonius and the Black radical, C. L. R. James, "of their standing outside the Western cultural tradition, however much they articulate the adversarial experience of colonial and / or non-Western peoples."[5] The same, with certain reservations, could be said of Rihani's writings. His fervent Pan-Arabism did not, however, require the anchorage of British or even American sponsorship, as was the case with Antonius and his compatriot, Edward Atiyah. In fact as a Christian, Rihani's independent identification with the majority Arab interest almost inevitably lays him open to the charge of searching out a security within the broader Arab Muslim community. Elie Kedourie goes so far as to accuse him of embracing a sort of surrogate "Islam without dogmas" in order to exchange the corruption of his native Christian Maronite sect for a new identity provided by the more powerful and confident Muslim majority.[6] This view is mistaken, however, for, as I hope to show, it ignores Rihani's goal of delimiting the borders of Arab consciousness within a larger space than that provided by any single existing Arab narrative.

The Making of a Pan-Arab Narrative

Starting from the general *mahjar* project to revive Arab culture, the balance of Rihani's sense of Arab nationality changed from the cultural to the political as time went on. The cultural radicalism of his early Arabic writings gave way to the political activism of the war period, when he undertook anti-Ottoman propaganda among his fellow Syrians in North America, and later to the Pan-Arabism expressed during his journey to the Arabian peninsular, and in his subsequent agitation, in both America and Lebanon, against the mandates. By the time of the Great War, Rihani's sense of nationality was already not confined to the Syrian nationalism which saw Damascus as its center, nor was he, as Albert Hourani put it, among "the advocates of independent Lebanon [. . .] [who] saw Lebanon as a Mediterranean country linked with western Christendom," although his Lebanese patriotism is as obvious as any of the other *mahjari*.[7] In *The Book of Khalid*, begun around 1907–8 and eventually published in 1911, Rihani had already comprehended Lebanese patriotism into a Pan-Arabist narrative that culminates in Khalid's vision of "a great Arab Empire in the border-land of the Orient and Occident, in this very heart of the world, this Arabia, this Egypt."[8] The text needs to be juxtaposed alongside Rihani's actual meeting with the political and military leader of the Wahhabis, Abdul-Aziz Ibn Saud, in whom Rihani found the living Pan-Arab hero to which the messianic message of his novel was attenuated. Completed a decade before Rihani met Ibn Saud, the book might be considered a first draft of a sort. Rihani's later earnestness about the Pan-Arab cause is presaged in burlesque form in Khalid's career as Sufi visionary and political messiah who promotes inner reform in order to effect an outward expansion of the Arabs into a great empire. *Sartor Resartus's* hazy German transcendentalism is replaced by Rihani's personal brand of Sufi mysticism implanted into a rhetoric of nationhood, that begins in Khalid's native Lebanon, and stretches outward into greater Syria, Egypt, and the Arabian peninsular, the original Arab home.

The first stage, centered on Khalid's hometown of Baalbek, and thrown into relief by his sojourn in New York, focuses on the character's supposed link with the Phoenicians, the ancient Semitic inhabitants of Mediterranean Syria. "A descendent of the ancient Phoenicians" and "this fantastic mystic son of a Phoenician", Khalid invokes the "super-stitious, honest, passionate, energetic" qualities of his ancestors – "my Phoenicians" – traders and perhaps first migrators of the Atlantic ocean – against the modern Syrians – "we, their worthless descendants." The inventions of the West, the enterprise of America, are for Khalid but reincarnations of the spirit of adventure and industry of the Phoenicians.[9] Echoing an argument employed by Muslim Arab reformers, Khalid asserts that the West has enslaved the East by a supe-rior technological know-how once taught the West by the East.[10] But Khalid's Phoenician myth is not used to underwrite a narrow Lebanese nationalism. The Young Turk Revolution thrusts him into the limelight as a political lecturer and causes him to re-form his address to suit the Muslim and Christian audiences who are responsive to the new revo-lutionary conditions. Khalid invokes "founders" and "ancestors", now linking Muslims and Christians together in an appeal to their joint reli-gious heritage. The danger of the moment was to borrow the worst features of the West and exclude the best. "The Mosque and the Church, notwithstanding the ignorance and bigotry they foster, are still better than lunatic asylums. And Europe can not have enough of these." The need was not for just a political revolution; "Ours is in a sense a theo-cratic Government [. . .] only by reforming the religion on which it is based, is political reform in any way possible and enduring."[11] But when Khalid delivers his ambiguous message in the Omayyah Mosque in Damascus, and ends up promoting Wahhabism as the only means of renewing Islam, he is hooted down for his religious "innovation" and "infidelity." What Khalid means by Wahhabism is evidently not the ancient faith of Abdul-Wahhab though. As he makes clear to his American mistress before his appearance at the mosque, the leaven to which he applies this name is in reality the genius of the Arab race itself:

The Turk must go: he will go. But out in those deserts is a race which is always young, a race that never withers; a strong, healthy, keen-eyed, quick-witted race; a fighting, fanatical race; a race that gave Europe a civil-isation, that gave the world a religion; a race with a past as glorious as Rome's; and with a future, too, if we had an Ali or Saladin. But He who made those heroes will make others like them, better, too. He may have made one already, and that one may be wandering now in the desert. Now think what can be done in Arabia, think what the Arabs can accomplish, if American arms and an up-to-date Koran are spread broadcast among them. With my words and your love and influence, in our powers united, we can build an Arab Empire, we can resuscitate the Arab Empire of the past [. . .] Wahhabism is not dead. It is only slumbering in Nejd. We will awake it; arm it; infuse into it the living spirit of the Idea.[12]

Khalid's parting message to the world before his last battle in Baalbek and his flight to the Egyptian desert and obscurity, hearkens back again to the cradle of the Arab race, and indeed of Arab religion. "It is because I will it, nay, because a higher Will than mine wills it, that the spirit of Khalid shall yet flow among your pilgrim caravans, through the fertile deserts of Arabia, down to the fountain-head of Faith, to Mecca and Medina."[13] In this mock heroic, mock-messianic parody, Rihani sets in place the basic ingredients of his Pan-Arab narrative; the myth of the author's native Lebanon, with its imagined Phoenician origins, Mediterranean vistas and Christian "people 'as one'", has encountered the "authentic" Arab narrative, in which the linear historical perspective traces its beginnings to the pre-Islamic tribes of Northern Arabia, and the greatest of all Arabs, the Prophet of Islam, is the founder of his people and the *umma* presents its unassailable claim of "cultural supremacy and historical priority."[14] Within this new cultural space Christians and Muslims could live as one. It was with this essential message that Rihani set out for the Arabian peninsular for the first time in 1922.

Pan-Arabist Traveller

> "I was told that the Ustaz (he meant me) is a spy for the British
> Government."
> "That may be."
> "Our rulers are, then, being deceived."
> "No one is infallible."
> "I heard also that he is in the service of King Husein."
> "That may be."
> "Are you going to Jaizan?"
> "*Inshallah.*" [15]

In Amin Rihani's report of his dialogue with "a man from Hadhramaut", two Arabic speakers meet on board ship en route to Jaizan in Asir, on the south western coast of the Arabian peninsular. Their short conversation encapsulates the different levels of ambiguity beneath Rihani's journeys in Arabia. Though a few paragraphs earlier he refers to his "anti-English" reputation, his interlocutor takes him to be a British spy and an agent of King Husain of the Hijaz. Rihani's cryptic replies seem to parry perfectly the charges of the would-be agent provocateur, whose own identity Rihani tells us soon afterwards is even more dubious than his, the Lebanese American's. He responds to his inquisitor's innuendo by playing on the man's evident taste for disguise and deceit. The discourse epitomizes the claustrophobic atmosphere of

Arabia following on the upheavals of the end of the Great War. Embedded in the conversation is an implicit understanding on the part of both speakers of the semantics of hidden treaties, obscure identities and double entendre, of local animosities acted out in a theater managed by the colonial impresario where anyone could be working for anyone. In one of his lectures in the United States, Rihani later contended that "the Arabs were obsessed with the nefariousness of British policy," and claimed that he had had "personal experience of this feeling, for many times [during his journey] he was suspected of being a representative of the British government." As for King Husain, Rihani had agreed to negotiate a treaty with the Idrisi of Asir (as well as with the Imam Yahya of Yeman), "only to have both treaties rejected by Hussein" because they did not recognize him under the rubric "King of the Arabs."[16]

In spite of, or perhaps because of this, Rihani determined to travel to Arabia as himself, strictly dispensing with the strategy of disguise adopted by the western travelers who had gone before him: men like Burkhardt, Palgrave, Burton and Doughty, all of whom he had read in the New York Public Library, and who had helped his "discovery of his Arabness in the distant West."[17] There would be that one essential difference between him, them, and the "Orientalist-as-agent", through whom, as Edward Said has written with due irony, "the Orient was made to enter history." The difference was race: an Arab could hardly have written, as T. E. Lawrence, "I meant to make a new nation," or as Lord Cromer: "I was talking to Crewe the other day at the Turf Club and he agreed with me that a few officers who could speak Arabic, if sent into Arabia, could raise the whole country against the Turk."[18] However, the terrain taken by the colonizer could also be reclaimed in the name of the colonized, and Rihani could adopt an idiom as markedly postcolonial as any "Third World" nationalist of the era of decolonization: "Arabism brings us together, Arabism unites us. Arabism it is which creates that strength which the Europeans respect, a strength which can never be defeated or brought low."[19] But more usually the tone is tongue-in-cheek, appropriately knowing, as in this passage describing his state of mind as he crossed between Egypt and Jeddah en route to meet the Arab kings:

> I was a traveller, a pious and believing traveller; and, with all the willingness in the world, I was ready to believe that the Red Sea for instance was at one time as red as carmine, and that East of Suez is, even in our day of grace, a moral murk, an absymal continent. For not only Orientals delight in romancing, be it remembered.[20]

(Here "the flippant superficiality [that] mars some really fine descrip-

tive passages" is on show.) On the other side of the coin was the matter
of Rihani the naturalized American. Along with the majority of Syrian
Arab immigrants in America his attitude towards his adopted country
involved him in playing up loyalty to the American flag. During the
Great War the Syro-Lebanese were able to harness their desire to appear
good American patriots to their virulent anti-Ottomanism. Rihani was
the vice-President of the Syria-Mount Lebanon League of Liberation,
and Khalil Jibran and Mikhail Naimy its secretaries. Rihani wrote to
Teddy Roosevelt on American entry into the war claiming this filled him
with joy and that he had never been so proud of being an American
citizen. He went on to offer his services, outlined his activities encouraging Syrians to enlist, and concluded: "Our first duty is toward our
adopted country, whose flag we honor, whose democratic principles we
uphold, whose political ideals will yet be the ideals of every nation in
the world."[21]

On his travels, Rihani made no effort to disguise his American citizenship, and this may have been because there was no need to. Irfan
Shahid notes the positive if generally amorphous profile the United
States held in the Middle East between the wars as an anti-imperialist
power, and, after Woodrow Wilson's declaration on the subject, as a
sponsor of national self-determination. The abortive King–Crane
Commission, sent to the region in 1919, at least gained for the United
States, momentarily, a higher profile among the Arabs than the old colonial powers. Rihani was able to represent his mission in a letter to
undersecretary of state Henry P. Fletcher as undertaken by a friend of
Islam and of Arabia "who desires to see her go forward hand in hand
with European civilization."

There was also the aim of bringing about greater understanding
between East and West – that foundation *mahjar* project had not been
relinquished, and Shahid is right to point out that at this stage Rihani's
"self-image" engaged himself as "the apostle of the new relationship
[. . .] the interpreter of the Arabs and Islam to the West, especially
America, and vice versa."[22] In an era when the space between competing
communities and nationalisms was not as narrow as it is now, Rihani
could still show himself at one and the same time as an Arab patriot and
an unofficial emissary of the United States, as can be seen in his activities in Mexico in 1917 promoting the cause of the Allies against the
Central Powers, specifically Turkey.

Throughout his journeys, Rihani projected the persona of the man of
good will, ready to promote the cause of Arab unity in whatever way
he could. King Husain responded to his Lebanese-American guest by
inviting the Syrians of America to come to live and trade in al-Hijaz
where they would be happy and help build "an Arab kingdom based

upon Arab unity."[23] In Sanaa, Rihani raised the topic of Pan-Arabism in his first meeting with the Imam Yahya, only to be rebuffed on the score of religion. Rihani replied:

> But race unites [. . .] and religion separates. The Christian of Syria is an Arab like the Muslem [sic], and this nationality is destined to unite firmly the two and keep them united. Religion separates the Syrian Christians from you, but the feeling of race will bring them back, is bringing them back to you.[24]

En route to Najd, he had to run the gauntlet of the British, who at first would not let him see Ibn Saud, sending him on to Baghdad instead. "In their political friendships, the British are extremely jealous. When they have a friend among the native rulers they are careful to keep him their own, and they carefully guard all access to him."[25] But although British officialdom made difficult Rihani's visits to the kings of Arabia he was never slow to win allies to his side where possible. In Baghdad he enlisted Gertrude Bell to plead his cause. No doubt the British too believed Rihani to be an agent of some sort, but he ended up offering to help mediate in the border dispute between Iraq and Najd, imploring the British High Commissioner, Sir Percy Cox: "Take me with you, [. . .] to Ibn Sa'oud and I'll serve you in what I can, in so far as you will permit, without any charge to you or the British Government." Not for the last time, we catch a note of self-parody beneath the surface naivete, as Rihani reports Cox's reaction: "He laughed and said something which I did not hear." In Najd at last, Rihani raised the issue of Pan-Arabism again, to be told by Ibn Saud:

> "Who are the Arabs? [. . .] I know them all [. . .] I have to be aware of my own people – the nearest to me. Treachery we have discovered among the closest of our allies. Let us not muddle our head with fine fantasies."[26]

But Rihani persisted in his efforts and was back in Arabia in December 1924 at the climax of the struggle for the Hijaz, fruitlessly endeavoring to reconcile Ibn Saud with Husain's son Ali, who had succeeded to the throne after his father's forced abdication and was held up in Jeddah before the besieging Wahhabis. He told the British consul in Jeddah:

> I am not inimical to European influence in the East, nor to English influence in Arabia. But I think it is a shame that the Allies, particularly England and France, who needed the Arabs during the war and were ready to take any treaty with them, should now abandon them and stand arms folded watching them slaughter each other.[27]

Neither, when it came to outlining succinctly the forces aligned against the Pan-Arab cause, was Rihani under any illusions. Foremost was the "secret diplomacy" of Britain and France. The Sykes-Picot agreement "was a fatal blow to Pan-Arab aspirations." On this he is even more scathing than Antonius: "Monsieur Georges Picot and Sir Mark Sykes completed their nefarious scheme of dividing Syria and Palestine into political and economic zones – blue and red and brown zones, which are all to-day, considering the national interests, black zones of despair."[28] As for British influence over the Arabian peninsular after the war, Rihani noted in a report to the American Government that Britain had pledged to assist the Arabs in forming a united state or confederation but would only do so if two or more of the Arab rulers asked for this:

> Which is almost impossible to-day; for if they agree to ask for England's assistance and appoint her as arbitor [sic] among them and she accepts, the Pan-Arab dream will be half-realized. But most of them have no faith in England: her policy in Arabia is never consistent. Whether her intentions are good or bad, the result is always the same. Her favor or her assistance is seldom if ever equally shared by all the rulers at once. It moves from one amir to another, and thus creates suspicion , discord, hostility. She is safe, therefore, in promising to help to establish a United States of Arabia, if all the Arab rulers ask for her help. She is not ignorant of the real situation, – division and discord everywhere, – for which she is partly responsible.[29]

This was only half the story though. There was also the matter of the Arab rulers. The Arabian peninsular proper was left out of the Anglo-French deception, but it was here that the Arab cause was weakened by an Arab – King Husain of the Hijaz – who in his preoccupation with Syria and Palestine, which he hoped to rule himself, lost sight of the foundations of the Pan-Arab dream which were in Najd and Al-Yaman and Asir. In failing to put down the rebellious bedouin tribes and to make common cause with the other Arab rulers in the peninsular, Husain lost the moral and political credibility to speak for the Arab cause. Ultimately, "Hussein's pan-Arab dream was unsuccessful because he was not able to win the other [Arab] rulers to him."[30] Husain's rule in the Hijaz has become the butt of easy ridicule. Reader Bullard, British first consul in Jeddah between 1923 and 1925, sent home letters and reports which abound with damning tidbits illustrating Husain's vanity and venality as seen in his exploitation of the pilgrims to Mecca, his blocking of British-led efforts to build an effective system of quarantine and regulations for pilgrim safety, and his inability to curb the excesses of the Hijazi guides and bedouins who preyed upon the pilgrim caravans. Rihani's account is knowing about all this without entirely exonerating the British, whom he pointed out also had a finan-cial interest in the pilgrimage, and, may have suspected, had an interest in deconstructing the credibility of their one-time ally. Bullard and Rihani present parallel readings of Husain, which diverge chiefly in their respective colonial and Pan-Arab encodings. No champion of the Hashimites, Rihani was nevertheless more alive to the ambiguities at the heart of Husain's multiple roles as standard-bearer of the cause of Arab independence, descendant of the Prophet and would-be caliph of Islam, and ruler of the Hijaz:

> He is, of all Arab Kings, the most kingly, if not also the most spiritual and the least clannish. Nor is this strange. For he is a descendant of the Prophet and he has lived twenty years in Constantinople. His charming person-ality, therefore, has two sources, innate and acquired – the Prophetic and diplomatic.[31]

But Rihani's chief criterion remains the Pan-Arab dimension: in spite of helping "the cause before he became King of the Hijaz [. . .] [Husain] would not [. . .] face the facts"; he refused to conciliate the other Arab leaders, chief among them his enemy Ibn Saud, and in the end "his self-delusion was sublime."[32] Husain was just too simple and unsophisticated in his logic in holding to the letter of the McMahon agreement entered into under the duress of war, and unscrupulous in his use of religion for political ends. For the colonialist Bullard, Husain stood for the despotic oriental ruler who refused British tutelage. Rihani though, assesses the King with characteristic detachment, abrogating the partial reading of the colonizer to see straight into the "human tragedy" of the man:

> King Husain was the most imposing personality among the Arab kings of his time as well as the oldest of them in age and the highest in religious rank. He was also the most devious in his political methods, the weakest in real authority, and the greatest in cares and sorrows.[33]

According to Rihani, he left the Hijaz with Husain's promise to cede his own claims of leadership in order to establish "a united Arabia, an Arab empire." To this end, he set out "in my national mission, seeking to pave the way for an understanding between His Majesty and the other ruling princes of Arabia."[34] There seems to have been nothing disingenuous in this – he did visit in turn the Imam Idrisi in Asir, the Imam Yahya in Yemen, as well as taking in the protectorates of Aden and the Gulf

Coast, before his final encounter with an Arab leader: Sultan Abdul-Aziz Ibn Saud of Najd. This fateful meeting made King Husain's parting speech nugatory, for Rihani at once came to the same conclusion as most of the other westerners who had met the two monarchs: Ibn Saud was not only the more impressive figure, he clearly also possessed the political acumen the King of the Hijaz patently lacked. Rihani wrote:

> I have now met all the Kings of Arabia and I find no one among them bigger than this man [. . .] I came to Ibn Sa'oud with an unburdened heart, bearing him neither hatred nor love, accepting neither the English view of him nor that of the Sherifs of Al-Hijaz. I came to him in fact with a hard heart and a critical mind, and I can say that he captured my heart at the first meeting [. . .] I have now a gallery of Kings for comparison [. . .] And I am glad I came last to Ibn Sa'oud.[35]

Pan-Arab Hero

Looking back from a decade or so later, Rihani drew what was by then the obvious conclusion: the eclipse of the Hashimites, Idrisis, and Rashidis, made Ibn Saud undisputed leader in the Arabian peninsular. But his increased prominence did not go unchallenged, especially given its Wahhabi base. The King had told Rihani during his visit that he "would accept the kingship of all Arabia," might join an Arab federation, but could not "accept the leadership of others."[36] In a lecture he gave in America in 1930, playing to an audience which would have had little sympathy with old imperialism British-style, and could hardly have understood Ibn Saud's loyalty to his western ally, Rihani identified the Saudi monarch as a potential threat to British interests:

> The great political dream of Ibn Saoud is now the great political problem of the British Government. Pan-Arabia, under his leadership, is fast becoming a reality. Two thirds of the Arabian peninsular are now under his control. But he avoids the pitfall that was fatal to ex-King Hussein; he does not call himself King of All the Arabs, but King of the Hejaz and Nejd and its Dependencies.[37]

For the Arab-American proponent of Pan-Arabism, whatever the niceties of his diplomacy, Abdul-Aziz Ibn Saud was nothing less than the Pan-Arab Idea on camel-back. The Saudi monarch had naturally taken over from King Husain the baton of Pan-Arab hopes – he had been "destined not only to grow steadily in power but in time to draw to himself as a magnet all the hopes fostered by the independently organized pan-Arab movement."[38] The key word was *independent*, for by the time he had got to know Ibn Saud, Rihani was well aware of the control the British exercised in the Arabian peninsular. Rihani met Ibn Saud, then the Sultan of Najd, for the first time at the Conference of Uqair in December 1922. The conference was a key moment in the evolution of the future Saudi Arabia, with Ibn Saud on the verge of breaking out of Najd and uniting with the Hijaz, but in so doing, in danger of causing a rift with the British, who had called the conference out of concern for the raiding activities of Ibn Saud's Ikhwan fighters across the border into Iraq. The conference was also of significance in the later development of Saudi Arabia's oil deposits; here, Rihani's involvement may have been crucial in preventing the British from obtaining control over the country's vast potential oil wealth.[39]

According to Irfan Shahid, Rihani had not heard of the Abdul-Aziz when he started out from the United States but by the end of the conference the two had established a firm friendship, based initially on Rihani's role as translator. His first impression was of "a tall, majestic figure in white and brown, overshadowing, overwhelming." The camp at the conference was divided into two sections, the Sultan's and his men on one side while on the other were the "British High Commissioner and the delegates of the Iraq Government. The first section was Arab, the second European: in the first we sat on the ground and drank coffee, in the second they sat at tables and ate with knives and forks." At the evening dinner held under a marquis in the desert, Rihani could not resist making a statement about his Arab identity: the British, and the Iraqi delegate wore dinner jackets; he was accoutered in Arab gear alongside his new hero. After dinner the two "strolled together [. . .], barefoot on the sand, [. . .] under the brilliant stars that seemed to come so near to us with their light of assurance and peace. There was of a certainty, something more than clothes and language that drew me to this man."[40]

More than thirty years later, after Ibn Saud's death, Philby wrote in his one volume history of Saudi Arabia: "a brilliant chapter in the history of the Arabs [is closed]; second in importance, perhaps, only to the Meccan episode of the early seventh century [. . .] Like the Prophet Muhammad, 'Abdul-'Aziz ibn Sa'ud was also a man of destiny."[41] Rihani himself is not as direct in his association of the two great Arabs, except, perhaps in its own way as telling, when he sums up the character of Ibn Saud – "a man with a big heart and a big soul – a real, rugged, unaffected Arab" – with epithets clearly borrowed from Carlyle's lecture on the Prophet. According to Carlyle, the Prophet had "a certain directness and rugged vigour," and was "a rough self-helping son of the wilderness; does not pretend to be what he is not."[42] That Rihani should

have adopted the language of the European to foreground key phras-
ings of his Arab narrative might undercut his credentials as an
anti-colonial writer. To speak of his having appropriated Carlyle's
language would be too portentous. The matter of western affiliation
remains, or to be more precise, however deeply layered the archetypes
might be in a more universal sense of epic, the attraction of a hero-
worship derived from western Romantic practices to the would-be
inventor of a new nation. For Rihani, the narrative of the Arab people
could be rewritten – for the westerner at least – in a borrowed, in part
hybrid language. It would employ notions of "beginning", "first",
"founder", "ancestor", "that which occurred earlier" all key terms in
Bakhtin's description of epic – "valorized temporal categories" corre-
sponding to the "reverent point of view of a descendent" – Rihani
himself.[43] Rihani's imagined Pan-Arab narrative starts out by recognizing the "hybridity of histories" and proceeds to reconcile the
Levantine periphery to the desert center, with Rihani himself the sophisticated Arab-American who is brought back to the Arab homeland to
discover the cradle of his race.[44] Here he has the fortune to come across
in person the archetypal Arab, the founder of his people – that is Abdul-
Aziz Ibn Saud. This explains the something more than clothes and
language which drew Rihani to the man.

To suggest, then, as Kedourie does, that Rihani was content to relin-
quish his Christian background, and indeed allow himself to be
patronized by Ibn Saud, for the sake of allying himself with the Islamic
Arab mainstream, is clearly a misreading of Rihani's purpose. However
much his potency as a leader of the Pan-Arab cause may have been
misjudged by Rihani, the Saudi monarch is valorized in Rihani's
discourse for his qualities as believing, dynamic, desert Arab leader; and
descendant by faith of the greatest archetype of the Arab race.[45] The
correlation is underscored in Ibn Saud's own words as reported by
Rihani: "I am responsible before Allah for them all [. . .] We the people
of Najd follow the Prophet, who recognized no differences in rank
among Muslems[sic]. And we would preserve, above all things, our religion and our honor . . . " And also in Rihani's own words:

> the Sultan Abd'ul Aziz is a Cromwell [again the validation from Carlyle
> and his chief hero] in the sense that he has made these people and fired
> them with inextinguishable enthusiasm for Allah and Najd [. . .] It is their
> faith, a living, glowing, flaming faith, which makes the blood of a brother
> fallen in battle sacred in their eyes.

But, as fits a nation's hero, Ibn Saud is set apart from all others, exalted
above his people – or at least the inhabitants of Riyadh. According to

Rihani, the Arab leader confided in him his feeling that he was "a stranger in his own Capital [. . .] Between them and himself there is no contact of mind or heart, not even of soul [. . .] He would not live in Ar-Riyadh a single day were he not the ruler of the country. He is, in truth, far above the ablest and the best: – a palm tree in a field of stubble – a lone pine in a wadi of brambles and thorns."[46]

In addition, underscoring the modernism comprehended in Rihani's brand of Pan-Arab narrative, which foregrounded not only the archaic and traditional, Ibn Saud represented progress, slow, but judicious. At Uqair: "Pointing to the British camp which they were approaching at a leisurely pace, Ibn Saoud said, 'Even though we walk slowly we are approaching civilization. Civilization is not going to run away from us.'" Ibn Saud's act of uniting the bedouin tribes under single leadership, and luring some of them into urban locations, meant the Arab national narrative was being inscribed both in terms of a mythology of the past, and a modernizing future.[47] Rihani might have endorsed John Glubb's view that the Saudi monarch would have risen to the highest political office in which ever country he had been placed, but what mattered to him, as an Arab nationalist, was that Arab race, the Arabian desert, and the Arabic language had made his hero what he was. The following fragment of a narrative describing one of Rihani's journeys with Ibn Saud typifies the magnetism the hero, the language, and the believing people held for the Christian secular Arab nationalist:

> The King then spoke, and the *imam*, or chaplain, took a book out of his saddlebags, opened it and began to read in measured accents. His voice was not , I must admit, particularly appealing; a good voice is rare among the Wahhabis of Nejd. Nevertheless, as this imam chanted his lines, he cast his spell even upon one who does not share the Moslem's creed. I was, in sooth, bewitched, not by the meaning – too often the words were meaningless or without any spiritual significance to me – but by the rhythmic splendor and the musical charm of the Arabic of the Koran. The intonations, the tonalities and the pauses that gave color, as it were, even to a voice devoid of quality, exercised a rare, ineffable fascination, especially in that desert setting, among the glistening golden dunes and under that dome of calm. Even the camels seem bewitched. Slowly and softly, with cadenced steps and gracefully swaying necks, they contributed to the harmony of the performance.[48]

Conclusion

When Ameen Rihani met Abdul-Aziz Ibn Saud in the Arabian desert in December 1922, it could be said that the Pan-Arab cause, alongside

Rihani's own Pan-Arab narrative, was still in the making. Rihani's personal career in the service of the cause was not terminated by the time his major accounts of his journeys in the Arabian peninsular had all been published by around 1930. He had yet ten more years to live and would continue to use his pen to assess the developments attending the emergence of an Arab nation: the question of Palestine, as one would expect, exercised him especially in his last years. He would not, however, live to see the tortuous courses his beloved cause would take during and after World War II. To compare Rihani's case with a parallel example of postcolonial struggle, the experience of the Irish poet, W. B. Yeats – the latter's disillusionment and bitterness would be spared the Arab patriot, by virtue of the fact of his not being around to witness the débâcle of 1948, or the demise of old-style Pan-Arabism as symbolized by the fall and death of Nuri as-Said ten years later.

But Rihani's contribution to remaking the self-image of the Arab people has perhaps yet to be fully acknowledged. Here Irfan Shahid's judgment repays restatement: Rihani's English writings on Arabia may have been overshadowed by those of T. E. Lawrence and H. St. John Philby, but, allowing for the fact that none of them were professional historians, Rihani's interpretation of Arab and Islamic history was the more perceptive, even though this is to be observed mainly in his Arabic works.[49] I have tried to show in this chapter how, particularly in his English writings, Rihani drew on western sources as well, not specifi- cally to appropriate them to make thorough-going postcolonial meanings, although colonial ironies are not missing from his works, but to enlarge the scope of his narrative and to foreground his heroes – notably Abdul-Aziz Ibn Saud, but also Khalid the fictive Baalbekian. And although Rihani's "imagined community" of the Arab people may itself be derivative of western romantic practices, it does still operate in that space in which, as Edward Said has written, the postcolonial writer is endeavoring to "restore the imprisoned nation to itself [. . .] to achieve solidarities on an essentially imagined basis."[50] That Rihani achieved this aim generously, eschewing the narrowness and divisiveness of much "nativist" writing, may indeed be in part due to his dual identity as Christain Arab and favored American, but it does not detract from the fact that, as Said says of Antonius: "Here at last [. . .] the Arabs, their leaders and warriors and thinkers, can tell their own story."[51]

4

Ameen Rihani: Decolonizing Arabia

> Every race should work for its own improvement without any ill intent towards others, and with the desire to co-operate. If we can co-operate, all to the good; if we cannot, then I say the nation that is more developed, and that has the instruments of progress at her hand, should look upon the weaker nations with a desire to improve them, not to enslave them.
>
> *Ameen Rihani* [1]

Ameen Rihani is sometimes referred to as an early figure in the Arab nationalist movement, usually in the context of discussion of the sectarian origins of the first Arab nationalists. The time may be ripe, however, for a wider assessment of Rihani's political writings. This chapter takes an aspect of his political thought – his statements on the need for Arab independence – and discusses it within the theoretical framework of postcolonialist theory; that is to say, the developing perspective, derived from the study of postcolonial literature, which accepts the reality of imperialism and of the liberation struggles that were its inevitable result, and seeks to build a common terrain which can accommodate the "overlapping histories" of colonizer and colonized viewed in a common light.[2] Such an approach appears to this writer to be a positive concomitant in the cultural realm to late twentieth-century moves toward reconciliation and peace in the world political order. Rihani's work, according to this postcolonial perspective, can be seen to be committed to re-writings of the experience of colonization at several levels. Where the writer sets out to create a new narrative for his people, Rihani can be seen to have made a series of Pan-Arab imaginings that had as their chief aim the uniting of the various traditions of the Arabic-speaking peoples. In addition to re-making the community on the imagined basis of its founders ancestors and modern heroes, Rihani, as political nationalist as well as writer, is a part of that impulse to "reclaim, rename, and reinhabit the land."[3] This activity proceeds within a specific stage of the historical process, in which the emerging Arab nation confronts the intrusive presence of the metro-

politan colonizing powers, and is located in the precise political conditions that obtained during Rihani's maturity, the period 1900 to 1939.[4]

The chapter begins with a brief outline of Ameen Rihani's involvement in Arab affairs during the period 1900–1939. A limited assessment
of the factors that helped toward the shaping of his Arab ideology is
then followed by a discussion of Rihani's ideas and statements on the
main issues concerning the decolonization of Arab lands and assertion
of national rights within the context of the international order of the
inter-War years.

Rihani's Involvement in Arab Affairs: an Overview

Rihani cut his teeth as an Arab radical in the overwhelmingly Christian
Arab emigrant milieu in the United States during the first decade of the
twentieth century. Each community had its own newspaper and leadership; Rihani's rejection of this narrow sectarianism was expressed in
his speech "On Religious Tolerance" delivered to the Maronite Society
in 1900. The negative response this received only strengthened his
resolve; several satirical articles in Arabic written between 1901 and
1904 attacking church authority resulted in his excommunication from
the Maronite Church.[5] Between 1905 and 1910, Rihani turned his energies to the wider forum of political debate, concentrating specifically on
the issue of how to liberate his native Syria from Turkish rule. These
years were passed mostly in his home village of Freike in the Lebanese
mountains, although he also spent time in Cairo where he opened
friendships with some of the chief figures in the intelligentsia, including
the men of letters, Hafiz Ibrahim, Ahmed Shawqi, and Khalil Mutran,
and the Islamic reformer and Chief Mufti, Muhammad Abduh. An
article of this period published in Michael Monahan's magazine,
Papyrus, shows Rihani already alive to the corrupting influence of colonialism on the native elites of the colonized countries. During a visit to
the Abdin palace he noted how well the Turco-Egyptian pashas got on
with the representatives of the British occupation.[6] In 1910 he was back
in New York arranging for the publication of *The Book of Khalid*,
(published in the following year) a novel in English with a Pan-Arab
hero and themes that epitomized the cultural radicalism of the Arab-
American *mahjar* movement.

In 1913, together with Najeeb Diab, Rihani attended the first Arab
Congress in Paris as a representative of the émigré Arabs of America.
At a time when Arab nationalist ideas were fissiparous to say the least,
Rihani already had a developed ideological stance.[7] During the war he
was able to work this out in practice by engaging in anti-Turkish agita-

tion on behalf of the Allies; by writing articles to encourage Syrians to volunteer to fight the Turks, and in 1917, in his capacity as chairman of the Syro-Lebanese committee to encourage enlistment, by traveling to Mexico to further the cause there (a move that resulted in his imprisonment by the Mexican authorities.) As a correspondent for the magazines *Bookman* and *Forum*, both published by *The New York Times*, he wrote key articles explaining to the Americans the contemporary developments in the Middle East, arguing as early as September 1917 against the establishment of a Zionist hegemony in Palestine. So by the end of the Great War, Rihani had a platform on Arab affairs that included the demand for Arab independence, warnings to the European powers against colonization of Arab lands, and the revoking of the Balfour Declaration.

Rihani found the immediate post-War conditions exceedingly propitious for spreading the Pan-Arab cause. With the defeat of Turkey and the collapse of the Ottoman empire, key sections of the Arab intelligentsia and military establishment had come over to the nationalist fold. The success of Arab armies in the Arab Revolt had raised the profile of Arab nationalism as Rihani had predicted in his wartime articles. No doubt emboldened by his own wartime activities, he was keen to engage in representing Arab interests in the councils of peace, and was able to attend several immediate post-War conferences on peace and disarmament in Europe and America in his journalist's capacity. In 1921, he embarked on his fruitful journey in the Arabian peninsular. His unconcealed agenda to promote the cause of Pan-Arabism led him to put himself at the service of each Arab leader in turn as an unofficial diplomatic go-between. He even offered his services to the British on the understanding that he might bring about better understanding between the various parties.[8]

This acquaintance with the colonial presence, which met him at almost every turn, and on more than one occasion threatened to subvert his itinerary, undoubtedly sharpened Rihani's awareness of the obstacles arrayed against his Pan-Arab dream. He had not started his journey in a state of naivete concerning the scope of imperial control in Arab lands; what undoubtedly was confirmed in him was the realization that, if the Arabs' so-called friends were a dubious asset, the need for Arab self-reliance and unity was paramount. In his representation to the West of Arab cultural identities and contemporary development agendas – as foregrounded in his publication of English versions of his Arabian travel narratives – Rihani became increasingly drawn into the political issues of the moment. The panoramic view of his war articles was shortened in the twenties and most of the following decade by the need to address the concrete conditions of the British and French mandates in

Iraq, Palestine, and Syria respectively. Criticism of the disguised imperialism these mandates represented crystallized over two main issues:
the ineptitude of British handling of the Palestine problem, and the
divide-and-rule tactics of France's administration of Syria and Lebanon.
As a counterweight, Rihani may have toyed with the idea of Ibn Saud
becoming Khalif of Islam and, fresh from uniting the Arabian peninsular, joining it with the fertile crescent in an all enveloping Pan-Arab
state. But he also knew too well the limited room for manoeuvre the
British and French had left the Arab rulers.[9] Here Rihani was ready to
invoke his dual nationality and address himself to a western audience
that was principally American. A member of the New York Asiatic
Society since 1918, he contributed frequent articles on the Arab scene to
its publication *Asia* throughout the twenties and thirties, in addition to
occasional features for *Travel* magazine. The extent of his involvement
in Arab affairs of a practical political character was exemplified by his
disagreement with Khalil Gibran over the latter's concern to follow literature exclusively and eschew politics.

On 7 September 1929, Rihani led an Arab-American delegation to
Secretary of State Henry L. Stimson to argue the abandonment of the
project of a Jewish homeland in Palestine in order to secure peace.[10] In
October, Rihani spoke in a public debate with M. W. Weisgal on the
subject of rights of Jews in Palestine. Further public meetings, lectures
and articles on the same topic ensued during the 1930s.[11] In 1932–3,
Rihani visited the newly independent kingdom of Iraq, where his
speech at the agricultural exhibition was broadcast over the radio. Back
in Lebanon, a speech critical of French policy in Syria in which he
compared the French High Commissioner unfavorably with Sultan
Abdul Hamid resulted in Rihani's banishment from his native land. He
went again to Iraq at the invitation of King Ghazi, returning to Lebanon
after pressure was placed on the French Foreign Ministry by Britain and
the United States. Increasingly outspoken in his Arab nationalism,
Rihani also succeeded in antagonizing the Shi'a of Iraq by statements
made in an article about his visit to Kerbala, and the Christian Lebanese
poet, Bishara al-Khoury, whose poetry he attacked for its fatalism and
implied acquiescence in the French occupation of Lebanon and Syria.[12]

In an era when travel between Arab lands was revolutionized, Rihani
was able to take advantage of the motor car to journey between Lebanon
and Iraq when earlier (in 1921) he had needed to go via Bombay and the
Arabian Gulf.[13] If horizons had widened incalculably, petty divisions
had also arisen to obstruct the cause of Arab unity. The drawing up of
political boundaries meant passports were required to cross hitherto
open spaces. The delimitation of particular Arab identities, a ploy of
colonialism in Rihani's eyes (he called the new boundaries the "inven-

tion of the Europeans"[14]) could mean, as he found out on his journeys in Iraq, preventing the bedouin from crossing a few kilometers into Syrian territory to search for water and pasture. But at the time his life was tragically shortened by an accident in 1940, despite the political upheavals in Iraq and the abortive attempts of Syria to throw off the French mandate, Rihani was still optimistic about the prospects for Arab unity. In the late thirties he continued to argue for an Arab federation insisting an Arab United States on the pattern of America was not far off.[15]

Factors Shaping Rihani's Arab Ideology

A full study of Ameen Rihani's politico-cultural ideology is beyond the scope of this paper; what follows is a brief survey of the salient factors behind his anti-colonial and pro-Arab statements.[16] Clearly the wider discourse of Arab nationalism would need to be taken into account in any such discussion; here, however, attention will be paid to analysis of Rihani's positions vis-à-vis the work done on the genesis and development of nationalist ideologies by scholars like Benedict Anderson, Ernest Gellner, and Eric Hobsbawm. First, however, reference can be made to the conventional approach to Arab nationalism of the type that stresses its sectarian and social formation. For example, Rihani's attack on Christian sectarianism and traditionalism in his early writings demonstrates a tendency common to Syrian Christian intellectuals in the period specified by Hisham Sharabi. With their pro-European thinking and detachment from traditional orthodoxies, these intellectuals were "a natural vanguard of change" in the Arab world. However, Rihani's radicalism, though it conforms to that of his fellow Syrian intellectuals in certain respects, is not perhaps as consistently rationalistic, and certainly not as materialistic in its philosophical implications, as the thought of writers like Shibli Shumayyil and Farah Antun.[17] It is noteworthy that the hero of *The Book of Khalid*, although for a while seduced by the blandishments of the "Temple of Atheism", eventually returns to the spiritual wellsprings of the East. What we can say for sure is that Rihani's portrait of Khalid the Lebanese émigré devouring European classics in a New York basement is a description of himself. He told a British audience in 1928: "Even as my spiritual heritage is in the main Oriental, my intellectual heritage is on the whole British, or broadly speaking Anglo-Saxon." Rihani's borrowings from western, predominantly Anglo-Saxon sources undoubtedly helped form his belief in political liberty and re-enforced his native Arab Christian intellectual's individualism, but he was critical of the belief in untrammeled individ-

ualism and freedom which he encountered during his years in the
United States.[18]

Seen in the traditional terms of analysis usually adopted by scholars
of Arab nationalism up to now, Rihani's fervent Pan-Arabism indeed
appears an aberration: the renegade Christian intellectual comes to be
viewed with suspicion on all sides. His Arabism disqualifies him in the
eyes of the Christians, yet, not being a Muslim, he does not belong to the
mainstream, while his counter-narrative to that of western imperialism
makes him suspect in the West too.[19] But if we view Rihani's nationalist
positioning according to the more recent perspectives on the phenomenon of nationalism worked out by the scholars mentioned above, it
escapes this narrow framing and he takes up his rightful place as an
innovator within the early schema of Arab nationalism. Starting from
Ernest Gellner's premise that "Nationalism is not the awakening of
nations to self-consciousness; it invents nations where they did not
exist," we can begin by placing Rihani within the project of inventing
the Arab nation.[20] Here mythic and modernizing constituents coalesce:
we are observing "the element of artefact, invention and social engi-
neering which enters into the making of nations." Rihani may be seen
to have assisted at the merging of two of the stages in the development
of nationalism proposed by Hobsbawm; that is, when the cultural,
literary and folkloric ingredients, having been articulated by scholars
and enthusiasts, cross into the beginnings of the political campaign for
the "national idea." Here Rihani emerges as both myth-maker and
modernizer: at the myth-making necessary to the creation of an imagined Arab nation he was an adept, but this should not obscure the fact
that his Arabism is reared on an understanding of the technocratic and
political exigencies of the new world order. Arabs must be empowered
to participate in this new reality, and to prepare them to do so, the necessary educational and political structures must be put in place, since
training "can only be provided by something resembling a modern
'national' education system." Rihani's call for a Pan-Arab polity above
all recognizes the functional need for a modern nation to emerge from
the ashes of the Ottoman empire, or, in Gellner's words, "it is *the objective need* for homogeneity which is reflected in nationalism."[21]

Rihani understood that such an Arab polity, whilst allowing for and
nurturing the past religious traditions of the Arab peoples, must be a
secular entity built around the solidarity of language and race. In this,
as a Christian Arab, he is at one with Sati' al-Husri, a Muslim Arab. Both
see the need "to articulate a doctrine of Arab nationalism and Arab unity
based on completely secular bonds of loyalty to and identification with
the concept of an Arab nation." Indeed, al-Husri's activities in Iraq as a
practical educator for Arab consciousness won Rihani's unqualified

praise.[22] Rihani, while alive to the emotive factors deriving from a love of Arabic culture and heroes, has as his primary urge as a nationalist the desire to see the Arabs take their place alongside the politically and technologically more advanced nations of the West. And while, as we shall see, he sympathized with the Islamic modernizers in their similar aims, he adjudged secularism to be the more effective means of reaching the goals of national unity and development.[23]

Out of Rihani's recognition of the necessity of building a strong independent Arab nation to operate and cooperate within the twentieth-century world of advanced nation-states, grew his assertion of the need to end colonialism and the hegemony of the dominant metropolitan powers. In this, he was in accord with the anti-imperialist spirit found pervasively at the close of the Great War. As Hobsbawm points out, this was associated, with the triumph of the "principle of nationality." The multi-national empires had collapsed and Bolshevism had arisen to challenge the western powers. In this situation the democracies saw the necessity of playing the "Wilsonian card" to try to win the allegiance of the smaller or less powerful emerging nations.[24] National self-determination, democracy and anti-imperialism were the demands of the day, even if the old European imperial powers had endeavored to smother the independence aspirations of the nations of the Near East at Versailles. This did not discourage Rihani, as it did anti-imperialists and pro-Arab westerners like Arnold Toynbee with whom it might seem natural to compare him. Rihani took a longer view, his convictions, it can be argued, being more profound than those of the liberal Europeans whom he mistrusted anyway.[25]

To summarize: the traditional assessments of early Arab nationalism that stress sectarian criteria fail to address the actual exigencies upon which that nationalism, like any other, would have to be built. The issue of whether Christians or Muslim reformers were the originators of Arab nationalism obscures the objective needs nationalism was intended to fulfill. Here, the contribution of the Arab-American, far from being aberrant or idiosyncratic, represented a comprehensive awareness of and answer to the demands of modern conditions upon the Arabs. In his dual project of imagining an Arab nation and mapping out its future needs, Rihani combines the myth-making and modernizing elements that recent theoretical study recognizes as part and parcel of the development of a nationalist ideology. And as a natural concomitant to this nationalism, his anti-colonial stance, both in respect of his early anti-Ottomanism, and later opposition to the encroachments of the mandates and of Zionism, completes Rihani's ideological response to the precise set of conditions confronting the Arab nation during the period specified.

Rihani on Arab Liberation

From one perspective, Rihani's involvement in Arab affairs can be seen as a continuous agitation against non-Arab hegemony over Arab lands. Though conducted in a spirit devoid of narrow partisanship, this activism was from the first committed and uncompromising. Where others came to Arab nationalism only after working through Ottomanism – or indeed never arrived there at all due to commitment to some particularism or other – Rihani's nationalist program was clearly developed from an early stage. It is evident in *The Book of Khalid* alongside a satirical treatment of the Young Turk Revolution of 1908–9. As a delegate to the First Arab Congress in Paris he already had a record of opposing Ottoman suzerainty over Arab lands. If we except the al-Fatat group, who according to Rihani's later gloss, were working at this time "for the liberation of Arabia from Turkish or any other foreign rule," his outright anti-Ottomanism would certainly have placed him in an avant-garde position vis-à-vis the other representatives at the conference.[26] As regards the question of Zionist activity in Palestine, Rihani was among the first Arab voices alerting the West to the dangers of creating a bitter future antagonism in that land, raising the issue with Theodore Roosevelt in 1917 and publishing the article "The Holy Land: Whose to Have and to Hold" in *Bookman* in September of that same year. This article, together with several others, form a major statement on Arab affairs toward the close of the Great War, which Rihani collected in the unpublished manuscript entitled "Turkey and Islam in the War".[27]

Here Rihani is writing for a western audience. In particular, the early pieces which treat the issue of the Arab revolt against Turkey are written in a vivid and heightened style in which a bitter attack on the record of the Ottoman empire is foregrounded. Indeed its anti-Turkish rhetoric probably needs to be viewed in the context of the executions of Arab leaders and notables carried out in Damascus and Beirut by Jamal Pasha in 1915 and 1916. Rihani charges the Turks with all variety of moral turpitude and a whole catalogue of policy failings, his aim clearly being to demolish any remaining credibility that might attach to the Ottoman empire as a cohesive unit. The Turks themselves, he is at pains to emphasize, were "responsible for the unbending antagonism of the Arabic-speaking people." To effect and complete the ideological separation of Arabism from Ottomanism Rihani recognized the centrality of the issue of Islam. Turkey has not only corrupted Islam, but, in the form of the Young Turks, who are atheists and skeptics at heart, effectively repudiated it. In proclaiming jihad against the Allies, the Ottoman Sultan did not have at heart the interests of Islam, and the only power this would benefit would be the Kaiser's Germany.[28]

For "the great nation of the Koran," Rihani reads the combined Arab peoples. The Turks had forfeited any right they ever had to speak in the name of Islam, and the notion that Morrocans and Indians could ever be embraced by a common Islamic political unit was an illusion. The Khalifate should be returned to the Arabs, whether to the Khedive of Egypt or the Sherif of Makkah. But his main fear was the direction Islam might take within the Arab lands. Here he was undoubtedly in favor of the reformers whom he identified with the progressive tendency: "their worldly ambition is to be abreast of the times with the Europeans and to become their equals. They are the torch-bearers of Islam." However, the danger was that the intervention of Europe – which was already in process – would strengthen the "passion of fanaticism", and fan "a conflagration" that would destroy the hopes of the educational and reform movement. In fact, the suspicion of Europe which was strong enough to keep the Arabs within the Ottoman fold for so long is well understood by Rihani even as he adjures the Europeans to help foster reform and desist from meddling in the politics of the region – a mostly forlorn hope as he well knew.[29]

Out of the confrontation with the Turkish empire, Rihani sees the future of Arabia emerging in struggle with a neo-imperialism, that of the western powers. "Turkey and Islam in the War" is therefore both a celebration of "the Arab awakening" and a warning to the West to support rather than distort Arab independence, if only for the sake of the West's own interests. A general process of revolution was spreading across the Orient, a revolution that would destroy the old backward customs and empower the nations of the East. "The sleepy-eyed Oriental" having woken from centuries of sleep no longer feared "the sinister spectre of Europe." Beneficiary of "the light of freedom and modern science," he would, "in spite of Europe," "overthrow his despotic government himself," and reform his social and "domestic life" of its "degrading customs and cants." Although Rihani knew that "in these days no European nation or Government will interest itself in any country or people unless for the purpose of exploitation," and the United States' newfound enthusiasm for national self-determination could as easily revert to her pre-war expansionism, it still seemed worthwhile to him to outline an international order in which colonialism and exploitative hegemony of one nation or nations over the rest would be replaced by the urge for mutual cooperation and liberty.[30]

As the significance of Turkey evaporated following her defeat, the other elements in "Turkey and Islam in the War" moved center stage. What would be the role assigned to the Arabs in the post-war settlement? How would the energies released by the Arab Revolt be channeled and – as Rihani already implicitly understood – contained by European imperialism. For a while these issues were allowed to fall into relief as he undertook his journeys in the Arab peninsular. These travels in turn provided him with the experience of high-level contacts with Arab leaders and first hand observation of Arab lands on which to base his later articles on the Arab scene. In addition, they opened the second stage of his ideological interface with imperialism. The impact of the British presence in Arabia after the Great War could hardly be missed by anyone, least of all by someone as sensitive to the nuances of the Great Game as Rihani. In terms of his own discourse on the topic of imperialism, this new stage marks a departure from the racial rhetoric of his anti-Ottomanism to a more deft, insouciant register that inscribes the new colonial presence by means of ambiguous asides, satirical cameos of British imperial agents and ostensibly detached political commentary. (On the other hand, Rihani's early writings were not bereft of the same qualities: he was capable of switching idioms at almost any moment in his writing career.)

The ironic tone is to be found in each work of the Arabian trilogy, but is especially pointed in *Arabian Peak and Desert: Travels in Al-Yaman*. The visit to Yemen was probably the least successful one Rihani made during his Arabian itinerary. To begin with, the Imam Yahya had been misinformed about his guest, and Rihani's letter of introduction from King Husain having omitted to mention him by name, meant he had to endure ten days of house arrest. The journey to Sanaa had been hazardous; in Aden, the British, believing him to be a spy or agitator of some sort, had presented every obstacle they could to prevent him actually getting into Yemen. "No, they would not let us make a step, the British authorities, without assuring themselves that it was safe for us to do so. They even did us the honour of having us shadowed in Arabia." There were also frightening moments when Rihani's personal safety would have been at risk if it had become known he was a Christian. He had little sympathy for the exclusivity of the Zaidi sect or the authoritarianism and political violence endemic to the country at that time. Here, if at any moment on his travels, Rihani might have felt himself entitled to switch into the superior register of the Orientalist, record the backwardness of the *bedu* and the hopeless recidivism of the local political culture, and virtually invite the healing ministrations of the British. But this would have been to suppress the inner duality that supplied the leitmotif for his entire Pan-Arab enterprise. Westernizer pure and simple he could never have been. Though he did promote the notion that King Husain of the Hijaz and the British might help modernize the country, and strongly advocated the need for education and development agencies to be set in place, the idea of diminishing

Arab sovereignty – even in so apparently dire a case – was foreign to him a priori. The passion behind his fervent attachment to Arab independence surfaces in his report of his own expostulation, addressed in a "moment of anger" ostensibly to the Sultan of Lahaj, who had promised an escort for Rihani to the Yemeni border. " 'And what do we want with the English? [. . .] We are satisfied with Arab protection, and if we are killed on the way, it will be for the love of the Arabs.'"[31] This to an ally of the British!

Among the *bedu*, he found elements who because they opposed the Imam had allied themselves with the British – "'The English are a necessity, ya Ameen [. . .] Of a truth, the Muslems are brothers, and the Ingliz are not Muslems: but the heart knoweth the brother ya Ameen, and the political interest knoweth only the necessity.'" Rihani makes no judgment; the embedded meaning is that Arab individualism and pride are proof against servitude to any imperial ruler, Turk or Briton.[32] Nor is there ridicule *de haute en bas* towards the diverse responses of pro-and anti-Imam *bedu* on seeing British airplanes overhead:

"the bombing planes are the winged heralds of victory – [. . .] send us some of them." "We are not afraid of the taiyarah [. . .] we will read the opening chapter (of the Koran) against it and it will fall to the ground in pieces."

Rihani's project was not to direct the recording lens and stand back in detachment: in Sanaa he did all he could to reconcile the Imam to his enemies on the principle that unity among Arabs was the solution to political alliances made with the colonizer. That achieved, good relations between Arabia and Europe might follow. As it was, the Imam Yahya appears at least to have been won over by his visitor's sincerity – "'You are of us now'" were his parting words to Rihani.[33]

Rihani's journeys in the Arabian peninsular encouraged him to try his skills further at mediating Arab disputes. He appeared to possess the necessary impartiality in Arab eyes, though his practical successes were few and far between. An advocate of the political project of Abdul-Aziz Ibn Saud, he nevertheless attempted mediation in the dispute between the Sultan of Najd and the embattled Hashimite Kingdom of Hijaz, and in Palestine between the ambitious Haj Amin al-Husaini and his opponents. In the next decade (1930s), Rihani returned to Iraq where he had briefly been present at the beginnings of the rule of King Faisal. Up to then no warm admirer of the Hashimites, he became, on his 1932–3 visit, not a belated convert to the Hashimite cause, but a strong supporter of Iraq as a newly independent Arab state that might form the nexus of an Arab federation in the fertile crescent and then throughout

Arabia. In giving his backing to the Iraqi experiment he was not identifying himself with a specific regime, warmly though he regarded its
leading light, Nuri as-Said, with whom he shared comparable aspirations toward an Arab federation, and in spite of the charges of Iraqi
opposition politicians. Rather he proffered his instinctive and active
good offices to strengthen an Arab polity that he believed might establish the necessary roots to survive. His lack of partisanship might be
considered naive, and his fulsome praises were certainly – probably
willfully – misconstrued by those who lacked his open spirit. King
Faisal, during his lifetime and since, has been blamed both for opposing
and acquiescing in the manipulation of Iraq by the British, and for laying
the foundations for its chronic political instability throughout its
Hashimite period. Rihani understood Faisal's dilemma better than
most, assessing the issues and players in this late colonial episode with
characteristic justice and detachment.[34]

"Iraq During the Days of King Faisal" is a hybrid work which
attempts to marry several different registers of writing which Rihani
had done before, but not in the same proportions. The travel compo-
nents suffer diminution as compared with the extended commentary on
matters political and cultural; the exposition of the Shi'ih milieu is
perhaps too long and does not mix well with the analyses of Iraq's
modern developments. Nor does the portrayal of Faisal constitute the
heart of the work as does that of Ibn Saud in *Ibn Sa'oud of Arabia*. Perhaps
this explains why the manuscript was never published. However, as a
text on the decolonization of Arabia, and as a document imbued with
the early spirit of Pan-Arabism, the work is an extremely valuable
record. Of all Rihani's writings it is the most replete with colonial
ironies, and closes the second stage of his ideological response to imperialism, in which his opposition is mostly refracted through satire and
disclaimers. This stage coincides with and presents a studied overview
of the period of Iraq's struggle to get free from the British mandate, itself
the western riposte to the Arab Revolt and the further revolts that
ensued in Iraq, Syria and Egypt immediately after the Great War. In
Rihani's version Iraq, and King Faisal in particular, come out of the
labyrinth successfully.

Rihani saw that the British mandate in Iraq was both disguised imperialism and proof of that imperialism's receding power. Fifty years
before Britain would have justified its presence by claiming moral superiority. Now it could only say "we are here because we are here." In King
Faisal, the British had as pliant a client as they could have hoped for, but
Rihani was also aware of the pressures Faisal worked under. Britain was
"universally distrusted and her representatives [. . .] [were] becoming
more and more unpopular." Her promises regarding Iraq's future

League of Nations membership were shifting. Faisal was therefore in
the difficult position of needing "to retain the friendship of the British
while striving to attain the confidence of the people of Iraq." While he
wanted the kingdom to succeed politically, Rihani was not blind to the
forces arrayed against it; lack of competent administrators, a factious
self-seeking cadre of politicians, and the legacy of imperialist manipulation of the minorities. He was specially contemptuous of the use of the
latter by the mandatory power as a wedge to weaken the creation of a
strong centralized state. In particular the inordinate attention given the
tribes by the British raised, not his ire, but his withering irony:

> Capt. Holt is not only a kurdish expert, but also an admirer of the kurds
> – and their loving brother. Even as Miss Bell was the loving sister of the
> Arabs. The chair of Oriental Secretary must always, it seems, ray out love
> in certain directions, must always cultivate and cuddle some minority
> [. . .] Herein lies the principal root of native suspicion.[35]

When Rihani chose to publish on his Iraqi experience in English,
however, he extracted the account he made of his visit to the
Agricultural and Industrial Exhibition (April 1932). The tone is upbeat,
Faisal and Nuri functioning as model heroes of the new, progressive
Arab state. The British barely feature, other than as a bogey invoked by
the opposition to try to discredit the exhibition. For Rihani, the poet and
lover of Arabic culture, the key moment is perhaps not the speech he
gave over the radio nor his presence among such distinguished
company. It is viewing the products of an Iraqi textile mill manufac-
turing "a cloth of native wool", albeit with foreign machinery; or the
"engine and power plant in miniature made by the students": each in
its way evidence to support his thesis that the Arabs could build a
modern nation. "The fact is significant in so far as it indicates that the
oriental mind, steeped in the poetry and the piety of resignation, is
acquiring new energy, is becoming mechanical."[36] Five years later,
Rihani was publishing another article on Iraq: the occasion was the overthrow of the government of Yasin al-Hashimi by military coup. The tone
is, not unnaturally, anxious, concerned; the issue, Rihani recognizes at
once, not merely the deposition of a corrupt and unpopular "old-fash-
ioned Turkish regime", but "why a military coup d'etat? Was
Constitutional government a failure in this Arab land?" After reviewing
the events and the reactions of prominent and ordinary Iraqis, he
concludes:

> Parliamentary machinery can never overthrow a government in Iraq,
> because it is in the government's hands. The government nominates the

representatives, who are elected inevitably [. . .] Here then is an organic
defect in the representative government of Iraq. And what happened in
the Yasin regime is likely to happen again.[37]

The turmoil in Iraq followed on the start of the 1936 uprising in
Palestine. Rihani had visited, and evidenced its temporary abating at the
call of the Arab Kings as "a significant sign of Arab unity." The deepening of conflict in Palestine and the classic postcolonial upheavals in
Iraq, together with the struggle against the French mandate in Syria,
presaged a new crisis in Arab affairs, one to which Rihani seems to have
reacted by becoming even more committed to what he construed as the
Arab cause. This final stage in Rihani's involvement in the issue of decolonization leads him to take up more overtly radical positions over
Palestine and Syria, dropping for the most part his satirical mask and
replacing it by the vocabulary of the liberationist. As he wrote around
1937:

> The Arabs, in their relations with each other, have attained a summit of
> peace; but in their mandatory or other denationalizing foreign relations,
> as in their struggle against foreign domination and foreign political inter-
> ference in their land, they are determined to uphold their rights and
> defend their national integrity to the end.[38]

Syria and Lebanon were steeped in the imperialist mire. The Turks had
bequeathed "effete institutions [. . .] a political morality which can be
made to serve any purpose [. . .] religious hostilities [. . .] sectarian
divisions [. . .] minorities [. . .] made to serve in recent times the colonial policy of divide-and-rule." A younger nationalist generation had
arisen with the determination of "joining in the struggle of the nationalists everywhere in the Arab world" – which meant an inevitable
collision course with the French mandatory power. The French record
in Syria prior to the Franco-Syrian Treaty of 1936 was one of abortive
attempts at introducing treaties allowing for limited constitutional
government followed by repression, riots and revolts. In order to stave
off widespread opposition to their authority they had adopted, beneath
a cover of impartiality, the typical imperialist ploy of cultivating the
minorities and special interest groups which they could then ferment
against any movement of national unity. "In treating the Christians and
Muslims alike with equal justice, and in being courteous and consid-
erate to them all, they insinuate themselves into the confidence of some
of the nationalists themselves and strengthen their hold upon the seces-
sionists, their opponents." In Syria's many religious minorities the
French found "a rich field for cultivation and development." Behind all

this was a barely disguised thirst for gain – in Jazirah, where the Jacobite Christians had been stirred to revolt against the Damascus government, the "Oil Divinity is astir." The minorities were the key to "the business of empire" and to "the rivalry of nations for oil": the "links in the chain" were:

> glorifying self-determination [for the minorities], agitating for independence [from the nationalist center], religious and mandatory wire-pulling, open revolt against native authorities, bloody conflicts between Christians and Muslims, the need of French protection, the perpetuation of French control – and the control of the oil fields.

The moral was a key nationalist text: "Unhappy is the country that has an oil well it cannot defend."[39]

On Palestine, Rihani's argumentation had time to develop according to the stages mentioned above. In 1917, he takes a long term view, pointing out that throughout its history the Holy Land had been occupied by one or other hegemonic power, usually with adverse results for all or part of the native population. Now the solution was to make it a special case, and internationalize it so that the further alienation of its indigenous inhabitants would be avoided. Above all, it was vital to understand that Zionism, as an imported presence with a hegemonic agenda, would be a disaster if allowed to establish itself in the area. "Keep the Arab and Jew at a safe distance from each other" was his conclusion at this time.[40] From the moment the Balfour Declaration was announced Rihani understood its fateful consequences. Not averse to the Jews being given a homeland, he was implacably opposed to it being sited in Palestine. He argued with cogency the disparity between Britain's obligations as the mandatory authority in Palestine to the overwhelmingly Arab population, and the promises she was making to the Zionists. But he recognized at the same time that British policy, backed by the United States, embodied the theoretic abstraction and arrogance on the ground that was typical of imperialism. The wishes of the indigenous population were cynically ignored and in the process the foundations were being laid for bitter confrontation in the future. In allowing Zionism the scope it demanded the western powers had let the genii out of the bottle, for those demands could never be satisfied. The Zionists would not be happy until they had pushed the Arabs into the desert; defense of a Zionist state would require a huge commitment of money and arms either from Britain or the United States, and the neighboring Arabs would not rest until they had expelled the Jews into the sea. Where Jews and Arabs had cooperated and lived alongside one another for a millennium, radical divisions were being created amongst them. The religious issue, invoked by the religious Zionists, could only call forth a commensurate hardening of the Islamic element in Arab nationalism. Inevitably, clashes would result, especially over contested holy sites such as the Temple Mount in Jerusalem.[41]

As time went on, Rihani increasingly spelled out on the one hand his disenchantment with British policy and its execution, and on the other his solidarity with the Palestinian Arabs. Together the Balfour Declaration and the mandate had created a "triangle of insuperable difficulties", a knot that could not be untied. "No matter how it is interpreted and enforced it [the declaration] will always be the cause of agitation and disturbance in the Holy Land." In order to keep its promises to the Zionists, the British government had placed the native Arab population "under a peculiar form of modern subjugation." "Zionism, with the British mandate as a shield and money as a weapon, is another form of conquest." The Zionists from Central and Eastern Europe were "the vanguards of a dream of conquest, a dream of empire which is being supported with American money and British bayonets."[42] Despite the strength of his convictions, though, Rihani did not resort to abuse or gross caricature of his opponents. He gave his support to the attempt of Arab leaders, led by Ibn Saud, to de-escalate the violence occasioned by the 1936 general strike in Palestine, recognizing that "a rupture [between Ibn Saud and the British] might mean a calamity to both the Arabs and the British."[43] At the same time, the issue of Palestine crystallized Rihani's aspirations for Pan-Arab unity. He instanced the support the Palestinians were receiving from ordinary citizens of neighboring Arab countries, as well as the independent governments of Saudi Arabia and Iraq. The sense of a common purpose was exemplified by the Palestinians themselves – both Muslims and Christians – "All the Arabs of Palestine are united today and are making sacrifices in blood and money to save their country from being absorbed by the Jews," he observed around 1937.[44]

The pointedness of Rihani's late statements on the dangers of the situation in Palestine, on which he had already spent so much time and energy to apprise the West, and, as a highly literate, bilingual Arab, on which his voice had to a degree been a lone one, brought him nearer than ever before to supporting the Arab struggle against what he saw as the outside colonizer.[45] How close had he actually come to crossing that boundary characterized by Edward Said in respect of George Antonius as being "honourably dependent on the West", to join the ranks of the anti-western liberation forces that sprang up so ubiquitously immediately before and after the World War II? To begin with, Rihani had never shared Antonius's high expectations of the British, although he gave credit where he thought it was due.[46] His satirical mask covered an ambivalence towards Europe in particular which is often hard to gauge. Any final assessment would need to balance Rihani's espousal of those areas of praxis in western political culture that he believed conduced to freedom, progress and development, against his will as an Arab to identify himself with his own people, who were partially under the yoke of the western colonizer. Rihani understood, as few others perhaps at that time, the underlying dilemma facing the western powers in regard to their relations with non-western nations and cultures. Western originated ideas of self-determination, liberalism and social justice could not be refused any people or nation that wanted them, or merely extended on condition. In other words, the ideals to which western civilization had given birth were now the property of all mankind; the stronger metropolitan powers would not only be working against their own first principles by exploiting the weaker nations, they would, in the long run, be undermining the entire human edifice, and with it their own invested interests. The East too demanded its "share in the fruits of this higher and nobler spirit of civilization."[47] Certainly, the warnings Rihani gave to the West of the turmoil and destruction that would pursue its policies in the Near East both predicate and foresee the tortuous liberation struggles to come: "Let me tell you [. . .] the most active and the most potentially devastating volcano in the East today [he writes in 1937] is that which is nearest to Europe."[48] The direction taken by radical Arab nationalism during and after World War II in respect of its anti-western astringency might not have been endorsed by Rihani a priori, but we can say it was foreseen by him. In one of his last articles for *Asia* magazine, he attacked the West for its interference in Arab affairs, arguing that the peoples of the fertile crescent had learned from their experience of the mandates that however advanced they might be in comparison with the Arabs of Najd and the Hijaz "even the highest culture and the most developed form of democratic government can become, in the hands of the foreigners in control, most effective instruments of tyranny and exploitation." The people of Syria, Palestine and Lebanon, were "beginning to look for salvation in every direction but the West."[49]

Conclusion

As a bilingual Arab, Rihani saw his task as representing the Arab cause to his fellow Arabs and to the West. There was no question in his mind that he should desist from such a mission because of its political implications, or out of regard for vague notions of universalism. But polemicizing Arab interests did not make him anti-western; his living

Arab heroes, Abdul-Aziz Ibn Saud and Nuri as-Said, were after all, each in their own fashion, prepared to work with the West while retaining as their core agenda the interests of their own peoples. Rihani himself, in a letter to Eleanor Roosevelt in 1937, denied he was pleading the Arab political cause, "but their cultural and racial resurgency."[50] Of course, there is a sense in which Rihani tempered his language to suit his audience. Indirect irony coexists in his writings on decolonization with a more stringent rhetoric of nationalism of the kind that got him expelled from Lebanon by the French in 1933. The latter strain could be directed against the hated Turk, or the western imperial powers that administered the mandates. In his later years, Rihani was perhaps more disposed to use charged language, and there is no mistaking the bitterness he felt towards the French presence in his native Lebanon in particular. It can certainly be argued that this sense of personal grievance against the occupation of Arab lands by the foreigner joins him with other Arab writers writing in Arabic on the same issue. But what distinguishes him from them is his cultural duality, from which he derives his cognizance of decolonization as an issue framed by the symbiotic relationship between the colonizing power and the colonized subject.[51] By joining the terrains of both the colonized and the colonizer, Rihani's political writings look forward to strands in postcolonial writing today, notably the work of Edward Said. Like Said, Rihani possessed a bicultural perspective on both western and oriental culture. His Pan-Arabism would seem idealistic and unrealistic today, and indeed discredited from having become the stale official narrative all over the Arab world. But his vision of an international order, secular but nurturing the various spiritual traditions of the human race, balanced by the respective talents of the people of the Occident and the Orient, but assigning for none the position of tutelage to a superior hegemonic force, should retain a resonance as we move towards the twenty-first century. Rihani was both of his time and forward looking when he argued: "Internationalism presupposes nationalism, is necessarily preceded by it. In the East we are still going through the first stage." The Arab genius, in particular, was "malleable, receptive, assimilative, inclusive." It had carried the torch of ancient civilization to Europe, and could today carry the same torch from West to East. Its destiny was to "attain the highest level of eclectic refinement and truth [. . .] But before this can be done, the Arabs must realize their national dream of unity and independence."[52]

---------------- *5* ----------------

George Antonius: Anglo-Arab Disjunctions

The Arab and British interests in this part of the world are so inter-woven that it is sheer folly to put such a strain on Anglo-Arab friendship, which, for myself, I regard as a sine qua non of peace.
George Antonius, letter to Sir John Richmond, 1936

It would be a jolly good thing for the Arabs if they had some more people equally-clear minded [as George Antonius] to put their case. As he says, the Arabs do lose from having no Englishman practi-cally competent to understand their point of view, and no Arab competent to express it.
Thomas Hodgkin[1]

A Greek Orthodox Christian of Lebanese origins raised in a successful commercial family in Egypt, George Antonius's roots were in the Syrian diaspora. Though fluent in Arabic, like his compatriot, Edward Atiyah, he wrote in English, having attended a British school and later Cambridge University. Of his own western education, part of which took place at the same school as Antonius, Victoria College, Alexandria, Edward Said writes in his introduction to *Orientalism*:

> Much of the personal investment in this study derives from my aware-ness of being an "Oriental" as a child growing up in two British colonies. All of my education, in those colonies (Palestine and Egypt) and in the United States, has been Western, and yet that deep early awareness has persisted. In many ways my study of Orientalism has been an attempt to inventory the traces upon me, the Oriental subject, of the culture whose domination has been so powerful a factor in the life of all Orientals.[2]

For Antonius too the domination of western culture was very great, although in *The Arab Awakening* it takes on a submerged, less conscious form than Said's disclosure of it in *Orientalism*. According to Said, Antonius wrote his book as a "partisan of both the Arabs and the British

– a classic case of interdependence if ever there was one."[3] To his Arab nationalism, Antonius, like the other Lebanese Christian Arab nationalists, brought an active commitment. Like Rihani, Antonius championed the cause of the Palestinian Arabs; although constructively from inside the British mandate in Palestine, rather than critically from outside, as in the case of the Arab-American. This accounts for the counterpoise Antonius set out to achieve in his only book, as well as in his activities as an erudite negotiator who worked with British officials and Arab leaders with equal ease.[4]

This chapter sets Antonius's Anglo-Arab discourse, as seen in *The Arab Awakening*, firmly within the context of his links with the British, both as their protege by virtue of his education and career in government service, and as their critic, as an advocate and defender of the Arab case in Palestine and inscriber of an Arab national narrative. The discussion starts with an overview of Antonius's relations with the British, then interrogates *The Arab Awakening* as an exercise in grand narrative, and ends by looking at the deepening Anglo-Arab disjunction over the impasse of Palestine.

Antonius and the British

Thanks to Susan Silsby's detailed research, from which the following account draws heavily, George Antonius's relations with the British can be reconstructed in the following terms. Expected to take his place in "an elite corps of European-educated Arabs whom they envisioned taking the reins of government one day," from the British point of view, by a combination of personal qualities, ability, and commitment to Arab interests, Antonius grew to be an object of jealousy and grudging respect. Developing an early interest in Arab politics, he attended the July 1913 Arab Congress in Paris and may already have had an "intimate dealing with organizations and secret societies working for Arab autonomy from Ottoman rule."[5] When war broke out in 1914, he joined the censorship department in Egypt, and enjoyed soirées with the likes of C. P. Cavafy, E. M. Forster, and Sir Bartle Frere. Already, his Cambridge don's manner and command of the nuances of the British political class's code, appeared to set Antonius out as a mediator between the British and the Arabs. To Thomas Hodgkin, a contemporary in the Palestine Government service, Antonius seemed to have "rather the manner of a young Fellow of All Souls." Years later, he spoke of Antonius's

genius for mediation [. . .] a role for which he was admirably equipped by his essentially rational way of looking at the world and belief in the rational solution of problems, the lucidity of his reasoning, his Henry-Jamesish sensitivity to the undertones and overtones of a complex situation, his imaginative power of grasping, and identifying with, conflicting points of view.[6]

But the jealousy that dogged his career right up to his resignation from government service sixteen years later was soon evident. His post-War association with the Milner Commission, role as lecturer to the Royal Colonial Institute, attachment to Amir Faisal's staff in London, together with his acquaintance with the likes of Henry McMahon and T. E. Lawrence, may, according to Silsby, have been partly responsible for the cooling of Antonius's friendship with Forster, with whom he had worked on the latter's *Alexandria: A History and a Guide*. More crucial, there began a series of career rebuffs. After three years involvement in helping to resolve inter-Arab territorial disputes, during which time he developed close relations with the likes of Ibn Saud, King Faisal, and Nuri as-Said, Antonius was recommended for honors by Sir Gilbert Clayton. Not only were these not forthcoming, he received little credit for his mediation, and the Colonial Office even refused to reimburse his expenses. Worse still, on his return to routine duties in 1927, Antonius was passed over in favor of a junior for the position of deputy director of the Palestine Department of Education. "If you hear me complain or if I appear bitter," he wrote Clayton, "it is not at all because of the absence of reward. It is simply because no matter how hard one may work, when it comes to the point one finds oneself in the intolerable position of a man on his knees asking for a favour." Transferred, and then effectively demoted, Antonius eventually quit, in Silsby's telling phrasing: "A victim of British discrimination against Arabs in which there was a parallel between Arabs denied key posts in the [Palestine] administration and Palestinian Arabs as a whole denied a representative, democratic form of government."[7]

Though he was now employed by Charles R. Crane's New York Institute for Current World Affairs as its interpreter of the Middle East, Antonius, who had become a Palestinian citizen in 1925, was able to dissociate his own personal history from that of Palestine. He was still convinced the British could be influenced by reason to see the justice of the Arab case. The 1930s saw him continue to act out the substance of this belief by submitting proposals on issues such as constitutional government in Palestine, maintaining friendships with sympathetic British officials and diplomats like Clayton, and testifying, in January 1937, to the Peel Committee on behalf of the Palestinian Arabs. At the same time he struck out on his own account as a lecturer on the Middle

East in both Britain and the United States, and as the author of a study on the Arab national movement which for the first time accessed the "jealously guarded chest" of documents in the hands of ex-King Husain of the Hijaz, and Amir Abdullah of Transjordan, concerning Britain's pledges on Arab independence. Antonius worked on the task of researching and writing this book with great single-mindedness, as a man with a mission, living like a hermit during the violence of the Palestinian uprising, still believing, against his own mounting criticism of the government's handling of the revolution, that a true presentation of the historical evidence might cause the British to change their minds.

The publication of *The Arab Awakening*, characterized by its author as "a bridge between two different cultures and an agent in the interpretation of one to the other," achieved at least one of his stated aims. It highlighted Britain's wartime pledges to the Arabs with such clarity that it was no longer possible for His Majesty's Government to refuse publication of the documents relating to the MacMahon–Husain negotiations and later British affirmations of Arab independence made to the Arabs. At the 1939 London conference on Palestine, Antonius was a leading Arab delegate and spokesman, drafting, translating, and editing the Arab side's statements to the conference, and taking the lead in the committee set up to investigate precisely those pledges he had done so much to foreground in his book. "Many British officials hastened to purchase the book because it contained all of the previously unpublished documents pertaining to the Palestinian claims to independence."[8] Arguably, the conference opened a window of light for Antonius's long cherished hopes of Anglo-Arab cooperation, for it went back on the Peel Commission's earlier recommendation of partition, made a pledge to accept an independent Palestine after ten years, and recognized the need to set a limit on Jewish immigration. In part, here was vindication of Antonius's own seemingly unwearying efforts. "The hurdles that remained between [the Arabs and the British]," he wrote in his notes, "were not large", and yet in spite of this statement he was not as satisfied as the non-Palestinian Arab delegates with the results which were published in the White Paper. He continued to oppose the sop of Arab appointments to positions in the Palestine administration, arguing instead for them to exercise legislative power first. He was, in the words of Malcolm Macdonald a "very hard bargainer", whose nationalism was founded on a hard-headed grasp of the bottomline: possession of the land.[9]

The window of opportunity represented by the London conference was soon closed: the Arabs went through the motions of rejecting it, but, on becoming Prime Minister, Churchill shelved the White Paper anyway. Antonius just as quickly lost his moment in the limelight. He spent the last years of his life in Beirut, isolated once again. On 25 September 1940, he went to see the British High Commissioner for Palestine, H.A. MacMichael, in the conviction that, owing to its policies in the region, Britain's position was threatened in the Middle East . He believed the British Government should formulate their policy toward the Arab world in a form that would counteract the promises being disseminated by the Axis powers. His own "Memorandum on Arab Affairs" was submitted to MacMichael on October 3. The covering letter to the High Commissioner revealed both its author's intentions in writing the memorandum, and the tenacity with which he still held to his belief in the Anglo-Arab relationship:

> I should like the Memorandum and the suggestions it contains to be read as being no more than an individual contribution from a student of Arab affairs who believes in the value of Anglo-Arab collaboration, not only for its own sake but also as a means towards the upholding of those principles of freedom and of the decencies of life, in the defence of which Great Britain is setting such a gallant example to the world. My knowledge of Arab affairs enables me to state, with the deepest conviction, that the Arabs are at heart as attached to those principles as any other civilised people, and that any effort that might be made to secure their collaboration in the right spirit would not be found to have been made in vain.

MacMichael's own covering letter to Lord Lloyd, Secretary of State for the Colonies, questioned Antonius's "intellectual honesty", and while recommending the memorandum's circulation, condemned it as "more of an essay by an ambitious writer, than a piece of constructive statesmanship." The British did not object to Antonius's main recommendation – that Britain make some sort of public declaration in favor of Arab unity – but were critical of Antonius's contacts with the exiled Palestinian leaders, and what MacMichael termed his silence on the Jewish problem.[10]

The Dutchman, D. Van Der Meulen, had first met Antonius in Jedda while he was Dutch consul there in the mid 1920s, and Antonius was acting as negotiator with Ibn Saud as part of the Clayton mission. When he came across him again in Beirut during the first years of the War he found Antonius older and weaker. "Here was a man utterly disappointed, forgotten by the British or, at least, not fully trusted by them, and allowed no chance to give his intellectual assistance to the Allied struggle."[11] Meanwhile, as Edward Atiyah would argue later, while the Arabs went on believing restitution lay with the British, the Zionists had already taken it upon themselves to take Palestine from the Arabs by force. It is difficult to avoid the conclusion that Antonius, who died in

1942, and therefore did not live to see the denouement, had backed the wrong horse in his insistence on an Anglo-Arab solution to Middle East politics, just as Atiyah would himself seem to fail later on in the same project.

The Arab Awakening and Grand Narrative

According to Edward Said, *The Arab Awakening* belongs to the category of grand narratives of emancipatory nationalism. This judgment of George Antonius's book is not the usual one however. It has been discussed mainly in terms of its status as a nodal point within the field of Middle East Studies. Albert Hourani's 1977 George Antonius Memorial Lecture to St Antony's College, Oxford, poses the question "how far the book can be regarded as a permanent and valuable contribution to our knowledge of its subject", and then goes on to review the revisions of Antonius's historical argument made by the likes of Sylvia Haim, A. L. Tibawi, Z. N. Zeine, and C. E. Dawn. Though Hourani problematizes Antonius's mixing of "political advocacy" with "historical narrative", it is as an essay in historical analysis that he is primarily interested in the work.[12] A recent reviewer, critical of the influence of Antonius on the study of Arab nationalism, is more concerned to refute what he calls the "Antonius paradigm" than to read *The Arab Awakening* for its function as a liberationist narrative.[13] A methodology which approaches any piece of historical writing and analyzes it according to its discourse, attitudes and alignments is itself open to criticism of the type that "what actually happens" (or happened) in societies like the Arab ones Antonius writes about, is not conclusively decided upon by analysis of "what people say and write about them."[14] It is my contention, however, that once the terms of its discourse have been established, and it becomes clear to us that Antonius's history like any other history is an articulation of events, rather than events as they happened, the reader should be in a position better to evaluate the tensions and disjunctures out of which his book was written.

In the foreword to *The Arab Awakening*, Antonius introduces his method as a continuous narrative of the origins and developments of the Arab Movement – "the story [. . .] never [. . .] told in full before" – balancing European and Arab sources by a unifying impartiality.

> I have tried to discharge my task in a spirit of fairness and objectivity, and, while approaching the subject from an Arab angle, to arrive at my conclusions without bias or partisanship.[15]

To the tone of conscientious, public-minded duty – "discharge my task" – with disclaimers of "bias or partisanship", is joined an honest disclosure of interest: the subject is to be approached "from an Arab angle." This segment, placed in apposition to the main clause, is nevertheless engaged in inseparable symbiosis with the declared method as expressed by the main statement. Antonius undertakes at the outset to adopt an Arab view while working within the larger frame of universality and objectivity, terms that belong to the standard code of British metropolitan discourse in fact.

This articulation of an Arab narrative in the language of the British colonizer can be seen as an expression of dependence, by which the rights of the colonized are argued from within the colonizer's discourse. To this extent it is filiastic, a continuation of the original imperial discourse. As Hourani put it:

> The readers to whom it was addressed were primarily British, politicians, diplomats, officials, journalists and scholars, members of the elite of a few thousand people who were seriously concerned about imperial policy and in a position to exercise some influence upon decisions.
>
> The relationship is one also of cultural dependence. The weaker party tries to assure the stronger that its essential interests will be safe even if its power is surrendered, and does so by demonstrating its own mastery of the culture and values of the stronger, and showing therefore that the transition to independence can take place without shock, and will not appear as radical change.[16]

It would be easy then, to categorize Antonius's work alongside the sort of nationalist criticism which "by failing to alter the terms of the discourse within which it operates, has participated implicitly or even explicitly in a discourse controlled by the very imperial power its nationalist assertion is designed to exclude."[17] But Antonius did not wish to exclude Britain entirely from engagement with any postcolonial Arab national entity in the Middle East. An alternative view is that the point about the western filiation of Antonius's discourse is not that it connoted inferiority, rather that it presaged liberation. "The narrated events," in *The Arab Awakening*, "were previously recounted by metropolitan witnesses," according to Said. Now, in Antonius's account, "at last, [. . .] the Arabs, their leaders and warriors and thinkers, can tell their own story." That this had to be done from within "that very European world of power and colonial domination [that] excluded, to some degree subjugated, and deeply disappointed" Antonius himself, was no more than a necessary evil. Yet the disjunction between the discourse of fairness and impartiality adopted by Antonius from the

British standard code, and the, to him, unfair and partial operation of British power over the mandated Arab territories, strains the symbiotic Anglo-Arab relationship mentioned above, with the result that "lodged at [the] heart [of *The Arab Awakening*] [. . .] is a complex of hope, betrayal, and bitter disappointment."[18]

The early chapters of the work borrow from the metropolitan histories by constructing a grand narrative with a teleological objective – the victory of the Arab national movement – only for this deserved end, tragically and ironically, to be stolen from the Arabs by the bad faith of those powers from whose culture the narrative derives. To argue that Antonius "essentialized the idea of Arab nationalism, which in his book took on the form of an indivisible *Geist* [. . .] maintain[ing] that Arab nationalism's modern incarnation was forged in the literary salons and secret societies of Beirut, Damascus and Istanbul, and was empowered by virtue of the Arab Revolt" may be an indictment of the work's contemporary value as academic history, but only confirms its grand narrative schema.[19] For Antonius, the history he was writing concerned the unfolding of an idea; his narrative method was not intended to embrace multiple meanings, nor dissonance of tone. If there is a counterpoint in *The Arab Awakening* it is between the major European powers and the emergent Arab nation, but the dissonance between the two is not built into the narrative structure per se, rather the disjunction occurs in spite of Antonius's attempts to maintain a resolution of differences. The parts which treat the Arab rebellion against the Turkish yoke presented no such difficulty; the account could be presented as a liberation narrative in a manner able to find approval in the European liberal conscience. It is as though Antonius were writing a history of the Greek Revolt or the Risorgimento. Opposition to the tyrant occupier, at first clandestine and surreptitious, formed around noble aspirations, gathers momentum, winning converts and throwing up heroes like the quondam Ottoman army officer turned Arab patriot, Aziz Ali Al-Misri. His arrest enables Antonius to record a union of Arab outrage and British good offices both aimed at the perfidious Turk:

> Early in April, it became known that 'Aziz 'Ali had been secretly condemned to death. The agitation became more vociferous, and wherever Arab officers gathered oaths were taken to avenge his death in blood. Fortunately for 'Aziz the voice of Europe and in particular of England, spoke in his defence. Kitchener moved the Foreign Office to act, Sir Louis Mallet made representations in Constantinople, and *The Times*, in a series of four leaders spread over six weeks, pleaded outspokenly in his favour.

A suitable nationalist lesson was drawn from the affair which ended in

Aziz Ali's release: "His trial had shaken the Arab world more profoundly, perhaps, than any single act of Turkish tyranny, and greatly hardened the Arab will to freedom, for it had moved the masses as well as the thinkers."[20] Since "the Arab will to freedom" would be at the expense of "Turkish tyranny", it could hardly fail to enlist the sympathies of European liberal opinion as well. The passage confirms Said's observation: Antonius shows "The Arabs are moved by ideas of freedom shared with Europeans."[21]

The climax of this mode of writing – and also one of the most moving passages in the book – concerns the relaying of the news to the Amir Faisal of the wartime execution by Jemal Pasha of twenty-one prominent Arabs in Damascus and Beirut:

> One of the Bakris read it aloud, and mournfully the twenty-one names rang out, to the mounting horror of the listeners, and lingered like the notes of a dirge in the still air of that spring morning in the orchards of Damascus. Long minutes passed in silence broken only by a prayer uttered in a low voice or a sighed invocation for the repose of the dead. One of the company recited the opening verse of the Qoran. Then, like one suddenly demented, Faisal leapt to his feet and, tearing his kufiya from his head, flung it down and trampled it savagely with a cry *'Tab al-maut ya 'arab!'*

There are echoes of Gibbon's account of the martyrdom of the Prophet's grandson, Husain, in the classic English prosody of this piece, which is heightened by Faisal's apostrophe in Arabic. Antonius gives a translation in a footnote, but only after a preface of a single perfect Augustan sentence pronouncing on its untranslatability, this underlining the formal separation of the two codes (English and Arabic) which Antonius maintains throughout the book.[22]

With the raising of the standard of revolt by Faisal's father, the Sharif Husain, the British move from cheerleaders on the sidelines to open, if equivocal sponsors of the Arab cause. The Anglo-Sharifian negotiations prior to this – so crucial to the entire polemic over Palestine in Antonius's time and since – are dealt with in chapter 9 headed, "Great Britain's Pledge: 1915", richly suggesting the burden of authorial emotions proposed by Said, which are all packed into the single chapter. The section as a whole is a grave test of the method Antonius outlined in his foreword; one which, in terms of the promise to eschew bias and partisanship, and balance both European and Arabic sources, he can only pass by a superficial impartiality that in part submerges difference only to leave a deep sense of disjuncture at the end.

Antonius places his bilingual expertise at the service of elucidating the controversy over the Arab territory – especially "that part of Syria

[. . .] mandated territory of Palestine" – that was to be included or excluded from the independent Arab state or confederation after the defeat of Turkey. Through his translation of the Arabic texts of the McMahon–Husain correspondence, "now, for the first time, available in English in full" and included in his book as an appendix, Antonius believed he had accomplished not merely a scholarly task, but had facilitated a better understanding of the contradictory Arab and British positions. These he summarizes with a terseness that proclaims his impartial method: "The Arab view is that Palestine did fall within the area of promised Arab independence. The British Government maintain the contrary."[23]

Given Antonius's project in writing *The Arab Awakening*: the unfolding stage by stage of the Arab national idea, it was perhaps natural that his nationalist sympathies would at least in part direct his scholarly impulses. As Hourani pointed out, Antonius was not the only historian to interpret the ambiguous British correspondence with her wartime allies in accordance with his political alignments.[24] However, it is clear from his text where the problem lay. To the extent that Great Britain could be represented as supporting the Arab cause, the historical narrative and political advocacy could proceed without disjuncture. When British interests and Arab interests appeared to be at one – as in the victory march of British and Arab armies into Damascus in October 1918 – there was not bifurcation. But where they were not – where Britain had other fish to fry besides her patronage of the Arabs – we can detect an underlying fracture in Antonius's narrative that he finds difficult to submerge by his professed impartial methodology.

When it came to accounting for British motives behind the promises she gave to her wartime allies, and her subsequent action on these, Antonius, who as one experienced in the world of diplomacy does not write as a blinkered partisan, affects a disingenuous agnosticism. Although ready to attribute the critical epithet here and there, he shrinks from following his discourse to its apparent conclusions, for that would mean inscribing disjuncture where, by virtue of his adoption of a grand narrative strategy, this needed to be repressed. McMahon's letters can be criticized for their use of absurd introductory "compliments and honorifics that are not English or Arabic, but a medley of Turco-Persian toadyisms, which someone on McMahon's staff had thought appropriate." The first note in particular is dismissed as "a curious example of official evasiveness" that made "foolish reading", partly "on account of its palpable insincerity", in contrast to the "single-mindedness" of Husain's.[25] But if Antonius was aware of British patronage – and what the King-Crane Commission termed her "colonial theory" which she might have found "difficult to give up [. . .] especially in [the] case of a people thought inferior" – he was not prepared to be more explicit. The insult could be dismissed, after all, as the work of "someone on McMahon's staff" rather than representing a standard British attitude.[26]

The momentum of Antonius's argument – that the British gave undertakings to the Arabs that were not carried out later – builds, via rejection of subsequent British interpretation supporting exclusion of Palestine from the area of Arab independence – "An examination of the text shows that the British Government's argument is untenable"; "No one who has had the text of the McMahon correspondence before him can legitimately hold such a view"[27] – only to be diffused before expression of irreconcilable difference can be reached. Antonius appeared to hope that the situation could even then be resolved on the basis of examination of the Arabic texts, divergent interpretation of which had already caused "a great deal of avoidable waste, suffering and bloodshed."

His contribution to the healing of the "present misunderstanding" had been to search out, collate and translate these texts – "It seemed a matter of public duty to make the Arabic texts known." In fact, according to Antonius, apparently unmindful of the colonial ironies(?), it was:

> open to any person with a knowledge of Arabic, who can obtain access to the files of defunct Arabic newspapers, to piece the whole of the McMahon notes together.[28]

Unvoiced is the possibility – one Antonius may not have wished to face up to – that the British had intentionally effected a closure on the interpretation of their wartime agreements; they had been divested of their plural meanings, largely at the expense of the Arabs, in order to satisfy great power arrangements in the Middle East. For all the diplomatic restraint and academic nicety of his discourse, Antonius could not entirely submerge his sense of British betrayal. It is refracted in his stated bewilderment at the refusal of the British Government to allow the text of the McMahon correspondence to be published – their invoking of the public interest as justification "remain[ed] a mystery" to him.[29]

As a coda to chapter 9 there is a portrait of Husain as Antonius saw him in exile in Amman in 1931. Ostensibly, the linkage is Husain's suggestion that Antonius "piece together the text of the McMahon correspondence." Husain is represented as a broken man near to death, whose earlier qualities of mind have been entirely taken over by "his old craving for self-justification [. . .] In his bitterness he ascribed all his misfortunes to the non-fulfilment of the promises made to him by Sir

Henry McMahon."[30] The chapter ends with the old man still harping on the perfidy of "Luweed Jurj", but the embedded meaning is not a rehearsal of Husain's failings. It is one of censure of the British Government for reneging on its "pledge", bewilderment over the reasons for this betrayal, and continuing bitterness over the resulting ramifications for Arab lives. Unable to give open expression to these emotions himself, as one restrained by the objective non-partisan character of his task, Antonius uses Husain as a mask, refracting his own criticism through this Lear figure, thereby placing a distance between his own bitterness and the personal anti-British recriminations of the old man.

Husain was an Arab leader who had accepted "British integrity" at its face value, and entertained a "solid belief in English standards of honourable dealing."[31] This was also true of Antonius, in spite of his first hand knowledge of the workings of the British mandatory authority in Palestine. His criticism of the unwelcome Anglo-French presence in the fertile crescent is conducted in the standard code of British discourse. Pros and cons are balanced with scrupulous fairness; the British receive praise for their constructive help to Iraq – "It was fortunate [. . .] that, in so many respects, Great Britain's interests marched with her own"; and the French reproof for the "vagaries of [their] administration in Syria and the Lebanon."[32] Even when discussing the elisions and omissions of the reports of British Royal Commissions on Palestine, Antonius lays out the case against with an undeviating precision that befitted his years of experience inside the British service. It is indeed a case of the colonizer indicted through his own discourse, though all to no avail.

Palestine: a Colonial Impasse

In spite of his personal experiences of discrimination, and the palpable fact that the British preferred Jews or Zionist sympathizers for key posts in the Palestine administration – a policy that, in the words of one British officer, "led to the final downfall of our reputation for fair play" – Antonius seems to have been unable or unwilling to face up to the colonial logic of the Palestine situation. This, though his pen portrait of Balfour, written ten years after he accompanied him on his 1924–5 visit to Palestine-Syria, shows a penetrating understanding of the colonial mentality, albeit in a mind as cerebral as Balfour's:

> Palestine was to him a game, a sort of historico-intellectual exercise and diversion, into which he found himself drawn by the flattery of a pausible and astute Jew. Of the Arabs he was at first not even conscious, except to

the extent to which he may be said to have been conscious of, say, the ground-lads who fielded the balls for him on the courts at Cannes. When the Arabs became vocal, he regarded them as a nuisance – hooligans who had never read Hume or Bergson and who must not be suffered to disturb the serene philosophy of his historical meditations or the delicate equilibrium of his fantastic experiment.[33]

In Silsby's account the question remains unresolved as to whether Antonius fully grasped the reasons behind his career frustration – ones which she adduces all too clearly from her personal interviews and delvings into the correspondence files:

> Stewart Perowne, who later worked in the Department of Education under Farrel, said simply, Antonius "did not fit in" [. . .] Farrel in an October 8, 1927 letter to Lionel Smith, said "he is no good to us," as from a British colonial perspective, he was not, being far too ambitious and desirous of reforms supporting the advance of Arabs. As Farrel said bluntly in an October 8, 1927 letter to Smith, "Being an Arab, he is ineligible to succeed Bowman."

She then continues in a footnote:

> While Antonius severed his ties with Bowman after his transfer, he may never have realized that from the start Bowman had first fancied that Antonius' contract would not be renewed after the first year and was also busy seeking to obtain "an Englishman not an Arab" as his second and to "fix it" that this Englishman be Lionel Smith as early as 1922.[34]

In his later lecture to the American Academy of Political and Social Science (1932), Antonius emphasized that Palestinians were without representation in the system of government and administration in operation under the British mandate, and he condemned the machinery of government in Palestine as bureaucratic and estranged from the public.[35]

In the United States, Antonius fell foul of the Zionist lobby, having an invitation of visiting professor retracted by Columbia University. But his progressive disillusionment with the British establishment was the most distressing, causing him to call into question British fair play, the closed nature of a pro-Zionist British press, and even his own role as mediator between the British and the Palestinian Arabs. Self-doubt extended to his position in Crane's organization; his defense of his credentials as "honest interpreter of events" was accompanied by a sense of having become "isolated and lost." It seemed that, the habit of mind which by "the circumstance of a Western education superimposed upon [his] Arab descent" had given him "a natural readiness to see something of the two sides of the questions affecting the relations of the East with the West," had diverted his mind from the glaring fact of colonial hegemonism.[36]

For example, he explained the problems of the mandated territories more in terms of the national character of the mandatory authority, than in line with the strict power relationship of colonizer and colonized. Even though he saw the unrest in British Palestine and French administered Syria as linked, devolving from the notorious Sykes-Picot agreement, he was ready to attribute French problems in Syria to the "psychological make-up of the French."[37] Once again, the dialectic of Antonius's argument on imperial meddling was padded by the lengthy periods of a balanced English prose, when he told an audience at Chatham House in March 1934:

> The feeling of disappointment and bitterness which was created in Syria and other Arab countries as a result of this occupation of Damascus, was not entirely directed against the French. One still hears harder things said of Great Britain for having allowed the French occupation to take place in violation of the pledges made by Great Britain to the Arabs, than one hears of the French for having actually committed the aggression.[38]

With the outbreak of War, aware of the problems Britain had created for itself among the Arabs on account of her Palestine policy, Antonius was still to be found arguing his former patron's corner. Given that all the great European powers were equally imperialistic, Britain was less harsh than the others in exploiting the weaker nations and more tolerant of their national aspirations. Palestine was "the blackest mark against her", but though there was some overt support for Germany, especially in Egypt and Iraq, an underlying preference for Britain still existed throughout the Arab world.[39]

Conclusion

Where Palestine was concerned, Antonius knew that an imperial enterprise was afoot. He indicted Britain's plantation of Zionism in a corner of the earth where she believed it might best protect her interests, by naming the policy the creation of another Ireland.[40] But perhaps the boundaries of Antonius's Anglo-Arab discourse are demonstrated most clearly in *The Arab Awakening* by his pained arraignment of the British record in Palestine – the land he believed had been promised to the

Arabs, but was now an arena of bloodshed among Arabs and Jewish settlers.

> Even now when, by steps which it did not take a prophet to foretell, their policy has turned Palestine into a shambles, they show no indication of a return to sanity, that is to say to the principles of ordinary common sense and justice which are held in such high honour in England.

The solution to the terror in Palestine, "the wise way to put an end to it", was "to remove the causes that brought it about."[41] The last years of Antonius's career were dedicated to persuading the British of the rationality of this position, as he argued vigorously against the creation of a Jewish state in Palestine, and for the cessation of Jewish immigration into that country. These beliefs were embodied in *The Arab Awakening*, and through that text, arguably, exerted an influence on the British attitude at the 1939 London conference. (Of course it might also be pointed out that by this time, with war approaching, the British had reassessed their strategic interests in the Middle East and had already turned towards a more anti-Zionist policy.) Whatever the case may be, Antonius's book represented the watershed of Anglo-Arab political discourse, written as it was at a time when the British still seemed to be the arbiters of the affairs of the peoples of the Middle East.[42]

Antonius can hardly be blamed for stopping short at the point where the struggle for decolonization begins. Due to reasons of filiation to British cultural codes outline above, the oppositional opening salvo of Fanon's *The Wretched of the Earth* would have been outside the parameters of his thought.[43] Antonius's work, as Hourani pointed out, prefigures without participating in "a new age of mass-politics."[44] He understood the marginalization of the Arab peasantry, realizing the 1930s revolution in Palestine was theirs, and by so doing essayed to give them a voice. His grand narrative of liberation was by its very constitution unable to shake off the discourse of the colonizer. Antonius himself belonged to a class of "notables superseded after the 1930s and 1940s by more radical, popular, and nativist writers in Arabic."[45] But his book remains a pioneering text on the struggle of a people for its freedom, and his life's commitment to resisting foreign encroachment on the land of the Palestinian peasantry still stands as the action of a true patriot.[46]

6

Edward Atiyah: Language and Colonization

"Does he write in French?"
"Don't insult him by supposing that he writes in Arabic! Mind you,
Arabic is such a difficult language to write in that it's just as well
it's unfashionable."

D. J. Enright [1]

The British education he obtained at Victoria College, Alexandria, and later at Oxford, ensured for the Lebanese writer, Edward Atiyah, escape from the constraining sectarian divisions of his native Beirut. Atiyah had become so Anglicized that even when, in his earliest years in colonial service in Sudan, he experienced at first hand British imperial arrogance, however deep the revulsion there was no question of rejecting British norms. Donning the *jalabiyya* was not an option. But the British presence took on a different character in Sudan, and more importantly, Palestine, from Britain's image as protector to the Christians of Lebanon. During his time as political agent in the Sudan Government in the twenties and thirties, and when he engaged in wartime work for the British in Lebanon, Atiyah maintained a position of constructive criticism towards British policy in the Middle East. This continued in London after the War, when, retired from government service, he involved himself in Arab concerns, first at the Arab Office, and later, more peripherally, at the Iraqi Embassy. According to Michael Atiyah, his father never aimed at becoming a political figure. However, his experience in Sudan, together with his outgoing, extrovert personality, brought him lots of friends, and plenty of opportunity to deliver his pronouncements on political affairs. He spent many years "fighting British policy in the Arab world", and his left leanings led him to sympathize with the Soviet Union which he thought could be of use to the Arab cause. But he was not impressed by the postcolonial Arab regimes.[2]

Atiyah's active writing career was concentrated into the forties and fifties, a period during which he supplemented his pension from the

Sudan Government by freelance writing and broadcasting for the BBC. His autobiography, *An Arab Tells His story – A Study in Loyalties* (1946), is still in print. His first published novel, *The Thin Line* (1951), a melodrama set in the Home Counties, was a modest commercial success in English and was translated into several other languages. The two novels on Arab themes, *Black Vanguard* (1952), and *Lebanon Paradise* (1953), were followed by an historical study, *The Arabs* (1955), concentrated largely on modern Arab affairs and drawing on *The Arab Awakening*, the classic narrative by Atiyah's friend and fellow aluminae of Victoria College, George Antonius.[3]

Starting from Atiyah's dual identity as British-educated Arab, this chapter juxtaposes the non-fictional prose of his autobiography, and the two novels on Arab themes, alongside parallel readings from the texts of other Arab writers writing on similar topics. It is hoped thereby to mark the western codes adopted by Atiyah's English texts as against those employed by writers who wrote in Arabic.

Ambivalence and Colonial Discourse

Edward Atiyah's autobiographical, political, and fictional writings are not as immediately fixable within colonial or postcolonial discourse as are the stridently anti-colonial writings of the likes of Franz Fanon or Tayeb Salih, or even the more moderate Ameen Rihani. He is of significance as a writer at the beginning of the postcolonial moment who is unwilling or unable to abrogate the constraining power of the metropolitan center, and forge outwards in the development of an independent literature. "It is characteristic of these early post-colonial texts that the potential for subversion in their themes cannot be fully realized."[4]

As a British-educated Arab demonstrating his mastery of the metropolitan language, Atiyah's declared task of foregrounding an Arab identity is undercut by his unwillingness to confront the cultural dominance of the colonial power. A close reading of Atiyah's prose will concentrate on the managed and restrained foregrounding of Arab meanings. A resultant slippage is discernible in his writings, which affiliate them to colonial discourse, fixing them as partial and incomplete. They raise the issue of ambivalence within colonial discourse, as theorized by Homi Bhabha when he writes of certain "instances of colonial imitation":

> What they all share is a discursive process by which the excess or slippage produced by the *ambivalence* of mimicry (almost the same, *but not quite*)

does not merely 'rupture' the discourse, but becomes transformed into an uncertainty which fixes the colonial subject as a 'partial' presence.

Bhabha intends the ambivalence to reside in the discourse of the colonizer, where colonial mimicry is, as he states in the paragraph above the passage I have just quoted, "the desire for a reformed, recognizable Other, *as a subject of a difference that is almost the same, but not quite.*"[5] I shall argue that in Atiyah's case, his schema for the emergence of a cadre of westernized Arab intelligentsia and administrators capable of leading their societies along the paths of modernization and secularization is, however unwittingly, cognate to this desire for a reformed, recognizable Other. The ambivalence of mimicry, almost the same, but not quite, underpins Atiyah's successful and failed exemplars of the western educated Arab. This ambivalence is exemplified in two narratives from his autobiography, which form Atiyah's normative notion of a representative colonized elite on the verge of decolonization, under the tutelage of the imperial power. Of the two narratives, one is polar, that is to say, it acts in binary opposition to the other normative exemplar of harmonious East–West encounter.

Moawiya Nur, once of Gordon College, then a graduate in English literature from the American University of Beirut, is Atiyah's "old pupil" and "greatest friend among the Sudanese." A flamboyant character, his career appears to encapsulate all the dangers of exposure to the culture of the colonizer. After a bohemian existence in Cairo he returns to Sudan only to be rejected as unsuitable for the sort of government post for which his education would seem to have prepared him. Moawiya then turns "out of pique rather than conviction" to writing anti-British copy for the Cairo press, and ends up losing his sanity. "He had become to a large extent a stranger in his own country, a lonely soul among his people and family [. . .] The gulf between his mental life and natural environment had become immense." Showing at a job interview greater knowledge of Dr. Johnson than the British interviewer, Moawiya seemed to court put down by the colonial power. In fact, as is usual with such examples of binary opposition, Moawiya's case is to be understood in terms of deviation from the metropolitan norm. The nationalist "pique" behind his articles attacking the colonizer (who had refused him a job) resemble Atiyah's own injured nationalist phase; but what makes him an object lesson to be feared is the terrible cultural recidivism attending his madness:

He put himself in the hands of a Fiki, a primitive, ignorant, half-religious and half-medical quack [. . .] He believed in his powers, in his superstitions. He had reverted to his native dress, and this change in his appearance, which at a normal time, would have made no impression on me, now seemed the symbol of a deeper reversion.[6]

The civilizing process had backfired; Moawiya's "deeper reversion" was to the darkness at the heart of the savage state, from which his metropolitan education had essayed in vain to uplift him. The fact that it was, in the first place, the colonizer who was to blame for rejecting Moawiya is just one of those unavoidable situations thrown up by the situation of colonization. The Sudanese only succeeded in making his Otherness, his difference, all the more apparent. According to Bhabha, this ambivalence (almost the same, but not quite) is the very condition of mimicry, "where the reforming, civilizing mission is threatened by the displacing gaze of its disciplinary double." The ambivalence embedded in Atiyah's discourse is all the more marked, since he had experienced himself rejection at the hands of the colonizer. The near phobic inscription of Moawiya's reversion to nativism is a sign of Atiyah's own fear of the "return of the oppressed – those terrifying stereotypes of savagery, cannibalism, lust and anarchy which are the signal points of identification and alienation, scenes of fear and desire, in colonial texts."[7]

In a telling transition, the polar narrative is juxtaposed alongside a normative personal history in which the conflicts that destroyed Moawiya are resolved, and a typology is sketched out for an emergent political class, embodying within itself the matter of the colonized and the form of the colonizer.

> While Moawiya lay insane in Omdurman, in part at least the Sudanese victim of the impact of the West on the East, that impact was leading another friend of mine, in different circumstances, to a consummation of glorious fulfilment. Amin Osman, Head Boy of the School and Captain of the 1st XI in my first year at Victoria College, had followed up those achievements with a distinguished career at Oxford and then entered the service of the Egyptian Government.

The reader has no difficulty in recognizing in Amin Osman the epitome of Atiyah's normative Anglo-Arab politico-cultural synthesis.

> A good Egyptian and a great admirer of those British values which had formed the basis of his education, Amin Osman's ambition had always been to bring into into harmony the relations between Egypt and England, to achieve a political synthesis between the two countries similar to the cultural synthesis he had achieved in his own mind and life.[8]

Where Moawiya was denied government service and succumbed to primitive superstition, Osman scaled the political heights by virtue of his public school and Oxbridge education (the embedded suggestion is that the American University of Beirut – which Atiyah himself had disdained to attend – fell that crucial bit short in preparing Moawiya for the consummation of a government career). But Osman had his own tragedy preparing: the 1936 Anglo-Egyptian Treaty of Friendship which he played so glorious a part in helping to frame, would within fifteen years be consigned to the dustbin of imperial history, but not before he was himself assassinated by Egyptian nationalists led by Anwar Sadat. According to Sadat, Osman was killed not because of his political influence with Egyptians, which was negligible, but because "he was more than friendly with the British, supporting their presence in Egypt with unprecedented fervor."

> Osman had declared that the relationship between Egypt and Great Britain was in effect a Catholic marriage, so that even if Britain chose to dissociate herself, Egypt could never do the same. The declaration was tantamount to a self-imposed death sentence.[9]

Moawiya, on the other hand, emerges from the role imposed on him, of victim of the East's disintegration under the impact of western penetration, to a self-empowering hero's status as an early symbol of the revolt of the colonized. Defined by Atiyah as a pitiful example of cultural recidivism, he stands for the colonized as a group, rather than the individual who has achieved assimilation, choosing to assert in the face of the metropolitan culture that has rejected him, "those differences [which], after all, are within him and correctly constitute his true self."[10]

On Hybridity

Having himself chosen the path of assimilation, Atiyah was unaware of the ambivalence we must now read into the colonial encounters he writes about. This is equally true for his novel, *Black Vanguard*, which is both an enlargement of Atiyah's own personal narrative, and a re-writing of the careers of the Muslim Arabs, Moawiya and Amin Osman. The novel is also a manifesto for the model decolonization Atiyah believed was in process in Sudan. As such, *Black Vanguard* invites a parallel reading with the Sudanese writer Tayeb Salih's, *Season of Migration to the North*, first published ten years after Sudan's independence, "a time which witnessed the high tide of Nasserism and the euphoria of anti-colonial Arab nationalism."[11] Works with a similar theme – their chief protagonists both return to their native Sudan following education in Britain – they, however, differ markedly in their treatment. Where Mustafa Sa'eed (*Season of Migration*) brings a legacy of murder and betrayal from his overseas interface with the colonizer's culture and womenfolk, Mahmud comes home with a mission of modernization and progress. Forced marriages occur in both novels: Sa'eed's young widow to an old man from his native village, and the Oxford student, Mahmoud, in absentia to his fourteen year old cousin. These congruent incidents both seem to be criticisms of the native culture, but Salih's reading of colonial and nativist formations is of an order of ambivalence almost entirely absent from *Black Vanguard*. In *Season of Migration*, the narrator's mixed feelings of guilt and relief on hearing of his friend's wife's marriage to the old man are of an order of ambiguity unknown to Mahmud when he first learns of his betrothal to his cousin:

> [Mahmud] looked up and down the rows of faces [at dinner in his Oxford college], and then at the high table, wondering what they would all think of him if they knew that he had just been married, without his knowledge, without any reference to his will, to a girl of fourteen! But he didn't have to wonder; he knew, and he felt like an impostor among these free individuals who were masters of their fate, whose personalities, whose wills, could never have such an indignity inflicted upon them. For the first time he felt inferior to them.[12]

Mahmud's struggle with his cultural hybridity, as one would guess from this extract, is all on the Sudanese side. He can only feel indignation and guilt for the backwardness of his people. "Love for the colonizer is subtended by a complex of feelings ranging from shame to self-hate."[13] Everything seems weighed against him back home: though he is temporarily reconciled to his wife, Badria, on account of her beauty, she is guilty of a "reversion" comparable to Moawiya's when she allows herself to be reabsorbed into the harem world of Sudanese women-only society. Mahmud is left to experience a deepening attraction to his wife's teacher, Jean Bannerman. When Badria has their baby daughter circumcised, an act which results in her death from high fever, Mahmud is so disgusted by this ultimate "barbarism" that he divorces Badria, only for his half-repressed love for Jean to come to nothing in a final meeting at Oxford.[14]

Conversely, the shortcomings of the colonizer are framed according to an optimistic finalism which assumes the eventual success of the British-led decolonization process. British Sudan was "nothing like the India E. M. Forster made his passage to." The country belonged "exclusively to its own people" and there was now "absolutely no inferiority attached to their status in it." The phrasing is the British First Secretary's, and it is addressed to the British fiancee of Mahmud's fellow Oxonian, Amin. The young woman is further assured that "no social inferiority is attached to the status" of an Englishwoman who marries a Sudanese.[15] Atiyah's reconstructed imperialism, based on the notion of trusteeship and partnership between the colonizer and the colonized, asks of the colonizer nothing. It is built on the assumption that the evils of colonialism have all but disappeared; that all the colonized have to do is put their primitivism away, avoiding any tendency to "reversion", in order to emulate their colonial masters, "free individuals [. . .] masters of their fate."

In this project the likes of Mahmud and Amin are the black vanguard upon whose shoulders rest their country's hopes of progression to a higher order of civilization. Unlike Mustafa Sa'eed, they are individuals whom the West has succeeded in civilizing. Amin settles down happily with a British woman, and Mahmud would dearly like to have done the same. Neither have any animus towards the British for having conquered their country – on the contrary, like Atiyah himself, they would, if asked, have expressed their belief in British rule in the Sudan, "seeing in it a close approach to the genuine mandatory ideal."[16]

This aspect of the text should be read contrapuntally alongside the anti-colonial message of *Season of Migration* as epitomized by Mustafa Sa'eed's activities in England. These begin with his declaration of war on arrival: "I have come to you as a conqueror"; continue through his seduction of a stream of susceptible white women, and end with his "destructive pursuit" and tragic killing of his wife, Jean Morris. Salih himself sees Sa'eed's entire embroglio with the British as a reversal of roles in which his protagonist returns to the West to visit on it the "disease" of violence it had first inflicted on his own society as colonial conqueror.[17] Curiously, this notion of retribution, which should be viewed in the context of the postcolonial return of the margins to the center, has a parallel in *Black Vanguard* in a brief incidence of dialogue. Mahmud's father is engaged in phatic conversation with his son's Oxford tutor:

> "It's been wonderful," said Sheikh Ahmed. "I can't tell you what a great impression your country has made on me, Dr. Andrews – greater even than I expected [. . .] That leaves you no excuse, no excuse whatever."
> "No excuse for what?"
> "For wanting to grab half the world, instead of remaining peaceably at home and being contented with what God has given you. Upon my life, Dr. Andrews, you English are a very voracious people! I shall forgive you

if you honour your word and leave our country when it can stand on its
own feet, as you say you will. But God help you if you don't, and I am still
alive, I should either fight you to the death or, better still, *come here and
colonise a little bit of England myself"* [18]

The phrase I have italicized is not a slippage from a rational ordered
colonial discourse to an oppositional postcolonial positioning. It is in
Season of Migration, that an antithetical re-writing of Sheikh Ahmed's
lighthearted threat ensures that a fight to the death does take place in
earnest, with Mustafa Sa'eed the one who returns to "colonise a little bit
of England" himself. *Black Vanguard* remains a novel written partially
from the colonial perspective. This is evident from the filial tenor of
Sheikh Ahmed's speech, as well as in the fear of reversion Mahmud
entertains towards his wife Badria and the world of the harem. At the
same time as he wishes to advance a nationalist discourse, Atiyah shows
no inclination to problematize the Western Enlightenment project, with
its "universalising will to knowledge" enabling its deployment of
power over non-western societies, by means of its "production of
knowledge as [. . .] negative: stereotyping, Othering, dominatory."[19]
Instead, he stages what is in effect a reversal of one of the standard definitions of postcolonial literature: instead of looking, as a member of the
colonized periphery, from the margin to the center, he has adopted the
view of the center towards the margin. It is in this respect that his writings scarcely manage to move beyond the category of colonial discourse.

Two into Three Won't Go: Palestine, Lebanon, Hollywood

By moving in his last novel, *Lebanon Paradise*, from Sudan to Palestine,
Edward Atiyah traversed the two poles of his political mapping of the
Arab world. His close personal involvement in the preparation of Sudan
for postcolonial government engendered in him an optimism for what
he believed was a key experiment in decolonization, but this optimism
could hardly be replicated in the case of Palestine. Atiyah's concern with
the issue of Palestine had become evident in his Sudan Agency reports
of the mid-1930s and resurfaced in his autobiography and political
lectures and pamphlets of the 1940s (see chapter 7). Palestine became a
far more ambivalent site of intersection than Sudan for his pro-western
schema of decolonization allied to Arab nationalism. In fact, as the title
suggests, in *Lebanon Paradise*, Atiyah re-sites the Palestine issue within
a Lebanese context shot through with resonances of later events he
himself never lived to see. Set immediately pursuant to the débâcle of
1948, it attempts both to account for this defeat and to construct an

agenda for the revitalization of Arab society. Besides the politics of Palestine, the novel foregrounds two across-the-barriers love stories which, after the success of his first novel, *The Thin Line* , show Atiyah experimenting with the potentially commercial formulas of Hollywood romantic melodrama. In fact the romantic interest is interwoven with both political and gendering concerns in an attempt to project a brave new world of secular, enfranchised Arab men and women set above the narrow channels of traditionally sectarian Lebanese and Arab society. At the same time, the novel unwittingly looks forward barely two decades or so to the dismemberment of Lebanon and the massacres of Sabra and Shatila.

Lebanon Paradise doubles as a comedy of manners and a manifesto for an Arab renaissance made essential by the defeat in Palestine. The narrative has two main locations: a hotel (the name in the title) used as a summer retreat by the high class citizens of Beirut, situated on the coast immediately above that city, and a Palestinian refugee camp outside of Sidon. The main array of characters are, with the exceptions of a Palestinian camp leader, a middle class Palestinian refugee woman, and a British female journalist, all Lebanese. The Palestinian refugees are themselves curiously marginalized and possess no real voice in the narrative. Their representatives are mainly mouthpieces for the politico-cultural agenda outlined above, which however laudable, is at best peripheral to the experience of the refugees themselves. Served with generous helpings of Chekovian dialogue, the novel represents the self-indulgent Lebanese idle rich on the verge of the Middle Eastern holocaust.

The wealthy Batrunis, a family of husband, wife, and five daughters, are the center of a satire of Lebanese manners, around whom Atiyah interweaves "representative" characters from high society and political life. The youngest daughter, Violette, is set to emulate her successfully married sisters by her engagement to Andre, a too polished and charming socialite from an excellent Beirut family. But Violette is marked with nationalist sympathies, shame at the recent humiliation over Palestine, and a proto-feminist streak that attracts her to Jennie Haydon, a British journalist who has recently been reporting the fighting in Palestine and now wants to visit the refugee camps. Violette's unlikely accompaniment of Jenny to the camp in Sidon, where she meets and is attracted to the Palestinian camp leader, Musa Canaan, links the two worlds of opulence and despair.

Through Musa Canaan, Atiyah ties the issue of Palestine into a Pan-Arab perspective that owes not a little to the work of his friend, George Antonius:

"I was in despair for a time, like many others [. . .] How could we not be? As Palestinians we had lost our country overnight. As Arabs we found we had been living on an illusion called the Arab awakening which, after filling us with pride and hope and self-confidence since we were school-boys, was suddenly exposed as a false dawn [. . .] Well, never mind. If it was a false dawn, the real awakening will yet come. This catastrophe ought to awaken us. Despair is a terrible experience, but it is something real. It takes you down to the depths, and from the depths a new life, equally real, may come [. . .] Perhaps if you have known despair, you will never again be taken in by the facile and spurious."[20]

By referring to the false dawn of the Arab awakening, Canaan discloses his western-filiated nationalism, and in pronouncing on the positive lessons to be learned from the loss of his land he is a mouthpiece for Atiyah's own program of Arab renewal. Though Atiyah may have had in mind his friend Musa Alami, the unofficial champion of the Palestinian refugees (to whom the novel is dedicated) when he named his chief Palestinian character, Canaan is nothing less than the political voice of the Anglo-Arab writer himself. The choice of Canaan implies a pre-Islamic biblical genealogy to the land of Palestine, but it is evident from the passage above that Atiyah's hero, a graduate of the American University of Beirut, a democratic socialist, and admirer of British administration, is neither a peasant guerrilla leader of the 1936–39 Revolution, nor a scion of the five or six families that constituted the pinnacle of Palestinian landowning notables. Given that the British perhaps bore primary responsibility for the loss of his country, Canaan displays remarkably little animus towards them. At moments – as when he expostulates to Violette on the refugees' habit of concealing deaths in order to get extra rations – he sounds curiously like one of the colonial governing class. "It is difficult to make them see [. . .] that they are stealing rations from others by doing this sort of thing."[21] At the end of the novel, we feel Canaan receives an appropriate reward for his British-style organizational efficiency when he is promoted to the UN relief agency's salaried roving inspector of refugee camps in Lebanon, Syria and Jordan.

In contrast to Canaan, the Palestinian refugees in the camp are figures of pity, with quaint mannerisms and a language that is colorful but quite useless for articulating their plight. They are signified in quasi-biblical terms as a "tribe" and a "multitude" who without Canaan would be unable both to represent and organize themselves. He alone has the language skills that enable him to switch with ease between their idiom and the educated register needed to converse with foreign visitors and people of Violette's class. In speaking to the refugees Canaan employs a biblical language, as when a boy burns himself on a cooking pot: "'Can't you hear this poor boy? [. . .] Where are his father and mother? Go to him, one of you; call his people.'" On Violette's arrival at the camp, Canaan slips into the colonial register:

> "We have a few helpers, but they're not educated [. . .] one or two girls from Sidon paid by the Red Cross, but all more or less in the servant class – no good for responsible work."[22]

Musa Canaan is another of Atiyah's strangely de-Arabized Arab heroes and constitutes an evident extension of the problem of colonial mimicry already seen in Atiyah's earlier writings. In articulating the Palestinian cause in the codes of Fabianism and British common sense, he seems to have climbed into the shoes vacated by the progressives in the Palestine Government of the mandate: "'something like English socialism; a programme that will abolish poverty and ignorance and disease [. . .] among the Arab masses in ten or fifteen years. This isn't communism, but only common sense and common decency. It's the only way to prevent communism.'"[23] The *déraciné* experience of bilingual Arabs, as represented by Canaan and Violette, both convinced Arab nationalists, is encapsulated in their use of written English to communicate with each other: "She wrote in English, because her Arabic was very inadequate and she never used it in correspondence [. . .] [This] helped to maintain the separation between the two worlds, in which she was now living."[24] By extension, the novel's attempt to render variant registers and codes, indeed discrete languages (colloquial Arabic, British colonial English, Hollywood American English, and a macronic conversational French), creates an effect of hotch-potch rather than linguistic richness. This is seen in the novel's second love relationship, between Violette's brother-in-law, Emile, and the middle class refugee, Fareeda Barradi, who he falls for while attending her son. The Muslim Palestinian woman and the Christian Lebanese doctor provide a central text for the novel: female emancipation, and a simultaneous reformation of the social character of both the mercenary and superficial Christians and the backward, custom-ridden Muslims. This in the name of an advanced, unifying Arabism. The fact that the love relationship that bears the burden of this ideological project is conducted in the manner of a Ronald Coleman movie severely limits the message's credibility. (At one point, Fareeda tells her lover: "I have sometimes dreamed of a love so great and magnificent that it would crush everything in its way," while in response to his offer to divorce his wife and convert to her religion, she exclaims: "No, I don't want you to become a Moslem [. . .] *Quelle ironie.* The very thing I am fleeing from.")[25] As for the Arabic language, it is rendered throughout the novel in an Ali Baba idiom located somewhere within the static construct analyzed by Said in *Orientalism*. "The racial tendency to eloquence" is shown to carry within itself a core semantics of half-truths, deception, and lies, as seen, for example, in the case of the Lebanese doctor from the refugee camp: "Like many Arabs he became intoxicated with the magic of his own words after hearing them for a few moments."[26]

Lebanon Paradise therefore summarizes the problems that attend the project of forming a discourse that sets out to handle Arab themes in an alien metropolitan language. Atiyah's *pedagogic* purpose is to construct from the static notion of a single unified Pan-Arab nation whose formative linear history is in the past (the Arab nation of *The Arab Awakening*), a new westernized entity which shows no slippage from its pure origins to its fractured present. This position differs markedly from Ghassan Kanafani's in *Men in the Sun*, a text which fills the absence opened in *Lebanon Paradise* by the latter's effective silence on the experience of the Palestinian refugees. The distinction resides in Kanafani's attempt to suggest the *performative* dimension of Palestinian dispossession, that is, to emphasize the liminality of the Palestinians within the Arab nation in terms of their dislocated, fractured *present*.[27] Kanafani's novella about three Palestinian men journeying inside an empty tanker across the desert to the borders of Kuwait, where they hope to obtain illegal entry, enacts the lived experience of Palestinians without commenting on the politics of their predicament. According to his English translator, in this novella, "unlike many committed writers, [Kanafani] refuses to impose an ideological scheme on his fiction in any but the most general terms."[28] The novella attempts to represent, in the words of Edward Said, the living out of an unstable present, "subject to echoes from the past"; a present that drives the men in the sun toward the future where "they will die—invisibly, anonymously, killed in the sun, in the same present that has summoned them out of their past and taunted them with their helplessness and inactivity."[29] It is clear, however, that the Palestinans in Kanafani's story must make their present for themselves, that is to say, whatever the helplessness of their fate, they are not creatures of passivity waiting on the correct ideological reactivation of the other Arab nations.

Conclusion

In writing about Sudan and the problem of Palestine in a popular form in English, Atiyah was certainly motivated by genuine concern to expedite the development of fellow Arabs. But by forcing the language and

behavior of his Arab characters – be they Sudanese students or
Palestinian refugees – into western codes, he succeeded in saying little
about them that could be considered recognizable to Arab experience.
His writings founder, as do other exercises in Anglo-Arab poetics, on
their author's decision to encode Arab themes in an alien metropolitan
language, where the codes of the adopted language are made to substi-
tute those of the writer's native culture. Atiyah's command of English
is deceptively fluent, covering the fact that behind the writing there
exists no shared speech community, no cultural connections between
author and readership. On the one hand, in spite of the Hollywood
dimension he attempts to build into his discourse, he knows too much
about Lebanon and its Arab tensions to produce texts disclosing
"universal" significations for a western readership. On the other,
barriers of a foreign language and alien codes close off the texts to a
monocultural Arab readership. But more serious is the contention that
Atiyah's writings are undermined by the "ambivalence of mimicry"
which Bhabha theorizes as a marking feature of colonial discourse. I
think I have shown above that, in substance, this is the case. Amin
Osman, Mahmoud, the Sudanese student, Musa Canaan, the
Palestinian: each bear the mark of colonial mimicry. Like their creator,
the Anglo-Arab writer, they are almost British but not quite, with a
resultant attitude towards their fellow Arabs which is condescending
and phobic at one and the same time. Their desire to reform the Arab
character in the image of the rational, progressive westerner is threatened by the fear of reversion to native ignorance and barbarism. Such
an ambivalent and partial vision unfortunately fatally undercuts
Atiyah's main purpose of embodying Arab themes within the English
language.

7

Edward Atiyah: The End of Anglo-Arab Politics

▬▬▬▬▬▬▬

A few of the colonized almost succeeded in disappearing in the colonizer group. It is clear, on the other hand, that a collective drama will never be settled through individual solutions.

Albert Memmi

The British authorities needed subordinate officials who spoke Arabic and understood the ways of the Near East, but who were also acquainted with Western methods of thought and administration. They found what they needed in the graduates of the Syrian mission-schools, who for half a century loyally and effectively filled a variety of positions in the Governments of Egypt and the Sudan [. . .] Being largely an urban middle-class community, partly Christian and suspected of an excessive attachment to Great Britain or at least to the West, the Syrian-Egyptians have not always been liked by the Egyptians.

Albert Hourani[1]

If George Antonius's monument is *The Arab Awakening*, his historical account of the Arab national movement, Edward Atiyah's most enduring piece of writing is his autobiography, *An Arab Tells His Story: A Study in Loyalties*. Although both figures undertook important translation work on behalf of the Arab cause, they wrote exclusively in English, underscoring the formative effect of their British education as well as their self-appointed roles as mediators between the Arabs and the West. The rough road of Anglo-Arab politics caused Antonius and Atiyah plenty of buffeting. While Antonius's credence in the link all but came to grief over Palestine, Atiyah's more positive experience working in the Sudan Government service only delayed the disillusionment which eventually came with Suez, the débâcle that destabilized pro-western Arab elites throughout the *mashreq*.[2]

Edward Atiyah belonged to the last generation of Arabs for whom the Anglo-Arab dimension to the development of Arab nationalist politics remained central to their thinking. Through interrogating the discourse of one of Britain's last proteges in the Arab world, this chapter will try to shed light on the stage of affiliation to western norms through which non-western nationalisms, initially framed within the context of colonialism, seem to have passed on the path towards decolonization and national liberation. Atiyah's formation in British codes, his production of an Arab self-identity, and his articulation of the issues of imperialism and decolonization in the context of the Middle East, are each factors in a discourse that eventually demands re-framing as a consequence of the breakdown of Anglo-Arab relations over Palestine and Egypt.

Atiyah, the British, and the Arabs

Edward Atiyah was of Greek Orthodox lineage, like his compatriot George Antonius, although Atiyah's immediate family had converted to Protestantism. Also like Antonius, Atiyah attended the British-run Victoria College in Alexandria, and then Oxbridge, which he left in 1925. Both took up careers as public administrators working for the British; but where Antonius had been employed in troubled mandated Palestine, Atiyah's posting was to the relative peace of Sudan. His later involvement in Arab affairs saw him Secretary of the Arab Office in London soon after the end of World War II.

Atiyah's attachment to Great Britain seems to have developed almost naturally out of the national vacuum that operated within the Ottoman domain known in the early part of this century as Syria. Ottoman Syria was divided into three main districts: Mount Lebanon, Syria, and Palestine. The Ottomans grouped their subjects according to religious affiliation, and it was the custom for people from the geographical area termed Syria to express their identity in terms of their church or mosque, rather than according to any racial or political criteria. As Philip Hitti put it:

> The Syrian is the man without a country par excellence. His patriotism takes the form of love for family and sect, and when expressed in inanimate terms, love for the unexcelled scenery of Syria with its glorious sunshine and invigorating air. Syrian patriotism has no political aspects.

Atiyah articulated this state of affairs succinctly in his autobiography:

> No attachment to the soil of Syria, no idea that Syria was the natural home

of the Syrians, ever developed in my mind. Rather it seemed that the best thing people who had been so unfortunate as to be born in Syria could do was to leave it as soon as they could, and adopt some other country.[3]

As a Lebanese Christian, Atiyah seems to have been predestined to adopt one or other western protector, and as his maternal grandfather was a convert to Protestantism, his opting for Britain was hardly surprising. His pro-British sentiments appear to develop credibly out of the factious Lebanese society of his childhood and early youth, in which, as he explains in his autobiography, Christians, Muslims and Druse entertained mutual prejudices and suspicions toward one another. While many of his fellow countrymen emigrated to Africa, North and South America, and even Australia, Atiyah's family followed a course adopted by the more able, professional classes, developing links with Egypt and Sudan, where they were employed by the British adminis-tration for the reasons outlined by Hourani above. But Atiyah's ardor for the British exceeded that of his parents who, though educated in English, did not "become in any way anglicized" and provided for him "a home influence [. . .] still strongly Arabic." His emotional attach-ment to the British was cemented by an incident in the Turco-Italian war of 1911 in which the Italian fleet bombarded Turkish ships in Beirut and the young Atiyah took refuge in the British mission school.

> The glories of the British Empire, of English power and dominion over one-quarter of the World (marked red) stretched out gratifyingly on every map I saw. With one part of this empire I was personally acquainted. I was indeed living in it most of the time, and could see from our house the British flag flying over the Government headquarters, that flag which had protected us from the Italian shells sinking the Turkish destroyers in Beyrouth harbour.[4]

Another way of fixing Atiyah's identification with empire is to see its formation as characteristic of minorities who disdain the majority of their fellow colonized, aspiring instead to join with the colonizer. Atiyah's case recalls another minority – the Jews of Tunisia – to which Albert Memmi belonged, and whose affiliation to France he signifies in similar terms:

> The Jewish population identified as much with the colonizers as the colo-nized. They were undeniably "natives," as they were then called, as near as possible to the Moslems in poverty, language, sensibilities, taste in music, odors and cooking. However, unlike the Moslems they passion-ately endeavored to identify themselves with the French [. . .] My own

relations with my fellow Jews were not made easier when I decided to join
the colonized, but it was necessary for me to denounce colonialism, even
though it was not as hard on the Jews as it was on the others. Because of
this ambivalence I knew only too well the contradictory emotions which
swayed their lives. Didn't my own heart beat faster at the sight of the little
flag on the stern of the ships that joined Tunis to Marseille?

An Arab Tells His Story could well be read as an exemplary text on the
desire for assimilation on the part of the colonized. That socio-religious
sense of superiority that caused the Syrian Christian to look down upon
his Muslim neighbor could without too much difficulty be translated
into near total absorption within the colonizer's mindset: "The first
attempt of the colonized is to change his condition by changing his skin.
There is a tempting model very close at hand – the colonizer. [. . .] The
first ambition of the colonized is to become equal to that splendid model
and to resemble him to the point of disappearing in him."[5] Atiyah
admits that this was true in his case. After barely a year at Victoria
College, he was ready to see the 1919 Egyptian revolution wholly
through the eyes of his English history master, Mr. Reed:

> my sympathies, in spite of my friendship with Egyptian boys, were not
> with the revolution. I did not really identify my Egyptian friends at school
> with this unattractive rabble shouting in the streets. My Egyptian friends
> were, like me, civilized boys. They discoursed on English history and
> quoted Shakespeare [. . .] Besides, if my going to Victoria College had
> brought me into intimate touch with Egyptian boys and made me like
> them, it had also strengthened my love of everything English, and the
> revolution was a movement against England. It was a challenge to Mr
> Reed and his political convictions; it was wrong. The Egyptians could not
> govern themselves. To parade in the streets and shout and smash
> windows was just stupid. There was no sincerity in the movement; only
> agitation and hooliganism. This, I was sure, was Mr Reed's view of it.

During his years at Oxford – where he courted the British girl he later
married – Edward Atiyah felt he had gained acceptance in British
society. But back in Sudan, as a master at Gordon College, he fell victim
to the hauteur of the British tutors who not only maintained a social
remove from their "native" colleagues, but also occupied superior
grades in the government hierarchy. "At the College they enjoyed the
prestige of rulers. Not the dignity of schoolmasters but the aura of sovereignty surrounded their every step." Atiyah's reaction to this new
experience of colonial exclusion was to embrace what he considered a
nationalist position, assertive of his Arab identity, critical of the British,
but basically, "what I wanted was to be accepted by them as an equal

and treated as a friend." He moved in this phase toward a declared sympathy with the colonized. The mentality behind his rejection of the Egyptian revolution of 1919 was transmuted by a new awareness of the sentiments of the colonized. If it was still not possible for him to hate the British as the Indians and Egyptians did, he "could understand now why they hated British rule." After he had moved from Gordon College to his new post in the political department of the Sudan Government (known as the Sudan Agency by the British), Atiyah could claim to have achieved a reconciliation between the two loyalties. "Not only had two warring ideals made peace in my mind, but indeed two parts of me, both real and inescapable, had fused into a harmony." But this would certainly not have been possible did he not feel that he had "been accepted by the British as an equal."[6] It is clear that Atiyah was an Anglophile first, and that his Arabism followed on and always played a muted second string; that is to say, the "Anglo" definitely preceded the "Arab" in his proclaimed synthesis of the two constituents of his identity. The sense is that the experience of British imperial arrogance at Gordon College was decidedly ante, triggering in Atiyah a nationalist riposte that otherwise would have been unable to sustain itself.

For a Christian Arab, proclaiming oneself an Arab nationalist meant having to come to terms with the Muslim majority of his race. From the prejudiced attitude towards Muslims imbibed from his childhood, Atiyah moved toward a qualified acceptance of the Arab heritage that maintained the proviso that the Arab future lay with cooperation with the West:

> Some of us achieved, or we thought we achieved, complete identification [with the Muslim Arabs], became Arab nationalists in the belief that Arab nationalism was a secular movement in which Moslems and Christians could equally share. But many of us felt that Arab nationalism was still mainly a Moslem emotion and movement in which we had no real place, however much we might sympathize with it. We wanted it to become genuinely secular, leaving religion, as the West had learned to leave it, to the domain of intimate personal experience [. . .] For the moral virtues of the Moslem religion, for the genius of the Prophet who founded it and for the great achievements of Arab civilization at its height, above all its toler-ance and its democracy in the days of the great Caliphs, we had a genuine admiration. Those of us who knew Arabic well cherished it and took a proprietorial pride in its treasures of prose and verse. But we felt that in the world of to-day the road of progress was the highway of Western civi-lization. We wanted the Moslem Arabs to join us on that highway not as casual sightseers, but as purposeful travellers determined to reach the same end as ourselves – full membership of the modern world.[7]

While recognizing the "spiritual conflict between Islam and Western civilisation," Atiyah trusted in the advance guard of educated Muslims "establishing a fruitful relationship with the life and thought of the West [. . .] once the problem of the political relations of the Arab world with the West [was] completely solved."[8] (This theme was taken up in his novel, *Black Vanguard*.) For Atiyah, the West's was a universal culture in relation to which Arab culture could only be subsidiary. In spite of the Arabs' past achievements, their civilization had failed to absorb humanism and the inquiring spirit from the West and therefore had remained suburban. The Arab awakening was the reanimation of the Arabs "by the twofold inspiration of [their] own past and of the message of western civilization which [they were in the last century] beginning to receive." But the factiousness and indiscipline of the Arabs which had militated against the maintenance of the Arab empire and allowed in the Turks, worked against the realization of a united states of the Arab world in modern times.[9] Atiyah might at times speak the language of the early Arab nationalists who also conceived of Arab nationalism in entirely secular terms, but his nationalist discourse was more accurately characterized by Herbert Bodman as "the partisanship [. . .] of a sophisticated Arab Christian" for whom Islam was less a religion, more the cultural achievement of the Arab nation.[10]

Atiyah on Imperialism and Decolonization

Atiyah's hopes for the Arabs rested on two shaky pillars: Arab partnership with benevolent western powers, preeminently Great Britain; and the Arabs' recognition that their own best interests lay in their adoption of western values. The success of such a project, what Atiyah called the Anglo-Arab synthesis, depended on the orderly progress of decolonization in the Arab East. Atiyah's faith in this prospect derived from his education and his experience as a political officer in the British administered Government of Sudan between 1926 and 1945 which he advanced as "the showpiece of British colonial policy in Africa (or perhaps anywhere, for that matter)."[11] Alive to the usual objections made against the British imperialist enterprise, especially in the Middle East, Atiyah still had faith in a happy ending as far as both the colonized peoples and the British colonizer were concerned. He held to a version of the trusteeship theory, the genealogy of which he traced back via Lord Lugard to Mr Reed's beloved Edmund Burke. According to this reading of British imperial history, in the long run, the implicit decency of the British character, of British institutions and statesmen, would crucially manifest itself. The civilized world of Alexandria College, of discourse on Shakespeare and British history, with the spirit of Mr Reed hovering over his pen, had taught Atiyah to believe in the ultimately benign influences of Great Britain.

> To the peoples of the British Empire the British Government seemed at times to be dishonest in its intentions, hypocritical in its professions, unwilling to recognize their growing up, or perhaps determined to prevent its final logical consequences. Yet, viewing the history of the last two hundred years from the vantage point of today, it is impossible to deny that British colonial policy has followed a course of gradual evolution from paternal imperialism towards the complete handing over of authority to democratically representative governments in the various parts of the Empire. That this final handing over (as indeed several stages of the way) had often to be fought for by the colonial peoples concerned does not alter the fact that it is the fulfilment of a policy initiated by Britain and inherent in the principles repeatedly proclaimed by her statesmen.[12]

The narrative style is that normally reserved for the metropolitan history with its rational ordering ("logical consequences"), grand vistas ("viewing the history of the last two hundred years"), unfolding idea ("a course of gradual evolution", "final handing over"), and territorial cohesiveness ("various parts of the empire"). The grand design omits, smoothes out ("seems at times to have been dishonest"), or elides ("had to be fought for") all the conflicts, hesitations, and attempts to reinterpret or renege on the part of the colonizer.[13] The perspective is that of an insider, for whom all dissonance, fracture and ambiguity must be smoothed out or reconstituted, and any alternative narratives – i.e. the histories of the oppressed – homogenized ("peoples of the British Empire") or put aside. Objections by the colonized to this historicist narrative of maturing gradualism are bracketed as emotional short-termism. If the populations of the Indian subcontinent, for instance, had known "the end [of the colonial experience] was [to be] happy, peaceful and honourable in so far as relations between Britain and [themselves] were concerned," they would have viewed the struggles of decolonization with greater equanimity. In the Middle East it was true the story had been different – British rule there had "scarcely justified itself", and had made for little development in the countries concerned. In Palestine imperialism had shown its "greatest failure", but by the early 1950s, Egypt was on the track to successful self-determination. Opposition there to Britain was now the residuum of "emotional or psychological force" given that British "'occupation'" was now no more than "a shadow." The bitter feelings of the colonized often amounted to little more than a wounded *amore propre*. In short, in addition to his "new loyalty to the cause of Arab nationalism", Edward Atiyah's "old loyalty to the British Empire" had been modified to meet the exigencies of the postcolonial situation.[14]

Palestine, Egypt, and The Parting of Ways

Atiyah published his last substantial work in English in 1955. *The Arabs*, an essay on Arab history which concerns itself largely with the modern period, appeared seventeen years after the publication of *The Arab Awakening*. Antonius had died in 1942 and the question of Palestine had changed its character from the festering wound in the Arab psyche that had caused Antonius almost to lose all confidence in his role as a mediator between the British and the Arabs. That Atiyah had been able to maintain his own faith in British friendship with the Arabs was partly due to his involvement in Sudan, and partly due to the congruence of his views on Anglo-Arab relations with those of certain British representatives in the Middle East. In 1936 and 1937, for example, in his capacity as political officer in the Sudanese Intelligence unit, Atiyah, together with his uncle Samuel, produced a series of reports on political attitudes towards Britain in the Arab world. These stressed the new Pan-Arab links then being established in the fields of higher education, the press, and politico-cultural exchange visits, and foregrounded the negative fallout Britain's Zionist policy in Palestine was having, particularly on Egyptian public opinion. Muslim Arabs generally were alienated from the West by the sectarian conflict in Syria which had been exacerbated by the French mandate, and by British support for the Jews in Palestine. The reports noted the strengthening of Pan-Arab sentiments by the Islamic organizations and painted a somber picture for British strategic interests in the region should another world conflict break out. In that event, the Arabs, Atiyah predicted, would take a purely opportunist line. They felt betrayed by Britain because of her non-fulfillment of her promises to support an Arab state or federation of Arab states after the last war. Now the appropriate policy would be to sponsor the creation of some kind of Arab federation. Above all, the Palestine issue needed to be addressed. The Palestinian Arabs – both Muslim and Christian – were united in their rejection of partition and would resist it to the utmost, because it gave the Jews practically everything worth having in Palestine. Attempts to force partition on Palestine would involve Iraq and Egypt and embarrass Britain in the event of another European war. Overall, Britain had suffered a decline of her reputation for international invulnerability.

As for her "internal" prestige with the Arab nationalists, there is very little

left of that. Confidence in her probity, respect for her word, have vanished
completely, while fear of her striking power is almost totally absent.[15]

The fact that these reports should have been officially circulated both in
London and the Middle East "indicated a certain degree of accord" with
the views they propounded, at least among the British representatives
in Cairo.[16] Even so, in war time Britain Atiyah found it impossible to get
a hearing for the Arab point of view on Palestine. Still, he was prepared
to submerge his frustrations by the need to support Britain's war effort,
in spite of the damage her policies on Palestine were causing her among
Arabic-speaking peoples throughout the region.

Atiyah felt the "fate of Palestine [was] [. . .] the decisive factor which
more than any other [would] determine the course of Anglo-Arab
relations in the years to come."[17] The Palestine question became an
official concern in 1945 when he became Secretary of the Arab Office in
London. Certainly, the post looked ideal for someone with his pro-
British credentials. Though he denied the Arab League was the creation
of the British, he agreed that they and it shared "common interests",
even though Britain's opposition to Arab Palestine's independence
would mean "no peace or genuine friendship between her and the
League" was possible.[18]

From now onward, the lectures and writings Atiyah produced on
Palestine, culminating in those sections dealing with the topic in, *The
Arabs*, show an undoubted firming of his stance on Arab nationalism.
But this still operated within the schema of Anglo-Arab harmony and
amicable decolonization outlined above. Though the logic of these
pronouncements took Atiyah's nationalist discourse substantially
beyond the circumscribed parameters of, *An Arab Tells His Story*, and as
a result, threatened to subvert the Anglo-Arab synthesis the text
promoted, Atiyah remained unwilling or unable to unravel the implications of the West's support for the colonization by Zionism of an Arab
land. He was able to maintain his Anglo-Arab allegiance by marking the
perfidious character of Zionism, and eliding the formative role of the
British in opening Palestine up to it. Immediately up to and after the
Balfour Declaration, Britain had been deluded by the Zionists' specious
presentation of their cause, and they had thereby gained a bridgehead
in Palestine from which to launch their final attack without her aid.
After the 1939 London conference, at which the British appeared to see
the error of their ways and agreed to put a final stop to Jewish immigration within five years, the Zionists took things into their own hands.[19]
Under the impact of Zionist terror the British stood by passively, guilty
less of deception than of a failure of will, buckling in under Zionist and
United States' pressure at the crucial point "play[ing] the part which

had been played once before in Palestine by a Roman proconsul who washed his hands [. . .] This was not neutrality but a dereliction of duty." Britain's policy in Palestine had been a "disastrous experiment" that had gone badly wrong.[20]

But it remained indisputable that the "unique and unprecedented act of aggression committed by the Zionist Jews against the Arabs in an Arab country" had been "supported, *wittingly or unwittingly*, by the western world over a period of 30 years." (The phrase I have italicized demonstrates the reluctance with which Atiyah faced up to the premise.) It was true that Western Christendom had given its support to "this pernicious movement of fanatical Jewish nationalism" – the British included. Still he hung back from drawing the anti-imperialist conclusion: despite his undoubted sincerity in arguing the Palestinian cause, the whole affair took on for him the character of an aberration. The more desperate matters grew, and when, after 1948, it was possible to distribute the blame more generally – on the United States, the Soviet Union, the United Nations, and the Arabs themselves – the more Palestine came to signify an inchoate "disaster" around which one might throw up the demarcation of a *cordon sanitaire*. From the point of view of the Arabs themselves, the débâcle of 1948 had exposed characteristic shortcomings. A lot of bombast had been indulged in, but when it came to the point, the Arab cause had been "crippled by a lack of unity." Upon the Arab League and the Arab leadership which had presided over the abortive attempt to defend the Palestinians militarily, a clear portion of the blame fell. For despite the forces arrayed against them, "the Arabs would have won the battle for Palestine had there not been something false or rotten in themselves."[21]

As if to throw the Palestinian problem into greater relief and thereby ensure its isolation, Atiyah declared its nature intractable, coming up with a position himself at least as hard-line as the mainstream Arab opinion of the time. Israel was an expansionist entity which, if the Arab states were unable to defend themselves, would "snatch another piece of Arab territory – in Jordan or the Gaza region – with impunity." To the question – would Israel be accepted and integrated into the region?

> The only honest and realistic answer [. . .] for any foreseeable future is an emphatic "No" [. . .] To the Arabs, Israel is an alien, hateful, and dangerous intrusion [. . .] the expression of a militant and fanatical nationalism which is incompatible with the existence and healthy development of the Arab community.

Though the West obviously favored a rapprochement, Atiyah's hope was that by a concerted boycott of the new state, in the long run "the imported plant with its roots in New York will die."[22]

But was there a correlation between the pro-western politics of the ruling elites in the Arab world, and the popular "discontent with the corruption of the *ancien régime*, which was in power everywhere when the Palestine catastrophe occurred, and which symbolized the political and social rottenness that had cost the Arabs Palestine"?[23] The final chapter of *The Arabs* makes it clear that Atiyah did not make this connection. He remained committed to the westernization of the Arab world, manifestations of which he saw everywhere, from the post-war oil boom, the secularization of Arab society and the emancipation of women, to the spread of western ideals of democracy, independence and national sovereignty. The western presence was passing from its "dominant and aggressive" imperialist phase to a "friendly and helpful" patronage. Decolonization – in spite of Palestine – seemed to be making orderly progress in the Arab East if not in North Africa. The Anglo-Egyptian agreement over Sudan (February 1953) recognized that country's independence and "removed one of the two major sources of discord between Britain and Egypt."[24] The second of these problems, British occupation of the Canal Zone, appeared to have been solved by the 1954 Anglo-Egyptian agreement to evacuate the Suez base. This was going to "cause a great difference in Arab feelings." Even the Arab League had recovered from the nadir of 1948 and continued to embody Arab aspirations "for some form of confederation." As they got their freedom, the Arabs' "alignment with the West [was] bound to be strengthened"; educational ties and aid ensuring a "more genuine cooperation between the parties."[25] The tide was still flowing in the appropriate direction. Omitted is the possibility that Britain would cease to be a major player in the region in the not distant future, as well as any linkage between Zionism and western manipulation of Arab regimes.[26]

The Arabs first appeared in 1955, shortly after the conclusion of the Anglo-Egyptian Treaty which appeared to bring to an end over seventy years of British control over Egypt. A second edition with an appendix appeared in 1958. This appears to leave the central thesis of the text unaltered. A disjunctive narrative is cobbled together from the Suez events, a denial of the finality of Nasser's rift with the West in favor of an alliance with Russia, the emerging conflict in Algeria, and endorsement of Tunisia and Morocco's decision to "proclaim their determination to align themselves with the West." One sentence only carries the burden of Atiyah's "feelings of shock and disillusionment" over Suez:

> The whole Arab world was profoundly outraged by the fact that Britain
> and France should not only perpetrate an act of naked military aggression

against an Arab country but that they should do so in collaboration with Israel.[27]

With the Anglo-Egyptian Agreement of 1954 now "a dead letter", and Britain guilty of using military force in conjunction with Israel against Egypt, the embedded structure of Atiyah's discourse had broken down. The Suez débâcle had brought to realization a radical Arab nationalism of which one of the chief planks was an anti-westernism that comprehended not only Britain and France, but also the United States. It was clear, as Joseph Malone wrote in his introduction to the 1963 reprinting, that Atiyah had felt "feelings of shock and disillusionment, typical of an educated Arab of his generation, with the policies of the West [. . .] After the 1958 edition appeared, the course of events in the Arab World drove home the fact that Arabs of his background and inclinations had become outsiders."[28] What is of significance here is not so much Aityah's reported disillusionment with the British – he had already absorbed a great deal of anguish over British policies in Palestine. It is rather that with Suez, Atiyah's favored brand of Anglo-Arab politics was now clearly anachronistic. The era when Arab nationalism could be filiated to any western power was finally over. The last vestiges of the old imperialism were being confronted everywhere, in a manner that excluded the participation of pro-western Arab elites. Atiyah was not alone in being shocked by the flaying acts of this dying imperialism. For him, as for his hero, Jawaharlal Nehru, the behavior of the British over Suez would have seemed an inexplicable aberration from the civilized principles his education had led him to expect Britain would uphold.[29] But there is no escaping the feeling that with Suez, in Atiyah's case, not only had an entire narrative been subverted, but the orientation of a whole life and career had been undermined.

Conclusion

It is natural to compare Edward Atiyah's Anglo-Arab politics with those of his Lebanese compatriot, George Antonius. Antonius's Arabism had as its starting point the Arabs themselves; for him, Arab national identity was self-empowered, and only afterwards enabled by British sponsorship. Antonius's notion of Arab nationalism could be called filiative without ceding its independence, whereas for Atiyah, without western support and guidance, the Arab lands would remain a cultural backwater. As the issue of Palestine became the cause of a deepening concern, it threatened to force a wedge between the Anglo-Arab cooperation that both hoped for. In Atiyah's case, as a result of Palestine his identification with Arab interests grew firmer, even if he failed to reach a decisive conclusion as to the culpability of the West in its support for Zionism. That Atiyah was more than a stooge or spy for the British is evidenced by his support for Palestine. Palestine was after all the litmus test that separated Arab nationalists – even pro-western Christian Arabs like Atiyah – from Arabia's Anglo "Arab" friends – such as Gertrude Bell, H. St. John Philby, and T. E. Lawrence, in whom "Orientalism and an effective praxis for handling the Orient received their final European form, before Europe disappeared and passed its legacy to other candidates for the role of dominant power." The record shows Lawrence and Philby on several key occasions failed to understand the intensity of the Arabs' objection to Zionism.[30] Edward Atiyah, in contrast, in the words of Albert Hourani, "never wavered in his belief that the Arabs of Palestine had been treated unjustly."[31] For this commitment he deserves a mention in that line of spokesmen for Palestinian rights, writing in English, which can be traced from Ameen Rihani and George Antonius, through to Edward Said.

   In achieving a near complete assimilation with the colonizer, however, Atiyah could not have appreciated that, as Albert Memmi pointed out, colonization is a collective drama that cannot be resolved by individual solutions. Atiyah's personal achievement was not replicable in the lives of the masses of the colonized, and the political mapping of his writings hardly stretches beyond the Anglo-Arab dimensions out of which they are for the most part constructed. His closeness to the British makes his nationalist discourse, including his statements on Palestine, strained and incoherent. There remains a significant gap between Atiyah's politics and those even of a British educated "Third World" nationalist contemporary like Nehru, still more from Atiyah and Anouar Abdel-Malek's call for a "thrust in self-reliance [that] is towards the mobilisation of all the potential of any given nation and national-cultural area" in order to block off the hegemony of the West.[32] But this gulf marks the separation of the elite nationalism of the period of immediate decolonization, in which Atiyah only partially participated, from that of anti-imperialist resistance that followed. Atiyah clearly belongs to the epoch of non-western cultural dependence on the West, in his promotion of an enterprise that, in the final outcome, still "preserved the nineteenth-century imperial divide between native and Westerner."[33]

8

The Politics of Anglo-Arab Discourse

Absolve me from things of pomp and state,
For the earth in its all is my land
And all mankind my countrymen.
Khalil Jibran

To achieve recognition is to rechart and then occupy the place in the imperial cultural forms reserved for subordination, to occupy it self-consciously, fighting for it on the very same territory once ruled by a consciousness that assumed the subordination of the designated inferior Other.
Edward Said [1]

The mediatory function of Anglo-Arab discourse between Arab and Western cultures begins with *mahjar* schemes for uniting East and West, Islam and Christianity, and feeds into the wider debate in Arab writing on the proper relations between the two cultural spaces. It is concerned less with strictly bilateral relations between Arab Muslims and Christians, more with the construction of structures around a secular Arab nationalism which is in turn related to the development of the modern world and the West's dominant position within it. The debate is not between Muslim and Christian Arabs, but Christians of Lebanese extraction who had undergone substantial, formative exposure to western norms and patterns of thought, and a western audience that was both specific and amorphous. Its outcome was from the Arab writers' point of view largely unsatisfactory, since the partnership with the West which they, to varying degrees, argued for, failed to sustain their warnings about the threat of Zionism, or to allay aggression by western states against the Arab nation. In addition, their impact on the broader movement of Arab nationalism was necessarily marginal.

Most of these outcomes are explicable in terms of the international order of the first half of the twentieth century, and the isolation of the Lebanese Christian intellectual within the Arab Muslim world. The great European liberal tradition, while managing to withstand the challenge posed by anti-democratic totalitarianism in the inter-war period, had still to undergo the fragmentation that set in after World War II. It continued to remain attractive to the intelligentsia of emerging nations, in spite of the fault-lines opened by the struggles for decolonization, largely because these intellectuals had been formed from within the boundaries of western liberal discourse. However, as these struggles intensified, and as the old elites were replaced by largely middle and lower middle class army officers and intellectuals formed outside the western liberal tradition, postcolonial dialectics threw up ideologies which were antithetical to the liberal nationalism of Anglo-Arab discourse.[2] In spite of Rihani's positioning close to mainstream Arab culture, and Antonius's engagement in the politics of Palestine, as Arab Christians they were never likely to make many inroads into the consciousness of the instinctively anti-western, monolingual Muslim Arab majority. As for Atiyah, the last user of Anglo-Arab discourse, he was left in an altered post-Suez landscape occupying a territory as isolated as that from which Rihani had set out in the opening decade of the century.

From Christian-Muslim Unity to a New International Order

In 1946 Edward Atiyah argued for a Lebanon that:

> might become a stronger link than it had ever been between the Arab world and the West, the interpreter of each to each and a stimulating example of that union between the two without which the Arab world must remain isolated and backward.

That same year, in a book that began a long and distinguished career of interpreting the Arabs to the West, the young Albert Hourani privileged the Lebanese "on account of their geographical situation [. . .] traditions and [. . .] [specific] characteristics," believing these qualified them to "serve as mediators of Western civilization to Arab Asia."[3] Lebanese mediation of western culture to the Arabs had a long genealogy stretching back to the establishment of the Maronite College in Rome in 1585. The transmission could operate in both directions, which is to say that the Lebanese might also be instrumental in apprising the West of Arab and eastern culture and thought. Rihani took on this task in his translation of Abu'l-Ala, and in his introduction of Abdul-Aziz Ibn Saud to western audiences. George Antonius used a broader canvas to foreground his narrative of the Arab national movement. The success won by Khalil Jibran's rewritings of the traditional wisdom stories of the

Arab Near East in English, or English translation, enabled his Lebanese admirers to claim that an Arab oriental had arisen as a teacher to the West.[4] Embedded in each of these projects of mediation was the seman- tics of Christian-Muslim unity. The authors concerned were light years away from the embittered medieval Arab Christians who peddled distorted images of Islam to their western co-religionists for the purpose of polemics, and from their modern-day descendants in Lebanon.[5] During their active years as *mahjar* writers, Rihani and Jibran spoke of collaborating on schemes to bring about Christian-Muslim unity, but while Rihani's efforts in promoting this cause took on an increasingly political form, Jibran incorporated it within his personal cult of prophet- hood. For his admirers, Jibran's credentials as a teacher were enhanced by his Lebanese identity, which privileged his encounter at first hand with the cultures of East and West, Christianity and Islam, the experi- ence of which he embodied in his pseudo-prophetic, oracular register. According to a recent editor, Jibran achieved in his writings a Christian- Muslim synthesis, joining the language of the Bible with the mystical philosophy of the Sufis. Add to this Jibran's conversance with strands of western romantic literatures, particularly Rousseau, Blake, Shelley and Nietzsche, and for some the resulting amalgam amounts, not merely to a new genre of writing, but an international tradition of the future.[6]

But Jibran's idealist universalism raises serious problems at a prac- tical level. At the core of these is its abstraction, its outright rejection of socially mediated discourse and programs of action. Khalil Hawi argued that Jibran's universalist statements have their roots in a romantic primitivism that denies social and political realities. He cites as an example of this, Jibran's inaugural speech to the only meeting of *al-Halqat al-Dhahabiyah* society which he tried to form in 1911. "True to his belief in the self as the source of all reform, he stressed his trust in the capacity of the individual, which led him to under-rate, if not to despise, political and national solidarity and autonomy. Even more meaningless to [his audience] would have been his belief in spiritual and moral freedom which could make a man free even in chains."[7] In his desire to escape from concrete power relations, and his claim for himself as a producer of truths that transcended such limitations, Jibran's writings run counter to postmodern notions about language, truth and power: "Truth is what counts as true within the system of rules for a particular discourse; power is that which annexes, deter- mines, and verifies truth. Truth is never outside power, or deprived of power, the production of truth is a function of power, and as Foucault says, 'we cannot exercise power except through the production of truth.'"[8] Jibran's message was more likely to be taken to heart by those who were themselves either detached from the struggle of oppressed communities, or were already positioned within a powerful, protecting national-culture. In arrogating for himself the role of truth's producer through an oracular function, Jibran might have been hoping to exercise power himself. Within his lifetime, his writings were already being packaged as the latest emanation from the perennial world-enlightening source of eastern wisdom. An aspect of their continuing vogue is the embedded claim some see in them to be another divine revelation from the East to the West. During his lifetime, this may be implied in Jibran's courting of acolytes like his hagiographer, Barbara Young, and in the reaction this drew from Mikhail Naimy in his de-mystifying biography of his compatriot.[9]

For the later Rihani, uniting the two main religious traditions of the Arab world had a secular, political object, above a spiritual one. But it is also true that he graduated to his secular Arab nationalism via a strong kinship with Arab spirituality, expressed in his personal version of a Sufi-style mysticism, and outlined in his essay "Of Church and Mosque", which concludes: "Come, my Christian Brother, – come with me to the mosque."[10] Ameen led by personal example, making Muslim friends and encouraging his traditional Maronite mother to overcome her sectarian fears and receive them as equals. The aberrant character of Rihani's nationalist position in the eyes of his own Maronite community perhaps still needs stressing. Other Christian idealists such as Ibrahim al-Yaziji and Adib Ishaq had extolled Arab unity out of a common love of fatherland that transcended religious affiliation. But, according to Sharabi, the first to give a "straightforward, unambiguous political (as distinct from cultural or linguistic) definition of the idea of nationality were the Christian expatriates Najib Azoury and Amin Rihani"; this at a time when "Christian sectarianism [among the Lebanese] turned its face toward the Mediterranean and Europe and its back to the desert and Islam."[11]

When Rihani told Imam Yahya that religion divides but race unites, he was articulating the classic position of the Arab nationalist Christian intelligentsia, one which Muslim nationalists of the time were ready to oblige. At the 1913 Arab Congress in Paris, the chairman, Abdul-Hamid Zahrawi, a Muslim, stated: "the religious bond has always proved insufficient in any attempt to create political unity."[12] Typical of Rihani's assertion of racial and historical identity as the main factors unifying the Arabs is the following statement from a speech in Arabic given in 1938: "The Arabs existed before Islam and before Christianity. The Arabs will remain after Islam and after Christianity. Let the Christians realize this, and let the Muslims realize it. Arabism before and above everything."[13] Being a Syro-Lebanese, Rihani could not fail to appreciate the many wedges that could be driven between Arabic-speaking peoples in the name of particularities of religion, race, and local territories. In an article written in 1934, "Who are the Syrians?", he concluded that the Syrian had mixed origins, but this "variety of strains [. . .] [made] his blood rich indeed." The weakness of the Syrian character though, remained a tendency to sectarianism: "a primitive and personal feeling about one's tribe and one's religion."[14] Rihani identified a further drawback in a speech in Beirut in which he berated the "tears and moaning" endemic to modern Arabic poetry. Although he quoted two lines from Bisharra al-Khoury to illustrate his point, his criticism could equally have been extended to writers like Jibran and Naimy. The politics behind Rihani's statement was of course not lost on his audience and a bitter debate ensued between pro-Rihani and pro-al-Khoury factions in the Beirut press.[15] Rihani's other brush with Arab sectarian attitudes in the 1930s was with the Shi'a Muslims. His account of a journey made to the shrine of Kerbala, first published in English in *Syrian World*, then in Arabic in the Beirut daily, *Lisan ul-Hal*, created (according to *Syrian World*) "a storm of protest from Shi'ite sources [. . .] What the objectors resented most was the author's reference to the unsanitary condition of what is commonly known as Howdh-ul Kurr, a basin found in the court of almost every house in Kerbala and used for a multiplicity of purposes." In a letter to *Syrian World*, Kamel Morowa accused Rihani of purposely writing "a sensational story to the Americans whose minds are widely [sic] open to accept such stories or legends." He went on to criticize Rihani for casting aspersions on the purity of the *howdh-ul kurr* and the Husainyah canal which Rihani had claimed was as sacred to the Shi'a as the Ganges was to Hindus. "Contrary to Mr Rihani's imputations, Kerbala is in many ways modern and clean, but [he] looked only at the reprehensible and black side."[16] Since Rihani had traveled the length and breadth of Arab lands and ingested most of the sights on offer, the charge that he had suddenly succumbed to playing the Orientalist seems unlikely. The argument with the Syrian Christians had been over adoption of a quietist Arab identity in the face of colonialism; with respect to the Kerbala affair, Rihani was marking both Arab tradition-alism and sectarianism at the same time, hence his stress on Kerbala as a place of pilgrimage (separate to Mecca) and his foregrounding of the drab, possibly unhygienic character of the place. What was at stake in both cases was what Rihani perceived as a diversity and recidivism harmful to the cause of Arab unity.

The creative aspect to Rihani's Arabism, on the other hand , was its imagining of an Arab nation with more than a single origin, and a projection into the future as well as into the past. In foregrounding both the myth of Phoenicia favored by Lebanese Christians, and the Muslim

story of the believing Arabs of the desert, Rihani generated a reconciliation of two hitherto inimical narratives, thereby adding a new afflatus
to the rarefied Arabism that was the usual menu for Christian Arab
nationalists. Rihani's advocacy of modernity and its embodiment
within the new Arab state, and his criticism of sectarianism and traditionalism, were the elements of realism that underscored his vision of a
revived Arabia. In the same breath as declaring himself a nationalist,
Rihani also claimed to be an internationalist. His aspirations for
Christian-Muslim unity were a part of an internationalist outlook that
found expression earlier on in *mahjar* universalism. Rihani's experience
of American political liberty strengthened his predictions of American
leadership of a future world civilization. This aspect of his thought can
be said to have framed his early nationalist discourse in *The Book of
Khalid* where he argued for Arab self-determination *pari passu* with an
enlightened international order led by the United States. But his understanding of the colonial realities with which Arab and other Asian
nationalisms would have to deal before liberation and national integrity
could be achieved led him to foreground the national struggle above
internationalism in the 1930s. Nothing worthwhile could be accomplished until the country was free of foreign domination.[17] If utopianism
had crept into Rihani's ideology, it is to be located in his belief that the
era of divisive religion and political sectarianism was receding firmly
into the past, that Christians and Muslims, and the different Arab
dynasties, were ready to bury their animosities in the cause of a common
Arabism.

George Antonius was certainly convinced, like Rihani, that
Christian-Muslim unity was a practical necessity for establishing the
foundations of a strong, united Arab polity. Antonius's notion of Arab
unity is inscribed in Hourani's definition of the kind of Arab nationalism Lebanese Christians were willing to support: "the idea of a secular
nationalism, which rests upon elements of unity other than participation in a common religion; which aims at building a Westernized laic
State; and in which therefore Moslems, Christians and atheists alike can
join on a footing of equality."[18] The thesis of Antonius's book – that
"contact with the West revived latent Arab nationality [. . .] among
Lebanese Christian Arabs, who led their compatriots in the movement
to base political and cultural life on nationality, not religion" – has
become a cause célèbre among scholars of Arab nationalism.[19]
Antonius's claims that "a positive union for national independence
[existed] around 1880" may have been "too sweeping" and lacking in
hard evidence.[20] One possible explanation for Antonius's emphasis of
the Christian role in the formation of Arab nationalism might be that he
was concerned with marking out a nationalist narrative in which

Christian Arabs would be seen to be standing shoulder to shoulder with their Muslim compatriots. Another is that his foregrounding of the Christian role in the early Arab national movement was motivated by a desire to claim precedence for the secular type of Arabism favored by intellectual Christians like Antonius's father-in-law, Faris Nimr The weakness of this construct was its elitest base: at the popular level, for Muslims, Arab nationalism and Islam were barely distinguishable. Around the time Antonius was writing *The Arab Awakening*, the emergence of the Muslim Brothers presaged a fundamentalist backlash against secular Arabism that was to find expression later on in Nasser's Egypt, translating in the 1970s into the politics of the Lebanese civil war, when Islamic fundamentalists and Christian extremists alike charged "what the Arab nationalists called Arab history was no more than a doctored version of the history of Islam."[21]

Antonius was aware of his liminality with regard to the overwhelming Muslim majority among the Arabs. He wrote to a friend in 1931, enclosing the precis of *The Arab Awakening*, which was then at the planning stage, that when it came to the question of his status as an honest interpreter of events: "I have not even the qualification of being a Muslim."[22] The text Antonius came to write ends with a cogent defense of the posture of the Arab masses of Palestine, showing that Antonius was genuinely moved by the struggle of the Muslim peasantry against British sponsorship of Zionism. However, the chapters that deal with Wahhabism, though laudatory of the achievements of Abdul-Aziz Ibn Saud and the cleansing of Islam of accretions in the Arabian peninsular, also present a litany of rigid Wahhabi practices, thus encoding an embedded critique of the religious mindset as an effective basis for a national movement. If, as one Arab historian has argued, "Arabism [after the Great War] was little more than a romantic notion whose full implications had not been carefully worked out," Antonius contributed through his book to a fuller imagining of Arabism in both genealogical and synchronic terms.[23] But he never encoded in extended written form his vision of a federation of Arab states stretching as far as the Arab countries of North Africa, beginning with the unification of geographic Syria, or the *bilad as-sham*, in a unitary Arab state. Antonius's view of the place of such an Arab federation within the larger international order went unexposited. Perhaps, with his empirical British training, he was not given to making universal projections, or it might be that he did not live long enough to construct a sequel to his re-invention of an Arab nation in *The Arab Awakening*. His framing of the issue of federation in the "Memorandum on Arab Affairs", written for the British barely a year or so before his death, foregrounds a mix of nationalism and empiricism typical of his Anglo-Arab grounding. Antonius wanted the

British to make a declaration favoring the aims of the Arab national movement "namely Independence and Unity, and their corollary trends towards Cultural and Economic Solidarity." Such a statement would recognize the "harm caused by artificial frontiers arbitrarily drawn across lines of national and economic intercourse." But it was equally important to avoid laying down a policy that might impinge on the sovereignty of existing states. Antonius was cognizant of the variant strategies animating the different Arab leaders and argued that it should be left to the Arabs to choose their own forms of government after the war. Even federation was a debatable term.

> When Arabs speak of *al-wahda al-'arabiya* [Arab unity] , they have in mind a somewhat looser association of separate states than is conveyed by the term Federation, an association which is to be achieved, first by the attainment of independence and the removal of artificial (*sc.* imposed) frontiers and divisions, then by the strengthening of cultural and economic ties, and lastly, in some more or less immediate future, by the conclusion of such political conventions between the separate independent Arab States as time and trial may show to be in the best interests of the collective family of Arabic-speaking peoples.[24]

This discursive statement on the mechanism of Arab unity politics shows Antonius holding, to the last, to the discourse of mediator/negotiator, a role already made defunct for him by British relinquishment of his services.

Equally, had he not died prematurely, Antonius would have been confronted with the radical Arab nationalism that had taken root by the close of World War II, and by the rapid eclipse of Britain as the arbiter of Middle East politics. Which is to say that Antonius would have had to address the same set of conditions faced by Edward Atiyah in the mid-fifties. For their part, Atiyah's writings revisit a number of the issues discussed above, building on a perspective of at least four decades of Lebanese writing on inter-confessional unity and East-West brotherhood. Atiyah's reading of Arab history accords with the standard Christian nationalist version in which the seventh-century expansion of Arab armies out of the Arabian peninsular privileges the Arabs over Islam itself.[25] In the modern period, Christian-Muslim Arab solidarity presupposes the development of the Muslims to a compatible level of culture and sophistication to the progressive, westernized Christian minority. The unity of Christian Arab and Muslim in Lebanon was only the stepping stone for a secularized Arab world, functioning independently under the umbrella of civilized values ultimately deriving from the West. Atiyah was responding to the developments brought about by the historical locomotive of World War II. On the Arab scene, Anthony Eden's Mansion House speech of May 1941 had apparently set Britain behind gathering moves towards Arab unity. Egypt had then taken the lead and initiated the creation of the Arab League in March 1945. The inauguration of the United Nations in the following year reflected a post-war idealism which had been gathering during the final rounds of the World War II. *An Arab Tells His Story* was written in the spirit of optimism animating the immediate post-war period, and in the closing chapters, Atiyah moves towards a postcolonial vision of sorts. The imperialist world of colonizing and colonized nations had been superseded but "the old concepts of nationalism and independence" had also to be relinquished. Arab independence itself was not an absolute goal. Atiyah placed his confidence in Arab "integration in [the] coming world order" through connection with Britain. In fact, it would be better if the Arab states remained within Britain's orbit, rather like the former nations of the empire soon to join up for the British Commonwealth.

Looking forward to the founding of a new international order, Atiyah foregrounded some of the key aspirations that had contributed to the creation of the United Nations. In place of national integrity and individualism, "new imperious realities" loomed; "the inescapable unity of the world, the need for economic coordination and collective security, the conception of an integrated human society." Individual human rights, and a program of action for the underdeveloped and socially oppressed, were, in the new order of things, linked to the advance of socialism under the leadership of the Soviet Union. The Soviet Constitution appeared to guarantee protection of smaller national communities which Atiyah believed could be brought along under the progressive Soviet schemes of socio-economic development.[26] In his readiness to take at their face value and fuse the ideologies of universalist socialist utopianism and progressive piecemeal liberal democracy, Atiyah not only occluded the growing threat of the cold war, he failed to grasp the persistence of neo-imperialism on the part of the large powers, thereby missing the resultant postcolonial struggle which, far from withering away, only deepened in the decades pursuant to the World War II. In addition, he omitted from his new order the forces of Islamic fundamentalism and Arab radicalism which, in their reports for the Sudan Political Unit, Atiyah and his uncle had deemed a threat to British interests in the Arab world. Atiyah's grand narrative view of history, which is rooted in his acquired British imperial training, and his partisanship of the kind of Arab nationalism typical of a sophisticated Arab Christian, account for the major part of these omissions.

Clearly then, a significant dimension to Anglo-Arab discourse, specifically its interest in Muslim-Christian unity and extension of this to take in wider, if vaguer schemes for world unity, derives from the Lebanese context out of which each of the four authors in question wrote. It is worth noting as a corollary to this, that 1958, the date which I have given for the closure of Anglo-Arab discourse, witnessed the first serious outbreak of sectarian hostilities in the Lebanese Republic. These were linked to the new Arab radicalism mentioned above, and in particular, to the spread of Nasserism through the Arab world. This helped the formation of the United Arab Republic, which in turn threatened the National Pact that had maintained a fragile balance between the various sectarian traditions of Lebanon.[27] Jibran encapsulated the sectarian dilemma of his fellow Lebanese when he wrote: "Pity the nation divided into fragments, each fragment deeming itself a nation."[28] The failure of Christian-Muslim reconciliation in Lebanon is no doubt to be located in the wider context of the struggle between the Palestinians and Israelis, and the conflict between western hegemonism and Arab nationalism. The tragic civil war in Lebanon, between 1976–1990, has added a special piquancy to the dimension of Anglo-Arab discourse that calls for, announces, or celebrates, the unity of Christian and Muslim in the name of a common nationality, and the providence of Lebanon's role as emblem of international unity and peace.

Anglo-Arab Discourse, the Arabs and Zionism

The one consistent factor within Anglo-Arab discourse that appears to jar with its internationalist orientation is its refusal to countenance an accommodation with Zionism. Rihani in the United States, and Antonius and Atiyah within the orbit of Great Britain, each encoded broadly similar messages on the dangers of Zionism. As convinced Arab nationalists, the trio of Arab writers in English offered their services with the pen to the cause of the Palestine Arabs. Although not Palestinians by birth, Antonius and Atiyah had intimate links with Palestine, through family in the case of Atiyah, or through prolonged residence there and adoption of Palestine citizenship, in the case of Antonius. Rihani merely devoted a great deal of time and effort to expounding the Palestinian Arab cause in America. Arguing early on of the threat to the balance of forces in the Middle East which would result from the plantation of Zionism there, Rihani proceeded to warn of greater disasters to come if the western powers continued with their colonial games. Rihani's dual Arab-American identity may have privileged him to some extent in the Arab world, but when it came to his anti-Zionist discourse in the context of Palestine, it clearly cut precious little ice with the American government (or the American public for that matter). The exoticism that attached to Rihani's writings on Arabian rulers and Arab culture transferred to his political pronouncements. He established some lines to the American political establishment, but the kudos of academic qualifications or organizational back-up was lacking. Rihani's anti-imperialist Arab-American voice may have penetrated some foreign policy circles in the United States, but only within severely limited parameters.

The 1928 address given by Rihani to the Central Asian Society in London, the series of lectures to the Chautauqua Institute in 1930 – a typically American Wasp organization – and those made on his travels in Arabia under the auspices of the American Foreign Policy Association, all evidence to the fact that Rihani could obtain a respectful hearing for his views on the Arab East – if little more. In his London Central Asian Society lecture, Rihani proposed Britain release its cordon of Protectorates around Aden, arguing that Britain could thereby build bridges with Imam Yahya:

> This best could be done [. . .] by putting an end to the unedifying pretence of a Protectorate in which the Sultans and Chiefs were corrupted by honours and subsidies while British authority was almost non-existent and handing it over to the Imam while retaining a slightly enlarged territory round Aden in full sovereignty.

The audience of diplomats and old Middle East hands listened respectfully, knowing Rihani was a man on his own.[29] When it came to the Americans, Rihani was able to utilize his dual American citizenship and Middle East origins, but the extent of his effectiveness as a lobbyist was, needless to say, circumscribed by government-perceived American interests. As leader of the group that met Secretary of State Stimson in September 1929 over the heating up of Arab-Jewish clashes in Palestine, Rihani made a connection that resulted in at least one further visit in 1931. In the latter instant, Rihani went to argue American recognition of Saudi Arabia, a policy in tune with American commercial interests as already represented on the ground by the oil prospector Kenneth Twitchell. Here Rihani could promote himself as both a friend of America and an advocate of an Arab political cause, since the interests of both sides coincided. He wrote to the State Department from Saudi Arabia in June 1931:

> Here [. . .] is a virgin market of great possibilities. I have done all I could to open it to American capital and enterprise. I myself, I repeat, have no axe to grind. Only an interest, purely sentimental, in my native country's

progress and in the enterprise of the country of my adoption – the two countries I love best.

Whereas the United States was not interested in hearing the Arab position on Palestine, where it had other interests at stake – in the developing market of Saudi Arabia – it was ready to listen to Rihani's views on the benefits of doing business with Ibn Saud.[30]

As sometime political servants of the British Government, Antonius and Atiyah were better placed than Rihani in that both had the ear of the British governing elite. Access to this arbitrating audience, and mastery of its codes, afforded Antonius and Atiyah a more direct, if limited influence, on Arab affairs than Rihani. They encoded their messages strictly within the discourse of the colonizer, adopting the appropriate register of the elite speech community, utilizing the form of memoranda and reports, and addressing the interests of the colonial power. In addition, they each published histories in the manner of grand historical narrative. Taking the moral high ground, Antonius endeavored to persuade the British of their disloyalty to their natural allies, the Arabs, as well as laying out before them the chaos their Palestine policies were causing in the Middle East. At almost exactly the same time, Atiyah delivered a variation on this message to his British political masters, stressing the strategic dangers that were fast accruing to Britain's interests in the region as a result of her sponsorship of Zionism in Palestine. That both Antonius and Atiyah had some initial success in this project is probably explained by the flexibility of British response to the Palestine problem in the late thirties, although Antonius's fall from grace after his summit of achievement at the 1939 London conference on Palestine demonstrated how loathe the British were to trust someone whose mastery of their codes equaled that of any Cambridge don, but who maintained lines of contact with perceived enemies like the Mufti of Jerusalem and Jamal Husseini. Antonius's "Memorandum on Arab Affairs" was received coldly in London and rejected in all its essentials, except in so far as its call for a British public declaration in favor of Arab unity coincided with a move in British thought that led to Eden's Mansion House Speech. But in Atiyah's case, although one individual objected to his reports, overall these were perceived to be depressingly accurate in their articulation of Britain's position in the Arab world on the eve of World War II.[31]

The obvious point about the relative weakness of all three writers in delivering the message of Arab opposition to Zionist settlement in Palestine to western ears is that, unlike Dr. Chaim Weizmann and other prominent Zionists, they had no organization behind them, wielded no economic power, and were backed up by no Arab influence within the respective British and American political establishments. After resigning from Palestine Government service, Antonius worked for Charles Crane's organization, which had an agenda as far as the Middle East was concerned which could be considered sympathetic to the Arabs. Rihani also had relations with Crane, but even if it could be shown that Antonius and Rihani coordinated their efforts and acted as a tiny pressure group under the umbrella of the Crane organization, this was not the same as belonging to a self-constituted independent body with the status of the Zionist Organization. The westernized Arabs could not tap the metropolitan status of a privileged pressure group which Zionism enjoyed, specifically in London and Washington, although in comparison with Palestinian representatives who came to the West to voice their cause in the early 1920s they were in a different league.[32] Both Rihani and Antonius delivered public lectures stating the Arab point of view with regard to contemporary developments in Palestine. Antonius gave evidence to the Peel Commission and participated at the 1939 London conference on Palestine. But they remained individuals with no official Arab backing. When the Arabs belatedly made an effort to get their public relations act together, Atiyah was able to command the prestige, for what it was worth, of being the first secretary of the Arab Office in London, even if he was, according to Michael Atiyah, disappointed that he was not in overall charge. As Musa Alami, Atiyah's recruiter and one of the chief organizers of these offices, put it: "We were just visitors sitting in a hotel, with no pressure groups at our disposal, no money to buy space in the press."[33] It was only too obvious that, unlike the Zionists, the Arabs could muster no effective support in the Westminster parliament or the US senate, or mobilize a bloc of Arab voters in either country. In the words of Walid Khalidi:

> The moral of all this is that, at least in normal times, pressure from a non-*colon* community (the Arabs in Palestine) is peripheral and therefore taken in the imperial stride as a nuisance to be suppressed in the interests of law and order. But pressure from the autonomous metropolitan base of an overseas *colon* community is part of the balance of power system at the decision-making centre – a different story altogether.[34]

Rejection of any settlement on the basis of recognition of a Jewish state in Palestine of any size whatever could easily be dismissed as an intransigence inconsistent with the espousal of liberal and internationalist ideas. But Rihani and Antonius, who were active in Arab nationalist affairs from the beginning, clearly believed the manner in which they engaged with Palestine during the 1920s and 30s was consistent with both secular liberal and internationalist perspectives. Rihani figured

Zionism not only as a threat to the Arabs and to the peace of the Middle East, but also as endangering the entire international equilibrium. From the outset he argued that political Zionism could not be confined within limits, as the Balfour Declaration seemed to suggest it could, and as western diplomacy during his lifetime consistently sought in vain to effect. Although not averse to a Jewish home of a purely cultural character being established in Palestine, Rihani always opposed any plan based upon partition or the creation of a separate Jewish state, and during the 1936–7 disturbances called for an end to Jewish immigration and purchase of land. At that time, he was deeply pessimistic about the likely escalation of relations between the two communities if the Zionists went on with their agitation to obtain a Jewish state. Consistent with his secular nationalist tenets, Rihani saw the struggle for Palestine in ideological terms: political Zionism and Arab nationalism were engaged in a deadly encounter which was fast becoming complicated by the recidivist admixtures of the respective religious nationalisms of Judaism and Islam. Not being guilty of the simplistic reasoning indulged in by both sides, that is, that the other had no call to formulate for itself a nationalist cause, Rihani's stance remained basically empirical, from his earliest article on Palestine in September 1917 – there was not room for two competing nationalisms in the Holy Land. Political Zionism had just as much right to exist as Pan-Arabism; only, for the sake of international order, it was saner not to bring the two together in a showdown over the land of Palestine. In his espousal of Pan-Arabism in the 1930s, Rihani probably overemphasized the solidarity of the Arab nation on a secular base, as well as the feasibility of schemes for Arab confederation, which he invariably presented in an upbeat mode, and which he believed, when constituted, would, without western forces coming to its defense, swallow up a nascent Zionist state, if and when it was established.[35]

Not surprisingly, Antonius concentrated his argument against Zionism on liberal, humanitarian lines. Palestine was already a populated country and it was immoral to ask one people to give up their rights to the land in order to facilitate its acquisition by another people coming from outside. Knowing Palestine intimately from his years of residence there, Antonius was even less sanguine than Rihani about the chances of a resolution of Arab-Jewish hostilities, perhaps because he had staked so much on an Anglo-Arab solution, the prospects for which seemed to reach their nadir during the revolution of 1936–9. For his part, Antonius was no less committed to a secular Arab nationalism than was Rihani. But as a negotiator on behalf of the Arab delegation at the 1939 London conference, Antonius was more aware than the Arab-American of the conflicting stances of the Palestinian and non-Palestinian Arabs.

He was also cognizant of the peasant base to the Palestinian revolution of 1936–9; in fact *The Arab Awakening* makes possible a reading of the Palestinian struggle separate from the Pan-Arabism of Rihani and other nationalists of the period, in which a nascent Palestinian nationalism has the possibility of forming around the notion of collective resistance to militant Jewish nationalism. The revolution of 1936–9 may not, as some have argued, have been nationalist at all but instead a revolt under a religious banner, with Islam the uniting force. Only with the creation of Israel, and the setting up of the PLO and Fatah in 1964, this argument runs, could a Palestinian national identity form around the notion of hitting back against those who first hit me. So, instead of the structural— sociological readings of nationalism propounded by the likes of Gellner and Benedict Anderson, which I have argued appear to fit Rihani's myth-making/modernizing version of Arab nationalism well, Antonius, by his closeness to Palestinian events as they developed, could be used to support the rationalization of nationalism as founded upon antagonism, of negation of a negation.[36]

Atiyah, too, worked within a broadly similar parameter to Rihani and Antonius, advocating the establishment of some kind of Arab confederation, in which presumably the existing Jewish community in Palestine would be absorbed, and arguing for the end of British support for Zionist claims to Palestine.[37] He was also either more acutely aware of Arab limitations than the other two, or more ready to articulate them. Living through the Arab tragedy and farce of 1948, he, at least in part, laid the blame for this débâcle at the feet of the Arabs themselves. While Britain survived Atiyah's mid-1930s warnings about the inroads made by the Axis powers into the Arab lands of its imperial constituency, her postcolonial image among the Arabs was irreparably damaged by the 1956 invasion of Egypt, thus putting to an end all hopes of a British-Arab rapprochement, and deepening the rift between the West and the Arabs opened up by Palestine. Atiyah's pre-Suez prognostications concerning Israel's expansionist tendencies were soon borne out by the military adventure of 1956, and by the wars of 1967 and 1982.

By the time Edward Said began postgraduate studies at Harvard in the 1960s, Anglo-Arab biculturality was under threat, compounded by Suez and the anti-western turn Arab nationalism had taken since that time. New Arab identities had also, in the interim, been in the making. While Said could talk of a 1972–3 visit to Beirut reminding him of his Arab cultural heritage, politically, as a member of the Palestinian dias-pora, he was building for himself the reputation of a cogent and persuasive arguer of a specifically Palestinian national cause.[38] Pan-Arabism, the creed for which Rihani, Antonius and Atiyah had devoted a substantial amount of their political discourse, was to all intents and

purposes intellectually defunct, if still alive as the shibboleth of politically bankrupt regimes, but "little by little the vocabulary of Arabism
was altered to accommodate ideas and concepts designed to highlight
regional difference and local particularity."[39]

Reciprocity or Cultural Dependence?

Rihani, Jibran, Antonius and Atiyah came of a generation of Christian
Arabs many of whom came to consider biculturality as a norm. Was the
cultural joining advocated in their Anglo-Arab writings before its time?
Dissociated from the stigma of subservience to the West, could the
orientations proposed by Anglo-Arab authors – partnership of East and
West based on genuine cultural and political reciprocity and respect –
be considered the way forward for international relations in the twenty-
first century? Did Jibran's phenomenally successful English writings
marry oriental and western forms in an international style for the
future? Put in a nutshell: in its pursuit of East–West reciprocity, was
Anglo-Arab discourse a window to intercultural breakthrough, or were
the universal dreams of its writers compromised from the start by filiation to western norms? To begin with, close scrutiny of the writings
concerned casts doubts on any coherent, unified project emerging from
Anglo-Arab discourse. The variant programs its authors espoused for
Arab unity and cooperation with the West are easily dismissed as strong
on idealism but weak on socio-political realities. Jibran's lofty
pronouncements are entirely unrooted in any program of action or realistic schema of development, while Atiyah's internationalism revisits
the earlier *mahjar* dreams of East–West rapprochement only to founder
on the postcolonial realities of western and Russian neo-colonialism and
"Third World" anti-imperialism. The grand narrative of Arab emancipation adopted by Antonius implies a coterminous emancipation of
other national movements too heavily under the tutelage of the
European enlightenment, while Rihani's dual Arab-American identity
led him to privilege American values of democracy and freedom as reju-
venating agents towards a new world order, on which the jury looks like
being out for some time.

   Indeed, the history of western power meddling in the region – such
involvement clearly dictated by national interest rather than concern for
any of its indigenous peoples and nations – has so far made it difficult
for anyone from the area to successfully attempt to synthesize the
terrains of colonizer and colonized. An obvious interpretation of
Antonius and Atiyah's efforts to do so would be that they were part of
a small elite, intentionally created by the colonizing powers from out of

the colonized nations, to promote the former's political interests. Their training in western norms in turn induced in them a strain of politico-cultural schizophrenia, particularly when the reciprocity to which they fervently adhered was not embraced by the metropolitan power. Antonius's career rebuttals and the continual frustration of his attempts at mediation between the British and the Arabs would represent more than adequate evidence for this conclusion. In spite of Atiyah's belief that the British had accepted him as one of themselves, the riposte to his Anglo-Arab synthesis was the showdown at Suez.

Rihani, who regarded Burke and the imperial enterprise from the point of view of a sceptical outsider, (partly perhaps wearing American anti-colonial as well as native-oriental tinted glasses) held the British in particular at a knowing distance, and was in a better position to read the velleities of the colonizer. At times, he appeared not to be without hope that the West would mend its ways. Along with his faith in the good offices of the United States, he adopted the realistic argument that both the West and the Arabs needed one another, whatever the price. It may have been his capacity to see beyond the British-Arab connection in the Middle East, which gave Rihani a longer view of the region's future. He advocated reciprocity between the Arabs and the West, foresaw turmoil, and canvassed tirelessly for Arab unity as a rock bottom requirement for the Arabs' survival. Easily dismissed as an idealist, Rihani was both a romantic and a realist, whose fervent commitment to Arabism meant the rhetoric of the liberation struggle was not alien to him, even as he plied the virtues (especially within America) of inter-cultural exchange. But it is apparent from his early years that Rihani possessed a self-belief and detachment that sustained him above the bitterness of cultural dependence. (Recent research on the position of Syrians in America in the early decades of this century would suggest that he might have been the object of racist bigotry himself.[40]) Rihani nevertheless smoothed over the humiliations of colonialism by adopting feigned subservience (for example, to the British High Commissioner in Iraq in 1921) that might have derived from oriental behavior patterns, but was probably enhanced by a self-confident bicul-turality available only to the favored ones in an epoch in which individuals believed they still mattered more than movements. He had mastered the different registers of English sufficiently well to appear both American patriot and Arab nationalist before cultivated American audiences (including government figures), and even Imam Yahya was convinced he was "one of us." Like Marcus Garvey, Rihani also enjoyed the large gesture. He was in his element traveling across continents for the national-cultural cause, appearing in the company of national leaders (as at the Baghdad agricultural exhibition), regailing a crowd, delivering an incendiary speech and getting arrested (Beirut, 1933), and writing polemical copy on the event afterwards. In spite of the inevitable flack he received from journalists and supporters of Arab politicians bent on personal political aggrandisement, Rihani traversed the various political camps incurring the distrust of very few.

With all their limitations, the writers who operated in the period of western dependency raised issues that are still with us. In spite of certain naive aspects of his political thinking, Atiyah understood that national struggle would, in time, need to give way to international reconciliation. In arguing in this way, Atiyah was of course remaining true to the tradition of mediation which we have seen was a character-istic of Anglo-Arab discourse. In the cases of both Rihani and Antonius, too, advocacy of internationalism or East-West reciprocity in the form of British-Arab or American-Arab bilateral understanding, was advanced at the same time as the call for Arab national self-determina-tion. Each may have had cultural roots in epochs that have now disappeared. Rihani's Arab-American status privileged him, setting him personally apart from what Said has called the "hermeneutics of suspicion" that belongs more appropriately to the postcolonial scholar and writer whose work strengthens a conviction of the "devastating, continuous conflict with the colonized society." According to Hourani, Antonius belonged to the cosmopolitan (imperial) culture that pre-dated the emergence of narrowly national sectarian identities, while Said sees in "the grand, nourishingly optimistic narratives of emanci-patory nationalism" favored by Antonius and C. L. R. James a community of culture now superseded by the necessarily astringent, deconstructive postcolonial methodology of the subaltern studies group.[41]

Difficulties therefore abound in making out a case for the Anglo-Arab writers as pioneers at the meeting point of what A. A. Malek termed the European liberal tradition and the emerging radical-national renaissance of the tricontinental intelligentsia.[42] Nevertheless, I have tried to argue in this book that Rihani and Antonius do indeed stand at the gateway of an era of postcolonialism and national resurgence in the Orient; that Rihani's credentials as a pioneer figure bestriding the colo-nial and postcolonial periods should be taken seriously, as George Antonius's have already been by Edward Said. Edward Atiyah too, though his occupation of pro-western territory will never endear him to postcolonial theorists, is one with Said in his conviction that solutions to the Arab predicament are not to be found by turning back to the seventh century, and in his identification of the backwardness of Arab political culture as a key factor in a succession of twentieth-century Arab political defeats. Crucially, all three took seriously the task of creating an Arab narrative, according to Edward Said, a task that has barely been begun.

> Our tasks as Arabs and Palestinians is to pay closer attention to our own national narrative, which is neither an idle aesthetic pursuit nor something that can be continually postponed. Without a history that needs to be painstakingly researched and put together as a coherent story, we are like orphans with neither parents nor a home that we can claim as our own. In addition, modern Western Orientalists are re-writing the history of Islam as a tale of anger and irrationality in their constructions, the Arab and Muslim component of Palestine is always portrayed as either subordinate or non-existent. We cannot accomplish our self-determination as a people unless we can write and tell our own history – from ancient times till the present. The struggle with Zionism is a cultural one, which we must seriously begin to address. For this task we need a national and intellectual leadership that is conscious of this dimension of our struggle, and is determined to get the job done. How much longer must we wait? And how can we interpret our own history when freedom of thought and expression are currently so limited?[43]

It would be possible to trace a line within Arab secularist thought that begins with Rihani, Antonius, and Atiyah, then passes on to the later radical liberationism of A. A. Malek and the developing post-Orientalism of Edward Said. With Rihani, strategies of national liberation are envisaged taking place partly within, and increasingly outside of western auspices; the search for a new international order is put off until the decolonization process is over, and national integrity realized in the "Third World." The resultant interregnum is the emerging post-colonial world of Rihani's maturity; the epoch and the space inscribed in A. A. Malek's writings as "the second wave of national liberation movements [that] started with the crisis of the 1930s, and continued through the break-up of Western hegemony after the 1939–45 world war, which so transformed the world scene."[44] That era, culminating in the ejection of the United States from Vietnam in 1973, is in turn radically restructured in the late seventies and eighties, with the resurgence of fundamentalist Islam, and the collapse of Communism. This latest phase is problematized by Edward Said in terms of what went wrong with the national-liberation movements after the resistance struggles against western colonialism had resulted in forms of national independence.

Said's work on cultural hegemonism has provided much of the framework for this study. It looks beyond liberation politics to the world of interdependent nations, cultures, and communities, that must forge a new politics of identity if mankind is to survive. Said proffers a postcolonial dialectic whereby anti-imperialist nationalism – what he terms "nativism" – gives way to a wider consciousness:

> There is first of all the possibility of discovering a world *not* constructed out of warring essences. Second, there is the possibility of a universalism that is not limited or coercive, which believing that all people have only one single identity is – that all the Irish are only Irish, Indians Indians, Africans Africans, and so on *ad nauseam*. Third, and most important, moving beyond nativism does not mean abandoning nationality, but it does mean thinking of local identity as not exhaustive, and therefore not being anxious to confine oneself to one's own sphere, with its ceremonies of belonging, its in-built chauvinism, and its limited sense of security.[45]

In a sense then, Said has re-framed a number of the basic orientations of Anglo-Arab discourse. As Antonius before him, Said resets the discourse of European humanism in a larger mold inclusive of the emergent territories of non-western peoples. The tools Said has used to re-form the discourse of the dominant imperial center were not available for Antonius. Biculturality privileges Said access to a radical postcolonial discourse in which the colonial dilemmas Antonius and Atiyah struggled with have been superseded by a wholesale critique of western hegemonism, a process for which Said himself is in part responsible. Building on "Third World" liberationist political discourse, in writings such as, *Orientalism* and *The Question of Palestine*, Said re-charts imperialist cultural modes on behalf of the hitherto subordinated and silenced colonial subject. In *Culture and Imperialism* , Said moves beyond the entrenched positions of *Orientalism* toward a synthesis of the imperialist and anti-imperialist terrains by accentuating the reciprocal impact of each upon the other (their "overlapping histories"). In genealogical terms, Said's present position can be said to reproduce aspects both of Rihani's anti-imperialist, anti-Orientalist discourse, and his hopes for a future post-liberation, reciprocally-based international order. While this position constitutes a considerable advance on the experimental hybridism of Rihani's early writings, in his projection of the experience of the exiled and marginalized, and his rejection of essentialist labels, purist identities, and attachment to particular homelands, Said can be said to have refined Rihani's aspiration to liberate the individual, and oriental and western societies collectively, at one and the same time, from the destructive limitations of cultural separatism.

Notes

Introduction

1 Hilary Kilpatrick, "Arab Fiction in English: A Case of Dual Nationality," *New Comparison* 13 (Spring 1992): pp. 46–55 discusses four novels published by Arab writers 1960 and 1983.

2 Albert Hourani, *Syria and Lebanon, A Political Essay* (London: Oxford University Press, 1946), p. 2.

3 David Birch, *Language, Literature, and Critical Practice* (London: Routledge, 1989), p. 131, 139. The statements quoted convey the views of the anthropologist, Bronislaw Malinowski, and the linguist, Michael Halliday.

4 Mary Louise Pratt, *Towards a Speech Act Theory of Literary Discourse* (Bloomington: Indiana University Press, 1977), p. 115.

5 Paul Riceour, *Hermeneutics and the Human Sciences* (Cambridge: Cambridge University Press, 1981), p. 202, quoted in Birch, *Language*, p. 168.

6 The debate is summarized in C. Ernest Dawn, "The Origins of Arab Nationalism," in *The Origins of Arab Nationalism* (New York: Columbia University Press, 1991), ed. Rashid Khalidi et al., pp. 3–30.

7 Theo D'haen , "Shades of Empire in Colonial and Post-Colonial Literatures," in *Shades of Empire in Colonial and Post-Colonial Literatures* (Amsterdam/Atlanta: Rodopi, 1993), ed. Theo D'haen and C.C. Barfoot, pp. 9–16, p. 12.

8 For example Tayeb Salih, *Season of Migration to the North*, trans. Denys Johnson-Davies (London: Heinemann, 1980) and Naguib Mahfouz, *The Cairo Trilogy*, 1. *Palace Walk*, trans. William Maynard Hutchins and Olive E. Kenny (New York: Anchor Books, 1990); 2. *Palace of Desire*, trans. William Maynard Hutchins, Lorne M. Kenny and Olive E. Kenny (New York: Anchor Books, 1991).

9 Mary Louise Pratt, "Linguistic Utopias," in *The linguistics of writing, Arguments beween language and literature* (Manchester: Manchester University Press, 1987), pp. 48–66, p. 59.

10 Sabry Hafez, *The Genesis of Arabic Narrative Discourse, A Study in the Sociology of Modern Arabic Literature* (London: Saqi Books, 1993), p. 37.

11 See Reed Way Dasenbrock, "Intelligibility and Meaningfulness in Multicultural Literature in English," *PMLA* 102 (1987): pp. 10–19; for a wider discussion of the language options open to postcolonial writers, see

Bill Ashcroft, Gareth Griffiths, and Helen Tiffin, *The Empire writes Back, Theory and Practice in Post-Colonial Literatures* (London: Routledge, 1989), chap. 2.

12 Benedict Anderson, *Imagined Communities, Reflections on the Origins and Spread of Nationalism* (London: Verso, 1983), p. 127.

13 Tony Smith, *The Pattern of Imperialism, The United States, Great Britain, and the late industrializing world since 1815* (Cambridge: Cambridge University Press, 1981), p. 55.

14 On Arab intellectuals' reaction to contact with the West, see Albert Hourani, *Arabic Thought in The Liberal Age,1789–1939* (London: Oxford University Press, 1970); Hisham Sharabi, *Arab Intellectuals and The West, 1875–1914* (Baltimore: Johns Hopkins University Press, 1970); Nazik Saba Yared, *Arab Travellers and Western Civilization* (London: Saqi Books, 1996).

15 Eric Hobsbawm, *Nations and Nationalism since 1815* (Cambridge: Cambridge University Press, 1990), p. 131.

16 Edward Said, *Culture and Imperialism* (London: Chatto & Windus, 1993), pp. 293–4, pp. 309–10, p. 331.

17 See Bassam Tibi, *Arab Nationalism, A Critical Inquiry*, eds. and trans. Marion Farouk Sluggett and Peter Slugett (London: Macmillan, 1981).

18 In addition to Benedict Anderson (*Imagined Communities*), see *Nation and Narration*, ed. Homi K. Bhabha (London: Routledge, 1991), particularly Timothy Brennan, "The national longing for form," pp. 44–70.

19 Jawaharlal Nehru, *The Discovery of India* (New Delhi: Oxford University Press, 1981), p. 52. According to Michael Atiyah his father was a great admirer of Nehru.

20 Edward Hodgkin speaking to Susan Silsby in, Silsby, "Antonius: Palestine, Zionism and British Imperialism, 1929–1939," Doctoral dissertation, 1986, Georgetown University (University Microfilms, Ann Arbor, Michigan), p. 54.

21 Jean-François Lyotard, *The Postmodern Condition: A Report on Knowledge*, trans. Geoff Bennington and Brian Massumi (Manchester: Manchester University Press, 1984).

22 See Fredric Jameson, *Postmodernism, or, The Cultural Logic of Late Capitalism* (London: Verso, 1991), pp. 301–13; for a discussion of Arab traditionalism, modernism, and postmodernism, see Saree Makidisi, "The Empire Renarrated: *Season of Migration to the North* and the Reinvention of the Present," *Critical Inquiry* 18 (Summer 1992): pp. 804–20, reprinted in. Patrick Williams and Laura Chrisman, *Colonial Discourse and Post-Colonial Theory, A Reader* (New York: Harvester Wheatsheaf, 1993), pp. 535–50.

Chapter 1: Ameen Rihani: Cross-Cultural Disclosures

1 Ameen Rihani, *The Book of Khalid* (New York: Dodd Mead and Company, 1911), p. 241.

2 On the influence of western writers on Rihani see "Arabia: an Unbiased Survey," *Journal of The Central Asian Society* 16 (1929): pp. 35–55, pp. 35–7.

On the western travelers see Irfan Shahid, "Amin al-Rihani and King 'Abdul-'Aziz Ibn Sa'ud," pp. 231–40, in *Arab Civilization, Challenges and Response, Studies in Honor of Constantine K. Zurayk*, eds. George Atiyeh and Ibrahim Oweiss (Albany, NY: State University of New York Press, 1988).

3   A comprehensive bibliography of Rihani's writings, published and unpublished, is still wanting. See Albert Rihani, *Where to Find Ameen Rihani, Bibliography* (Beirut: The Arab Institute for Research and Publishing, 1979); Walter Edward Dunnavent, "Ameen Rihani in America, Transcendentalism in an Arab-American Writer," Doctoral thesis, Indiana University, 1991.

4   Hisham Sharabi, *Arab Intellectuals and The West, 1875–1914* (Baltimore: Johns Hopkins University Press, 1970), pp. 15–18.

5   On the economic and other reasons behind the Lebanese emigration see Samir Khalaf, "The Background and Causes of Lebanese/Syrian Immigration to the United States before World War I," pp. 17–36, in *Crossing The Waters, Arabic-Speaking Immigrants to the United States Before 1940*, ed. Eric J. Hooglund (Washington, DC: Smithsonian Institution Press, 1987); Charles Issawi, "The Historical Background of Lebanese Emigration, 1800–1914," pp. 13–31, in *The Lebanese in The World, A Century of Emigration*, ed. Albert Hourani and Nadim Shehadi (London: Centre for Lebanese Studies with I. B. Tauris, 1992).

6   Rihani, *Book of Khalid*, p. 41.

7   Albert Rihani, *Where to Find Ameen Rihani*, pp. 18–21; see also Nadeem Naimy, *The Lebanese Prophets of New York* (Beirut: American University of Beirut, 1985), p. 15.

8   Beverlee T. Mehdi, *The Arabs in America* (Dobbs Ferry, NY: Oceana Publications, 1978), pp. 7–8. See also pp. 12–13 for details of later Arabic newspapers and journals for the period 1910–11. It was not until *The Syrian World* appeared in 1926 that the American Syrian community possessed an English language publication. Its editor was Salloum Mokarzel, whose older brother Naoum Mokarzel edited *al-Huda* and, according to Albert Rihani (*Where to Find Ameen Rihani*, p. 18) was Rihani's tutor and one of his two companions on emigration to the United States. Rihani, Jibran, and the Harvard Lebanese scholar, Philip Hitti, were among the contributors to *Syrian World*. See John G. Moses, *Annotated Index to The Syrian World, 1926–1932* (St. Paul, Minnesota: University of Minnesota, Immigration History and Research Center, 1994).

9   Ameen Rihani, *Myrtle and Myrhh* (Boston: Gorham Press, 1905); "The Coming of The Arabian Nights," *Bookman* (June–July 1912): pp. 366–70, pp. 503–8; "The Renans in Syria, the Writing of 'The Life of Jesus,'" *Bookman* (February 1912): pp. 599–611. Rihani and Monahan shared a common interest in the Renans. See the latter's piece on Henriette in Michael Monahan, *Adventures in Life and Letters* (New York: Mitchell Kennerley, 1912), pp. 339–51. I am indebted to Professor Miles L. Bradbury for uncovering Rihani's early American literary connections.

10 Mary Louise Pratt, *Towards a Speech Act Theory of Literary Discourse*

(Bloomington: Indiana University Press, 1977), p. 87.

11   Werner Sollors, *Beyond Ethnicity, Consent and Descent in American Culture* (New York: Oxford University Press, 1986), pp. 249–50.

12   Hooglund, introduction to *Crossing the Waters*, p. 11.

13   Rihani, "Arabian Nights," p. 506, p. 370, p. 505, p. 507, p. 508.

14   *The Quatrains of Abu'l-Ala* (New York: Doubleday, Page and Company, 1903), p. vi, p. xv.

15   Ibid., pp. xviii–xi.

16   Ameen Rihani, *The Luzumiyat of Abu'l-Ala* (Beirut: Albert Rihani, 1978), p. 35. It is interesting to compare Rihani's use of al-Ma'arri in his developing discourse of Arabism with that of the Syro-Lebanese poet and critic, Ali Ahmed Said (Adonis), who places him within his own debate on the perennial elements of traditionalism and modernism in Arab culture. See Adonis, *An Introduction to Arab Poetics*, trans. Catherine Cobban (Texas: Austin University Press, 1990); Mounah Khouri, "Criticism and the Heritage: Adonis as Advocate of a New Arab Culture," in *Arab Civilization*, eds. Atiyah and Oweiss, pp. 183–204; Edward Said, *Culture and Imperialism* (London: Chatto & Windus, 1993), pp. 378–9.

17   Ameen Rihani, *A Chant of Mystics and Other Poems*, eds. S.B.Bushrui and J.M. Monro (Beirut: The Rihani House, 1970), p. 17. For the monorhyme scheme see sect. 4, p. 111.

18   See *Defining American Literary History*, ed. A. L. B. Ruofl and Jenny W. Ward (New York: Modern Language Association, 1990), particularly, Paul Lauter, "The Literatures of America: A Comparative Discipline," pp. 10–34; and Harold H. Kolb, Jr, "Defining the Canon," pp. 35–51.

19   *New York Evening Post*, 12 March 1921; quoted in introduction, *A Chant of Mystics*, p. 16.

20   "From Concord to Syria," *Atlantic Monthly* (February 1913): pp. 284–6. The article was reprinted in *The Path of Vision: Pocket Essays of East and West* (New York: White, 1921) and was a reworking of an earlier piece, "A Syrian Symbolist," *Papyrus* (February 1908): pp. 18–22.

21   "From Concord to Syria," p. 286.

22   Quoted in Sollors, *Beyond Ethnicity*, p. 243.

23   *Bookman* (September 1911): pp. 21–2. Rihani was not the first to publish fiction in English set in the Syrian Quarter of New York. The Canadian journalist and writer Norman Duncan published a number of short stories with this setting in *Atlantic Monthly*, and *McClure's Magazine*. See also Norman Duncan, *The Soul of The Street, Correlated Stories of The New York Syrian Quarter* (New York: McClure, Phillips and Company, 1900).

24   S. B. Bushrui, "Arab American Cultural Relations in the 20th Century: The Thought and Works of Ameen Rihani with reference to his works in English," Fifth Annual Philips Lecture, University of Maryland, 12 December 1990 (unpublished typescript).

25   On nation and the novel, see Timothy Brennan, "The national longing for form," *Nation and Narration*, ed. Homi K. Bhabha (London: Routledge, 1990), pp. 44–70. For a reading of *Zaynab* that incorporates contemporary critical thinking on narrating the nation, see Elliot Colla, "Between Nation

and National Subject: Speculations on National Allegory," *Proceedings, The Third National Symposium on Comparative Literature, History in Literature* (Cairo: Department of English, Faculty of Arts, 1995), pp. 263–70.

26   Mohammad Hussein Haikal, *Zainab, the first Egyptian novel*, trans. John Mohammed Ginsted (London: Darf, 1989).

27   Sollors, *Beyond Ethnicity*, p. 244. According to Martin Seymour-Smith, "Amin Rayhani initiated the Arab prose poem, but, like Nuayma, has not written novels." *Guide to Modern World Literature* (London: Macmillan, 3rd edn, 1985), p. 181.

28   Andrew Gibson, *Reading Narrative Discourse, Studies in the Novel from Cervantes to Beckett* (London: Macmillan, 1990), p. 14. The author is paraphrasing Julia Kristeva (*Revolution in Poetic Language*, trans. Margaret Waller [New York: 1984]) on intertextuality.

29   Rihani, *Book of Khalid* , p. 129. On Rihani and Carlyle, see Geoffrey P. Nash, "Amin Rihani's *The Book of Khalid* and the Voice of Thomas Carlyle," *New Comparison* 17 (Spring 1994): pp. 35–49.

30   *Book of Khalid*, p. 36, p. 40.

31   Ibid., p. 48, p. 42.

32   Ameen Rihani, *Muluk al-'Arab* (Arab Kings), quoted in Ameen Rihani, *The Path of Vision, Essays of East and West*, eds. S. B. Bushrui and J. Monro (Beirut: The Rihani House, 1970), p. 15.

33   Bushrui, "Arab American Cultural Relations"; *Book of Khalid*, pp. 113–14. See also *Path of Vision* (Beirut edn), pp. 124–5.

34   *Book of Khalid*, p. 84.

35   Ibid., p. 284. The Iranian spiritual teacher, Abbas Effendi, also known as Abdul-Baha, visited America in 1912 when Khalil Jibran made his portrait.

36   Ibid., p. 239.

37   Ibid., p. 303. Rihani would have been aware that the Baha'i Movement began as a modernizing trend within Islam, but subsequently produced its own legislative texts claiming to supersede the Arabic Koran. The first Baha'i missionary to America, Ibrahim Kheiralla, was a Syrian. See Rihani's obituary, "Dr I. G. Kheiralla Dies in Syria," *Syrian World* (May 1929): pp. 49–50.

38   Ameen A. Rihani, in a letter to this writer.

39   A. L. Tibawi, *Arabic and Islamic Themes, Historical, Educational and Literary Studies* (London: Luzac, 1976), p. 151.

Chapter 2: Khalil Jibran: From Arab *mahjar* to Consumerist Prophet

1   Khalil S. Hawi, *Kahlil Gibran, His Background, Character and Works* (Beirut: Arab Institute for Publishing and Research, 1972), p. 111.

2   Philip Hitti, "Gibran's Place and Influence in Modern Arabic Literature," *Syrian World* (February 1929): pp. 30–2, p. 31.

3   M. M. Badawi, "Perennial Themes in Modern Arabic Literature," *British Journal of Middle East Studies* 20 (1993): pp. 3–19, p. 6.

4   Fredric Jameson, *The Political Unconscious: Narrative as Socially Symbolic Act*

(London: Methuen, 1981), p. 53. Jameson is referring here to a criticism of the Hegelian notion of Absolute Spirit by the Marxist philosopher Georg Lukacs.

5   Terry Eagleton, *Literary Theory, An Introduction* (Oxford: Blackwell, 1983), p. 60, p. 64.
    Eagleton is discussing the Phenomenological criticism of Husserl of which the central tenet – like much Jibran criticism – is that the language of a literary work is a transparent expression of its inner meaning.

6   Fredric Jameson, *Postmodernism, or, the Cultural Logic of Late Capitalism* (London: Verso, 1991), p. 306.

7   Ibid., p. 307, p. 312.

8   Mikhail Naimy, "Introduction to the Pen-bond Society." Quoted in Radwa Ashour, *Gibran and Blake* (Cairo: The Associated Institution for The Study and Presentation of Arab Cultural Values, 1978), p. 11.

9   Jameson, *Postmodernism*, pp. 312–13; Ameen Rihani, *The Descent of Bolshevism* (Boston: The Stratford Company, 1920). Rihani dedicated his study to his friend, the journalist and advocate of socialist ideas, Michael Monahan. His short book does not extend a very satisfactory analysis of the subject, and leaves the question open as to Rihani's own identification with socialist theory.

10 Ameen Rihani, *The Book of Khalid* (New York: Dodd, Mead and Company, 1911), p. 91.

11 "The Mesmeric Genius of Reinhardt, Max Reinhardt Hypnotizing The World," *Current Literature* 52 (March 1912): pp. 337–8, p. 337: see also "Max Reinhardt, The Maker of a New Mimic World," *Current Literature* 51 (September 1911): pp. 311–15; Ameen Rihani, "Deserts of Fact and Fantasy," *Syrian World* (December 1929): pp. 5–9, p. 7. For the western taste for the exotic Orient supplied by "The Sheik" , see Sari J. Nasir, *The Arabs and the English* (London: Longman, 1979), pp. 146–9.

12 "The Christian, uprooted and on his own, not only gained distance from the traditional background but plunged into a wholly different world of life and experience. The Christian simply had to fall back on his own resources, develop his own powers, and so try to face the world on its own terms." Hisham Sharabi, *Arab Intellectuals and The West, The Formative Years, 1875–1914* (Baltimore: Johns Hopkins University Press, 1970), pp. 15–16.

13 Kahlil Gibran, *Nymphs of the Valley*, trans. H. N. Nahmad (London: Heinemann, 1972), pp. 1–7, 35–56; *Spirits Rebellious*, trans. H. N. Nahmad (London: Heinemann, 1973), pp. 1–23, pp. 56–112. For an assessment of Jibran's early stories in the context of the development of the Arabic short story see Sabry Hafez, *The Genesis of Arabic Narrative Discourse, A Study in the Sociology of Modern Arabic Literature* (London: Saqi Books, 1993), pp. 138–40.

14 Hawi, *Gibran*, p. 101.

15 Suheil Bushrui, *Kahlil Gibran of Lebanon* (Gerrards Cross: Colin Smythe, 1987), p. 38. Jibran's description of himself as Syrian might itself contain Syrian nationalist overtones. According to Hawi, Jibran spoke "of Syria as a nation, dissociating it from the world of Arab nationalism." Jibran's

achievement was praised by Antun Sa'ada, founder of the anti-Arab, Syrian Social Nationalist Party, as a true expression of "the genius of the Syrian nation." *Gibran*, p. 155.

16   For Naimy's contribution to *mahjar* poetic theory, see M. M. Badawi, *A Critical Introduction to Modern Arabic Poetry* (Cambridge: Cambridge University Press, 1975), p. 186.

17   *An Anthology of Modern Arabic Poetry*, eds. and trans. Mona Khouri and Hamid Algar (Berkeley, CA: University of California Press, 1974), p. 11.

18   Barbara Young, *This Man from Lebanon* (New York: Alfred Knopf, 1956), p. 102.

19   Kahlil Gibran, *A Self-Portrait*, trans. Anthony R. Ferris (London: Heinemann, 1972), pp. 15–16.

20   Hawi, *Gibran* , p. 115.

21   Kahlil and Jean Gibran, introduction , Kahlil Gibran, *Lazarus and His Beloved* (London: Heinemann, 1973), p. 8.

22   Jean Lecerf, "Djabran Khalil Djabran et les origines de la prose poétique moderne," *Orient* 3 (1957): pp. 7–14. Reprinted in *Kahlil Gibran, Essays and Introductions*, ed. S. Bushrui and John Munro (Beirut: The Rihani House, 1970), pp. 47–59, p. 54, p. 56.

23   Bushrui, *Gibran of Lebanon*, p. 65.

24   Kahlil and Jean Gibran, *Kahlil Gibran: His Life and World* (New York: New York Graphic Society, 1974), p. 284. For a summary of the writing of *The Prophet*, including Mary Haskell's contribution, based on her own and Jibran's letters and journals, see Kahlil Gibran, *The Prophet*, Introduction and Annotations by S. B. Bushrui (Oxford: One World Publications, 1995), sect. 2, pp. 12–25.

25   Hawi, *Gibran*, p. 281. See pp. 91–6, p. 108 on Jibran's likely mistresses of this period.

26   Ibid., pp. 112–13.

27   Hafez, *Arabic Narrative Discourse*, p. 64. See chapter 1 for a theoretic discussion of the Arab writer's relationship with new narrative forms and the developing Arab audience.

28   Edward W. Said, *Orientalism, Western Conceptions of the Orient* (London: Routledge, Kegan Paul, 1978), pp. 113–15.

29   Kahlil Gibran, *The Forerunner* (London: Heinemann, 1963), pp. 58–9.

30   Letters of Kahlil Gibran and Mary Haskell, quoted in *The Prophet*, ed. Bushrui, p. 16.

31   *The Prophet*, p. 67, p. 72, p. 73.

32   Edward W. Said, *The World, The Text, and The Critic* (Cambridge, Mass.: Harvard University Press, 1983), p. 227.

33   *The Prophet*, p. 101.

34   Jameson, *The Political Unconscious*, p. 49.

35   Catherine Belsey, *Critical Practice* (London: Methuen, 1980), p. 58. "We have made it part of our task to interview as many as possible of Gibran's American admirers and followers in Britain and Lebanon, and found that most of them were ill adjusted to life, and bewildered by its complexities, lacking the strength of nerve and mind either to tolerate or to try to simplify

it, and that they found a welcome escape route in Gibran's primitivism, disguised, as it is, in the shape of prophecy and oracular wisdom." Hawi, *Gibran*, pp. 280–1.

36 *The Prophet*, p. 152.

37 Ibid., p. 164, n. 39; Hawi, *Gibran*, p. 267.

38 Jean and Kahlil Gibran, "The Symbolic Quest of Kahlil Gibran," In *Crossing the Waters, Arabic-speaking Immigrants to the United States Before 1940*, ed. Eric Hooglund (Washington D.C.: Smithsonian Institution Press), pp. 161–71, pp. 168–9.

39 *The Prophet*, p. 118.

40 Ibid., pp. 133–4; J. and K. Gibran, "Symbolic Quest," p. 169.

41 Ameen Rihani, *The Path of Vision, Essays of East and West*, ed. S. Bushrui and John Munro (Beirut: The Rihani House, 1970), p. 30.

42 J. and K. Gibran, " Symbolic Quest," p. 169.

43 Khouri and Algar, *Anthology*, p. 11.

44 Badawi, "Perennial Themes," p. 4.

45 K. and J. Gibran, *Lazarus*, pp. 10–11.

46 Jacques Berque, *Cultural Expression in Arab Society Today* (Langages arabes du present), trans. Robert W. Stookey (Austin: University of Texas, 1978), p. 42.

47 Eagleton, *Literary Theory*, p. 210.

48 According to the *New York Times* (Book Review, 10 June 1934; quoted in Bushrui and Munro, *Essays and Introductions*, p. 179):

> Kahlil Gibran was that rare phenomenon, a mystical philosopher [. . .] who was also a poet [. . .] In the pages of his books there is an unworldliness reminding one of Gautama and the philosophers of the *Upanishads*; there is a lyric manner and picturesqueness that recalls the best of the old Hebrew prophets; and, at the same time, there is an epigrammatic pithiness of utterance that makes many of Gibran's saying not unworthy to be placed side by side with those of older sages of the Orient.

Chapter 3: Ameen Rihani: Pan-Arab Imaginings

1 Rihani, "Turkey and Islam in the War," American University of Beirut, MS: 956 R572t, p. 108. Edward Said, "The politics of memory," *Al-Ahram Weekly*, 26 September–3 October, 1996.

2 Elizabeth Monroe, *Britain's Moment in the Middle East, 1914–1971* (2nd edn, London: Chatto & Windus, 1981), p. 71; A. P. Thornton, *The Imperial Idea and its Enemies* (2nd edn, London: Macmillan, 1985), pp. 165–7.

3 P. W. Harrison, Review, *Around the Coasts of Arabia, Moslem World* 21 (1931): pp. 89–90.

4 Ameen Rihani, *Ibn Sa'oud of Arabia: His People and His Land* (London: Constable, 1928); *Around the Coasts of Arabia* (London: Constable, 1930); *Arabian Peak and Desert: Travels in Al-Yaman* (London: Constable, 1930).

5 Edward W. Said, *Culture and Imperialism* (London: Chatto & Windus, 1993), p. 299. On Sati' al-Husri, see Bassam Tibi, *Arab Nationalism: A Critical*

Inquiry (London: Macmillan, 1981), pp. 93–4.

6   Elie Kedourie, *The Chatham House Version and Other Middle-Eastern Studies* (Hanover, N.H.: Brandeis University Press, 1984), p. 324.

7   Albert Hourani, *Arabic Thought in the Liberal Age, 1789–1939* (London: Oxford University Press, 1970), p. 287.

8   Ameen Rihani, *The Book of Khalid* (New York: Dodd, Mead and Company, 1911), p. 303. Rihani was perhaps unusual in that he included Egypt within the scope of his imagined "Arab empire": the pre-1914 advocates of Arabism excluded Egypt and the Arabic-speaking nations of the *maghreb* from the Arab nation. See Tibi, *Arab Nationalism*, p. 85.

9   *Book of Khalid* , p. 130, p. 71, pp. 139–40. Rihani is careful to avoid the cruder theory of Phoenicianism, popular among Christian proponents of Lebanism, "that Lebanon was none other than ancient Phoenicia resur-rected." He might have agreed with a recent historian of Lebanon, that "what makes the modern urban Lebanese so much like the Phoenicians of old is geography, not history." Kamal Salibi, *A House of Many Mansions, The History of Lebanon Reconsidered* (London: I.B. Tauris, 1988), p. 172, p. 178.

10   *Book of Khalid*, pp. 271–2; see also Hourani, *Arabic Thought*, p. 236.

11   *Book of Khalid*, p. 289, pp. 319–20. According to Ameen A. Rihani (letter to Geoffrey Nash): "One explanation for Rihani's support for political Wahhabism is perhaps his belief that this movement could end up, like Protestantism, by separating the State from the 'Moslem Church'. Wahhabism could have been a first step towards a secular state in Arabia." Rihani was not alone in this: the Lebanese Druze writer Amir Shakib Arslan had the same belief. See Nazik Saba Yared, *Arab Travellers and Western Civilization* (London: Saqi Books, 1996), p. 191.

12   *Book of Khalid*, p. 303.

13   Ibid., p. 326.

14   Homi K. Bhabha, "DissemiNation, time, narrative, and the margins of the modern nation," pp. 291–322, in *Nation and Narration*, ed. Homi K. Bhabha (London: Routledge, 1991), p. 304, p. 307.

15   Ameen Rihani, *Around the Coasts*, pp. 177–8.

16   "Three Kings in Arabia," report of a lecture by Rihani, *Chautauquan Daily*, 23 July 1930.

17   Irfan Shahid, "Amin al-Rihani and King 'Abdul-'Aziz ibn Sa'ud," in *Arab Civilization, Challenges and Responses: Studies in Honor of Constantine K. Zurayk*, eds. George Atiyeh and Ibrahim Oweiss (Albany, NY: State University of New York Press, 1988), p. 232.

18   Edward Said, *Orientalism, Western Conceptions of the Orient* (London: Routledge, Kegan Paul, 1978), p. 240; T. E. Lawrence, *The Seven Pillars of Wisdom: A Triumph* (London: Cape, 1973), p. 4; Monroe, *Britain's Moment*, p. 26.

19   Quoted in Kedourie, *Chatham House*, p. 325.

20   *Around the Coasts*, p. 4.

21   Ameen Rihani to Theodore Roosevelt, 20 April 1917, Theodore Roosevelt Papers, Library of Congress, Series 1.

22   Shahid, "al-Rihani and ibn Sa'ud," p. 231, p. 237. Rihani supplied the

American Consul in Beirut with irregular reports on his travels in Arabia. These read for the most part like digests of the books he was in the process of writing. See *Documents on the History of Saudi Arabia*, vol. 1 *The Unification of Central America Under Ibn Saud, 1909–1925*; vol. 2 *The Consolidation of Power in Central Arabia Under Ibn Saud, 1925–1928*, ed. Ibrahim al-Rashid (Salisbury, NC: Documentary Publications, 1976), "A Report on Arabia," 1, pp. 113–37; "My Peace Mission in Al-Hijaz," 2, pp. 24–43.

23 *Around the Coasts*, p. 20.
24 Rihani, *Arabian Peak and Desert* , p. 96.
25 "Three Arab Kings."
26 Rihani, *Ibn Sa'oud* , p. 10, p. 39.
27 "Peace Mission," p. 40. See also Reader Bullard, *Two Kings in Arabia: Sir Reader Bullard's Letters from Jeddah*, ed. E. C. Hodgkin (Reading: Ithaca, 1993), pp. 70–1, p. 73; for H. St. John Philby's part in the same cause, see Elizabeth Monroe, *Philby of Arabia* (London: Faber, 1973), p. 143.
28 *Around the Coasts*, p. 115.
29 "Report on Arabia," p. 114.
30 *Around the Coasts*, p. 116; "Three Arab Kings."
31 *Around the Coasts* , p. 17.
32 Ibid., p. 117.
33 Ibid., p. 105.
34 Ibid., p. 119.
35 Rihani, *Ibn Sa'oud* , pp. 40–1.
36 Ibid., p. 236.
37 "The Future of the Near East," report of a lecture by Rihani, *Chautauquan Daily*, 26 July 1930.
38 "The Pan-Arab Dream," *Asia* (1938): pp. 44–7, p. 44.
39 At Uqair, Rihani recommended to Ibn Saud that he accept the bid made for exploration in what later became known as the al-Hasa oil-fields by a consortium led by Major Holmes in preference to the Anglo-Persian Oil Company in which the British Government had a large share-holding. Holmes's consortium later allowed the concession to drop, so letting in Standard Oil of California. Leonard Moseley (*Power Play, Oil in the Middle East* [Baltimore, Maryland: Penguin Books, 1974] p. 51): "Had it not been for the fact that [Rihani] backed the wrong man and persuaded an Arab king to do likewise, today the richest oil fields in the world would be in British rather than American hands." See also H. St. J. B. Philby, *Arabian Oil Ventures* (Washington, D.C.: The Middle East Institute, 1964), pp. 55–68.
40 "Report on Arabia," p. 125; *Ibn Sa'oud*, p. 38, p. 56.
41 H. St. John Philby, *Sa'udi Arabia* (Beirut: Librairie Du Liban, 1955), p. xi.
42 *Ibn Sa'oud* , p. 58; Thomas Carlyle, *On Heroes, Hero-Worship, and the Heroic in History* (London: Chapman and Hall, 1897), p. 68, p. 72.
43 Mikhail Bakhtin, "Epic and the Novel," in Bakhtin, *The Dialogic Imagination, Four Essays by M.M. Bakhtin*, ed. Michael Holquist, trans. Caryl Emerson and Michael Holquist (Austin: University of Texas Press, 1981), p. 13.
44 Bhabha, "DissemiNation," p. 319.
45 Contrary to Rihani's optimistic assessment of Ibn Saud's potential as a

focus of Pan-Arab sentiments, the King was invariably opposed to any move towards greater Arab unity, which he took to be instigated by his Hashimite enemies, and believed might endanger his treaties with Great Britain. See Yehoshua Porath, *In Search of Arab Unity, 1930–1945* (London: Frank Cass, 1986).

46   *Ibn Sa'oud* , p. 46, p. 209, pp. 138–9.

47   "Three Arab Kings."

48   Rihani, "More Deserts Than Are Dreamt Of," *Asia* (1933): pp. 554–61, p. 556.

49   Shahid, "al-Rihani and ibn Sa'ud," pp. 235–6.

50   Said, *Culture and Imperialism*, pp. 259–60; Benedict Anderson, *Imagined Communites, Reflections on the Origins and Spread of Nationalism* (London: Verso, 1983), p. 74.

51   *Culture and Imperialism*, p. 303.

Chapter 4: Ameen Rihani: Decolonizing Arabia

1   Rihani, "Arabia: An Unbiased Survey," *Journal of the Central Asian Society* 16 (1929): pp. 35–55 , p. 54.

2   For a summary of the debate on the sectarian contributions to Arab nationalism see C. Ernest Dawn, "The Origins of Arab Nationalism," in *The Origins of Arab Nationalism*, ed. Rashid Khalidi et al. (New York: Columbia University Press, 1991), pp. 3–30. For a postcolonial reading of nationalist discourse, see Edward W. Said, *Culture and Imperialism* (London: Chatto & Windus, 1993).

3   Said, *Culture and Imperialism*, p. 273.

4   "This was the period of imperialism triumphant," Samir Amin, *The Arab Nation*, trans. Michael Pallis (London: Zed Press, 1978), p. 33. See Albert Hourani , *A History of the Arab Peoples* (London: Faber, 1991), Part 4, "The Age of European Empires" (1800–1939); George Antonius, *The Arab Awakening, The Story of The Arab National Movement* (London: Hamish Hamilton, 1938; reprinted Beirut: Librairie du Liban, 1969), which covers almost the same period.

5   The offending articles were, "The Triple Alliance in the Animal Kingdom," and, "The Muleteer and the Monk." See Elie Kedourie, *The Chatham House Version and other Middle Eastern Studies* (Hanover, NH: Brandeis University Press, 1984), p. 322.

6   Rihani, "A Night in Cairo," *Papyrus* (February 1905): pp. 24–8, p. 25.

7   "For most of its adherents, Arabism was not yet Arab nationalism, nor did it entail a demand for separation from the [Ottoman] empire." Khalidi, *Arab Nationalism*, p. 62.

8   Rihani, *Ibn Sa'oud of Arabia, His People and His Land* (London: Constable, 1928), p. 10; *Arabian Peak and Desert, Travels in Al-Yaman* (London: Constable, 1930), p. 5.

9   The British vice-consul in Jedda heard Rihani deliver a speech to Ibn Saud in April 1926 in which he concluded by saying "he had had the honour of

visiting Ibn Saud by two doors, first by the door of the Persian Gulf, secondly by the door of the Red Sea, and he sincerely hoped that soon he would have the honour of visiting His majesty by the third and most glorious door, that of the Mediterranean Sea and Syria and Palestine." The vice-consul adds the comment: "This from Rihani came rather as a surprise, as I had previously considered his efforts, though decidedly pan-Arab, to be concentrated on the success of Ibn Saud in the Hejaz. It may be that recent events in Syria has [sic] brought about a change of attitude on his part." *The Jedda Diaries*, vol. 2, compiled with an introduction by Robert L. Jarman, 4 vols (Farnham Common: Archive editions, 1990), p. 383. On the recent events in Syria Rihani wrote in a letter of 26 May 1926: "It is Spring; the Syrian Revolutionists are still fighting the French; greater Lebanon has been declared a Republic – a nice little French republic with a colonial ring around her neck – and all's well with the world." Letters of Ameen Rihani, *Al-Kulliyal* 24 (Autumn 1949): pp. 16–18.

10   "Arabs Ask Stimson to Aid Palestine," *New York Times*, 7 September 1929. Stimson saw Rihani again: he records in a diary entry of 23 January 1931 (*Diaries of Henry L. Stimson* [Yale University Library, 15: p. 44]):

After Cabinet Meeting I received Mr Ameen Rihani, an American citizen of Arab descent, who came to ask for recognition of Ibn Saud, king of Nejd. He was a smooth-appearing gentleman who made a good argument.

11   "Rights in Palestine of Jews," *New York Times*, October 27, 1929; "Palestine Arabs Claim to be fighting for National existence," *Current History* (November 1929): pp. 272–8. Rihani's articles and lectures on the Palestine issue are collected in part in *The Fate of Palestine* (Beirut: Rihani Publishing House, 1967). For a summary of Rihani's writings on the Palestine issue, see Walter Edward Dunnavent, "Ameen Rihani: Transcendentalism in an Arab-American Writer," unpublished Doctoral dissertation, Indiana University, 1991, pp. 178–93.

12   Rihani, "The Passion Play of the East," *Syrian World* (March 1931): pp. 5–17; "Shiites Protest Rihani's Criticism," *Syrian World* (September 1931): pp. 25–8; "Rihani stirs A Hornets Nest," *Syrian World*, 11 August 1933.

13   Hourani, *The Arab Peoples*, p. 338.

14   Rihani, "The Pan-Arab Movement," American University of Beirut, MS: 320.54 R572p, p. 53. According to Rihani (ibid.) these boundaries were intended "to strangle the Arab [. . .] The desert is one, and it knows nor Syria nor Iraq [. . .] The desert is the land of the Arabs. What right have the Europeans or other foreigners in it?"

15   Rihani, "Pan-Arab Nationalism – Is It A Myth?" *Asia* (1939): pp. 452–5.

16   A comprehensive account of Rihani's thought is to be found in Ameen A. Rihani, *The Philosopher of Freike* (Beirut: Dar Al-Jeel, 1987) (Arabic).

17   Hisham Sharabi, *Arab Intellectuals and the West, The Formative Years, 1875–1914* (Baltimore: Johns Hopkins University Press, 1970), p. 69, p. 71.

18   Rihani, "Arabia: an Unbiased Survey," *Journal of The Central Asian Society* 16 (1929): 35–55, p. 40. "It might be said that the masses in the East are blind slaves, while in Europe and America they are become blind rebels. And

which is the better part of valour, when one is blind – submission or revolt?" Rihani, *The Book of Khalid* (New York: Dodd Mead and Company, 1911), p. 112.

19   "Ameen Rihani is still in the shadow in the Arab world, being a non-Muslim writer; [. . .] in Lebanon, among Christians, being a Pan-Arab writer; and in the West, being anti-orientalist [. . .] an Arab-American who wrote about Arabia with a 'counter-mission.'" Ameen A. Rihani, in a letter to Geoffrey Nash.

20   Ernest Gellner, *Thought and Change* (London: Weidenfeld & Nicholson, 1964) p. 169, quoted in Benedict Anderson, *Imagined Communities, Reflections on the Origin and Spread of Nationalism* (London: Verso, 1983), p. 15.

21   Eric Hobsbawm, *Nations and Nationalism since 1870, Programme, Myth, Reality* (Cambridge: Cambridge University Press, 1990), p. 10, p. 12; Ernest Gellner, *Nations and Nationalism* (Oxford: Blackwell, 1983), p. 46. Italics mine. Gellner is arguing against Elie Kedourie's view that nationalism was imposed on the nations of the deceased Ottoman Empire by Europe; see Elie Kedourie, *Nationalism* (London: Hutchinson, 1966); Edward Ingram, introduction, *National and International Politics in the Middle East, Essays in Honour of Elie Kedourie*, ed. Edward Ingram (London: Frank Cass, 1986), p. 2.

22   William L. Cleveland, *The Making of an Arab Nationalist, Ottomanism and Arabism in the Life and Thought of Sati' al-Husri* (Princeton, NJ: Princeton University Press, 1971), p. x, p. 66.

23   Rihani was closer to "the official theory of Arab nationalism, such as it came to be after the First World War, [which] abjured any exclusively religious criterion." Sylvia Haim, *Arab Nationalism, An Anthology* (Berkeley, CA: University of California Press, 1976), p. 55.

24   Hobsbawm, *Nations and Nationalism*, p. 131.

25   "Liberals and conservatives and radicals are much alike [. . .] when the question is one of imperial, colonial, or mandatory control; and many of them [. . .] are shining examples of mental ineptitude, when it is a question of racial psychology reaching down to the hidden springs of a political movement." "The White Way of the Desert," American University of Beirut, MS: 892.78 R572w, p. 103.

26   Rihani, "The Pan-Arab Movement," p. 28; see Antonius, *The Arab Awakening*, p. 111, p. 115, and Khalidi, *Arab Nationalism*, p. 62.

27   For Rihani's remarks on a disappointing interview with Roosevelt, see Ameen A. Rihani, *The Philosopher of Freike* , p. 91. The following articles include material later built into "Turkey and Islam": "The Holy Land: Whose to Have and to Hold," *Bookman* (September 1917): pp. 7–14; "Germany and Islam," *World's Work* (January 1915): pp. 302–5; "Young Arabia," *Forum* (March 1915): pp. 315–26; "The Revolution in Arabia, I. Internal Causes and Purposes," *Bookman* (April 1917): pp. 121–6; "II. Political Considerations," *Bookman* (May 1917): pp. 283–8; "III. Social Forces: Its Destiny," *Bookman* (June 1917): pp. 495–501.

28   "Turkey and Islam," pp. 10–11, pp. 18–20.

29 Ibid., p. 15, pp. 20–3, p. 26, p. 49, p. 72.
30 Ibid., pp. 15, p. 108.
31 Rihani, *Arabian Peak*, pp. 8–9, p. 15. But Rihani did recommend (ibid., pp. 236–7) the British to the Imam Yahya as the least of evils in the unavoidable choice as to which European power he should enter into political agreement with – "the English [Jekyll-and-Hyde], even though more selfish and deliberate, is better than the Italian or the French."
32 Ibid., p. 27; under the Turks the Arabs maintained themselves "in a state of semi-independence"; the *bedu* took Turkish bribes "with a sneer, and always rejected [the Ottoman empire's] political yoke," "Turkey and Islam," p. 54.
33 *Arabian Peak*, p. 28, p. 40, p. 221.
34 Rihani's assessment of the political realities that hemmed Faisal in are more clearly expressed in his Arabic account, *Faisal the First*. See Philip K. Khauli, "Christian Poet Sings Paeans To an Arab King," *Syrian World*, April 27, 1934. For an extraordinarily negative account of Faisal in Iraq, see Kedourie, *Chatham House Version*, pp. 240–3, and for a more sympathetic assessment, Antonius, *Arab Awakening*, p. 360. On Nuri, Arab Unity and the question of an Arab federation, see Majid Khadduri, *Arab Contemporaries, The Role of Personalities in Politics* (Baltimore: Johns Hopkins University Press, 1973), p. 28; cf. Rihani, "The Pan-Arab Movement," pp. 46–7, and "The Pan-Arab Dream," *Asia* (1938): pp. 44–6.
35 Rihani, "Iraq During the Days of King Faisal The First," American University of Beirut, MS: 956.704 R572i, p. 166, 295. Gertrude Bell claimed in 1918 that the Arabs themselves preferred a British administration: "they can't conceive an independent Arab government [. . .] There is no one here who could run it." Elizabeth Burgoyne, *Gertrude Bell: From Her Personal Papers, 1914–1926* (London: Ernest Benn, 1961), p. 78.
36 Rihani, "The Young Nation on the Tigris," *Asia* (1932): pp. 603–9, p. 606.
37 Rihani, "Coup D'Etat in Baghdad," *Asia* (1937): pp. 436–8, pp. 436–7.
38 Rihani, "Pan-Arab Movement," p. 19.
39 Rihani, "The New Syrian Republic," *Asia* (1938): pp. 51–4.
40 Rihani, "Holy Land," p. 14.
41 Rihani, *The Fate of Palestine*, p. 26, pp. 70–1, pp. 78–9.
42 Ibid., p. 91, p. 27, p. 21, p. 23, p. 25.
43 Rihani, "Pan-Arab Dream," p. 46.
44 "Pan-Arab Movement," p. 18. Paradoxically, according to Edward Said, the Pan-Arabism favored by Rihani and George Antonius may have aided the Zionists in portraying themselves as "a civilization of sweetness and light out of the black Islamic sea." *The Question of Palestine* (New York: Random House, 1980), pp. 24–5.
45 On the deficiencies of the Arabs in putting across their cause on Palestine between the wars see *The Arab Awakening*, pp. 388–9.
46 *Culture and Imperialism*, p. 297. Rihani had generous words of praise for the penultimate British High Commissioner in Baghdad, Sir Gilbert Clayton, see "Young Nation on the Tigris," pp. 607–8.
47 "Turkey and Islam," p. 132.

48   Rihani, "Pan-Arab Movement," p. 19: "Even if the European Powers swear eternal friendship and peace among themselves, the continuous disturbances in the Near East will draw them into the vortex and eventually plunge them into a war, not with each other perhaps, but with the Eastern Powers around the scene of the conflict."

49   "Pan-Arab Nationalism," p. 454. To the Post-War slogans – "anti-imperialism, anti-Zionism and Arab solidarity" should now be added a fourth (always inherent in the formation of Arab nationalism) – Arabism and Islam are One. Roger Owen, "Arab Nationalism, Unity and Solidarity," in *Sociology of "Developing Societies," The Middle East*, pp. 15–22, ed. Talal Asad and Roger Owen (London: Macmillan, 1983), p. 19; Rihani may be said to fall into the stage of classic nationalism, as described by Edward Said, even as he foresees the "liberationist" stage. *Culture and Imperialism*, Chap. 3, "Resistance and Opposition," pp. 252–340.

50   Letters of Ameen Rihani, *Al-Kulliyal* 24 (Autumn 1949): pp. 16–18, p. 18.

51   Nazik Saba Yared (*Arab Travellers and Western Civilization* [London: Saqi Books,1996]) has placed Rihani within this Arab context. She accuses him of having a split personality, and of compensating for his aggrieved sense of Arab humiliation by the West by adopting a Utopian internationalism. The failure to understand his biculturality is one of the chief weaknesses of her reading of Rihani.

52   "The Pan-Arab Movement," pp. 12–13.

Chapter 5: George Antonius: Anglo-Arab Disjunctions

1   Antonius to John Richmond, quoted in Susan Silsby, "Antonius: Palestine, Zionism and British Imperialism, 1929–1939," Doctoral dissertation, 1986, Georgetown University (Ann Arbor: University Microfilms, 1986), p. 208. Thomas Hodgkin, *Letters from Palestine, 1932–1936*, ed. E .C. Hodgkin (London: Quartet Books, 1986), p. 82.

2   Edward W. Said, *Orientalism, Western Conceptions of the Orient* (London: Routledge, Kegan Paul, 1978), p. 25.

3   Edward W. Said, *Culture and Imperialism* (London: Chatto & Windus, 1993), p. 298.

4   See Albert Hourani, "*The Arab Awakening* Forty Years Later," in *The Emergence of the Modern Middle East* (London: Macmillan, 1981), pp. 193–215, pp. 196–7.

5   Silsby, "Antonius," p. 11, p. 13.

6   Thomas Hodgkin, *Letters*, p. 33. The longer quotation is from Hodgkin's 1981 George Antonius Lecture, St Antony's College, Oxford.

7   "Antonius," p. 40, p. 51.

8   Ibid., p. 227, p. 245.

9   Ibid., p. 280, p. 272.

10   Antonius, "Memorandum on Arab Affairs," FO 371/27043, E53/53/65. Antonius's memorandum is summarized in Yehoshua Porath, *In Search of Arab Unity, 1930–1945* (London: Frank Cass, 1986), p. 187.

11   D. Van Der Meulen, *Don't You Hear The Thunder, A Dutchman's Life Story* (Leiden: E.J. Brill, 1981), p. 121. According to the Dutchman, Antonius asked if he could help him to re-open lines with the British, specifically with Gilbert Clayton, who trusted Antonius. Van Der Meulen contacted Clayton's brother in Egypt but nothing resulted. He mistakenly concludes (ibid., p. 91) that Antonius then turned to writing *The Arab Awakening* at this time.

12   Albert Hourani, "*Arab Awakening* Forty Years Later," pp. 199–200.

13   James Gelvin, Review of *The Origins of Arab Nationalism*, ed. Rashid Khalidi et al. (New York: Columbia University Press, 1991), *British Journal of Middle East Studies* 20 (1993): pp. 100–2, p. 101.

14   Fred Halliday, *Islam and the Myth of Confrontation, Religion and Politics in the Middle East* (London: I.B. Tauris, 1996), p. 201.

15   George Antonius, *The Arab Awakening, The Story of the Arab National Movement* (London: Hamish Hamilton, 1938; reprinted, Beirut: Librairie du Liban, 1969), p. x.

16   "*Arab Awakening* Forty Years Later," p. 196, p. 212.

17   Bill Ashcroft, Gareth Griffith and Helen Tiffin , *The Empire Writes Back, Theory and Practice in Post-Colonial Literatures* (London: Routledge, 1989), p. 18.

18   Said, *Culture and Imperialism*, p. 304.

19   Gelvin, Review, p. 101. On grand narrative, see J-F. Lyotard, *The Postmodern Condition: A Report on Knowledge*, trans. Geoff Bennington and Brian Massumi (Manchester: Manchester University Press,1984), pp. 31–40.

20   *Arab Awakening*, pp. 120–1.

21   *Culture and Imperialism*, p. 310.

22   *Arab Awakening*, pp. 190–1; see Edward Gibbon, *The History of the Decline and Fall of The Roman Empire*, vol. 5 (Oxford: Oxford University Press, 1920), pp. 462–3.

23   *Arab Awakening*, pp. 176–7.

24   "*The Arab Awakening* Forty Years Later," p. 212.

25   *Arab Awakening*, pp. 165–8.

26   Ibid., p. 454. Antonius may have been aware that the letter in question was the work of Ronald Storrs and his "little Persian agent" and translator, Husain Ruhi. See Storrs, *Orientations* (London: Ivor Nicolson and Watson, 1939), p. 157, p. 161; Elie Kedourie, *In the Anglo-Arab Labyrinth, The McMahon–Husayn Correspondence and its Interpretations 1914–1939* (Cambridge: Cambridge University Press, 1976), p. 15, p. 20, pp. 70–1.

27   *Arab Awakening*, pp. 178–9.

28   Ibid., p. 180.

29   Ibid.

30   Ibid., pp. 182–3.

31   Ibid., pp. 174–5.

32   Ibid., pp. 367–68.

33   "Antonius," p. 36. The British officer was Thomas Hodgkin's brother, E. C. Hodgkin.

34 Ibid., pp. 52–3.
35 Antonius, "The Machinery of Government in Palestine," *Annals of The American Academy of Political and Social Science* 164 (1932): pp. 55–61, p. 57, p. 59.
36 "Antonius," p. 115, p. 118. Antonius was far more wary when it came to exercising his mediating skills between Jews and Arabs. On his aloof response to the anti-Zionist Dr. Judah Magnes's invitation to join him in Arab-Jewish cooperation, see Silsby, p. 115; on Antonius's response to Ben-Gurion's soundings regarding a Jewish state associated with an Arab federation, see Yehoshua Porath, *In Search*, p. 62.
37 Antonius, "Syria and the French Mandate," *International Affairs* 8 (1934): pp. 523–39, p. 534.
38 Ibid., pp. 527–8.
39 Antonius, "Memorandum on Arab Affairs."
40 Regarding Jewish colonization of Palestine, Dr. Chaim Weizmann suggested: "[The British felt] it might be valuable to have a friend in need, to have a European people, in this part of the world." But "so far, as I hope it will also be in the future, never has there been any attempt direct or indirect to dispossess an Arab of his land." "The Zionist Movement Under The Palestine Mandate," *Journal of the Central Asian Society* 17 (January 1930): pp. 23–42, p. 27, p. 31.
41 *Arab Awakening*, p. 398, p. 409.
42 Kedourie (*Anglo-Arab Labyrinth*, p. 300) takes the British to task for using Antonius's book as a pretext "to get rid of the Zionist embarrassment." See ibid., pp. 280–308, for a hostile – and therefore affirmative – assessment of the influence of *The Arab Awakening* on British thinking at the time of the London conference on Palestine.
43 "Decolonization, which sets out to change the order of the world, is, obviously, a programme of complete disorder. But it cannot come as a result of magical practices, nor of a natural shock, nor of a friendly understanding. Decolonization, as we know, is a historical process, it cannot become intelligible nor clear to itself except in the exact measure that we can discern the movements which give it historical form and content." Frantz Fanon, *The Wretched of The Earth*, trans. Constance Farrington (Harmondsworth: Penguin Books, 1967), p. 27.
44 "*Arab Awakening* Forty Years Later," p. 213.
45 *Culture and Imperialism*, p. 311.
46 On the Palestinian peasant revolution of 1936–39, which sought in vain to find a leadership among the urban notables, see Rosemary Sayegh, *Palestinians: From Peasants to Revolutionaries* (London: Zed Press, 1979).

Chapter 6: Edward Atiyah: Language and Colonization

1 D. J. Enright, *Academic Year* (London: Secker and Warburg, 1955), p. 51.
2 Michael Francis Atiyah, interview by Geoffrey Nash, 19 September 1996.
3 Edward Atiyah, *An Arab Tells His Story, A Study in Loyalties* (London: John

Murray, 1946); *The Thin Line* (London: Peter Davies, 1951); *Black Vanguard* (London: Peter Davies, 1952); *Lebanon Paradise* (London: Peter Davies, 1953); *The Arabs* (Harmondsworth: Penguin Books, 1955, reprinted. Beirut, Librarie du Liban, 1968).

4   Bill Ashcroft, Helen Tiffin and Gareth Griffith, *The Empire Writes Back, Theory and Practice in Post-Colonial Literatures* (London: Routledge, 1989), p. 6.

5   Homi K. Bhabha, *The Location of Culture* (London: Routledge, 1994), p. 86. Italics in text.

6   Atiyah, *An Arab Tells His Story*, pp. 177–81. On the rare occasions Atiyah imports transliterations of Arabic words into his discourse – such as fiki – these are usually denotative of "nativist" occupations or habits of which he disapproves. (See also note 12).

7   Bhabha, *Location of Culture*, p. 86, p. 72.

8   *An Arab Tells His Story*, p. 181.

9   Anwar el-Sadat, *In Search of Identity, An Autobiography* (New York: Harper & Row, 1978), p. 59. Amin Osman was instrumental as a go-between in the triangular relations between the British, King Farouk, and Nahas Pasha, leader of the nationalist Wafd Party, in the political crisis in Egypt of 1940–1942. He became Finance Minister in Nahas's government. See Hoda Gamal Abdel Nasser, *Britain and the Egyptian National Movement, 1936–1952* (Reading: Ithaca Press, 1994), pp. 65–85.

10   Albert Memmi, *The Colonizer and the Colonized*, trans. Howard Greenfeld (London: Earthscan, 1990), p. 198.

11   Hani Al-Raheb, "Two Invasions and One Tragic End: the Dialectics of North and South in Conrad's *Heart of Darkness* and Salih's *Season of Migration to the North*," *New Comparison* 17 (1994): pp. 50–66, p. 50.

12   Atiyah, *Black Vanguard*, p. 13.

13   Memmi, *Colonizer and Colonized*, p. 187. Compare Atiyah's own boyish fears: "What would Mr Reed or Mr Lias think if they came to see us one day and found my father in his caftan, like any Egyptian Omda, like Zakariya the laundryman at school? What would they think of me if they arrived when we were having lunch and saw me eating Kobeiba with raw onions?" *An Arab Tells His Story*, p. 65.

14   In addition to Tayeb Salih's work, the novels of Ngugi wa Thiong'o offer further postcolonial re-writings of the colonial mindset of *Black Vanguard*. For instance, *The River Between* (London, Heinemann, 1965), squarely faces the female circumcision issue. Ngugi does not defend the practice but places it in its traditional cultural context, seen by its Kikuyu defenders as a bulwark of their tribal identity against the civilization of the white colonizer. "Circumcision was an important ritual to the tribe. It kept people together, bound the tribe [. . .] Circumcision of women was not important as a physical operation. It was what it did inside a person. It could not be stopped overnight. Patience and, above all, education were needed." p. 68, p. 142.

15   *Black Vanguard*, pp. 158–9.

16   *An Arab Tells His Story*, p. 175.

17   Tayeb Salih, *Season of Migration to the North*, trans. Denys Johnson-Davies
     (London: Heinemann, 1980), p. 60; Joseph John, "A Dialogue with Mr
     Tayeb Salih on *Season of Migration to the North*," *Islamic Quarterly* 36 (1992):
     pp. 207–18, pp. 208–9.
18   *Black Vanguard*, p. 50.
19   Patrick Williams and Laura Chrisman, *Colonial Discourse and Post-Colonial
     Theory, A Reader* (New York: Harvester Wheatsheaf, 1993), p. 8.
20   Atiyah, *Lebanon Paradise*, p. 158.
21   Ibid., p. 88.
22   Ibid., p. 81, p. 82, p. 88.
23   Ibid., p. 157.
24   Ibid., p. 186.
25   Ibid., p. 164, p. 163. Fareeda Barradi's words could be compared to Garbo's
     who in "Queen Christina" declares: "I have dreamed of happiness . . . " The
     novel contains other direct references to film, such as Fareeda's compar-
     ison of her husband's possible amnesia to Ronald Coleman's in "Random
     Harvest", a film she had seen twice.
26   Ibid., p. 179, p. 128.
27   This discussion draws on the distinction between pedagogic and perfor-
     mative aspects of narrating the nation made by Homi Bhabha in his article,
     "DissemiNation, time, narrative, and the margins of the modern nation,"
     pp. 291–322, in *Nation and Narration* (London: Routledge, 1991), pp. 297–9.
28   Ghassan Kanafani, *Men in the Sun, and Other Palestinian Stories*, trans.
     Hilary Kilpatrick (London: Heinemann, 1978), p. 7.
29   Edward W. Said, *The Question of Palestine* (New York: Random House,
     1980), pp. 152–3

Chapter 7: Edward Atiyah: The End of Anglo-Arab Politics

1   Albert Memmi, *The Colonizer and the Colonized*, trans. Howard Greenfeld
    (London: Earthscan, 1990), p. 192; Albert Hourani, *Syria and Lebanon, A
    Political Essay* (London: Oxford University Press, 1946), p. 34.
2   "The Arab leaders who had co-operated with the British and the French
    were now fatally tarred as collaborators with the Israelis. Suez ultimately
    proved to be the kiss of death for Nuri Pasha." W. M. Roger Louis and
    Roger Owen, introduction, *Suez 1956, The Crisis and its Consequences*, ed. W.
    M. Roger Louis and Roger Owen (Oxford: Clarendon Press, 1989), p. 14.
3   Philip Hitti, *The Syrians in America* (New York: George H. Doran, 1924), p.
    25; Edward Atiyah, *An Arab Tells His Story, A Study in Loyalties* (London:
    John Murray,1946), p. 27.
4   Atiyah, *An Arab Tells His Story*, p. 35, pp. 27–8.
5   Memmi, *Colonizer and Colonized*, pp. 12–13, p. 186.
6   *An Arab Tells His Story*, p. 61, p. 138, p. 170, p. 149, p. 183. For a contrapuntal
    text on Egyptian attitudes to the British occupation of their country, see
    Naguib Mahfouz, *Palace Walk*, trans. William Maynard Hutchins and Olive
    E. Kenny (New York: Anchor Books, 1990).

7   *An Arab Tells His Story*, p. 188. Some Christians "identif[ied] themselves with the Islamic past, in the sense that Islam was what the Arabs had done in history [. . .] [but] the Islamic basis of Arab nationalism made many of them uneasy." Albert Hourani, *The Emergence of the Modern Middle East* (London: Macmillan, 1981), p. 187.

8   Atiyah, "Prospects of the Arab Renaissance," *Quarterly Review* 285 (July 1947): pp. 471–83, pp. 480–1.

9   Ibid., p. 473; *An Arab Tells His Story*, p. 186; *The Arabs* (3rd edn, Beirut: Librairie Du Liban, 1968), p. 217.

10 Herbert L. Bodman, Review of Atiyah, *The Arabs*, *Middle East Journal* 10 (1956): pp. 30–1.

11 Atiyah, *What is Imperialism?* (London: The Batchworth Press, 1954), p. 23.

12 Ibid. Atiyah was not alone among Arabs in believing in the good faith of Britain. This sentiment even stretched to the Turks. Faidy Alami, father of Atiyah's friend Musa Alami, found that in 1918 "even Talaat Pasha, to whom he confided his doubts about the Balfour Declaration, had robustly declared that Britain (his enemies) were 'too honourable to give Palestine to the Jews' and would at worst put it under some sort of international regime in which everybody's rights would be respected." Geoffrey Furlonge, *Palestine is My Country, The Story of Musa Alami* (London: John Murray, 1969), p. 63.

13 "Of course there is the mistake, encountered in the works of Britons especially, of seeing in retrospect a grand design for decolonization which in fact did not exist. Closer inspection commonly reveals the British to have been following Burke's sage counsel to reform in order to preserve: London made concessions more often to subvert opposition to British rule than to prepare for its demise." Tony Smith, *The Pattern of Imperialism, The United States,Great Britain, and the late-industrializing world since 1815* (Cambridge: Cambridge University Press, 1981), p. 96.

14 Atiyah, *What is Imperialism?* p. 26, p. 19, p. 30; *An Arab tells His Story*, p. 183.

15 Atiyah, "Report on the Pan-Islamic Arab Movement," 14. 2. 1936, FO 371 / 19980, E 1326/381/65; "Note on Near Eastern Affairs, " 17.12.36, FO 371/19980, E 8028/381/65; "Further Note on Near Eastern Affairs," 13.9.1937, FO 371/20786, E 5360/351/65.

16 Yehoshua Porath, *In Search of Arab Unity, 1930–1945* (London: Frank Cass, 1986), p. 228. See ibid., pp. 228–30, for the response of British officials to the Atiyahs' reports. (Porath, incidentally, repeats the mistaken Foreign Office assumption that the Atiyahs were brothers.)

17 *An Arab Tells His Story*, p. 225.

18 Atiyah, "The Arab League," *World Affairs* 1(1947), pp. 34–47, pp. 42–3: The question of Palestine was "extraneous" to Anglo-Arab mutual interests "in the sense that Zionism is not a genuine or legitimate British interest."

19 Atiyah, *The Palestine Question* (London: Diplomatic Press and Publishing Company, 1948), pp. 6–7. "The White Paper of 1939 served notice on the Jews that Great Britain had now definitely refused to carve out any 'national home', or Zionist state, by force of British arms. The desired end, therefore, could now only be attained by force of Zionist arms [. . .] The

Arabs made an error, in that they did not grasp that such was the Zionist outlook, and such the Zionist blueprint for the future." A. P. Thornton, *The Imperial Idea and its Enemies* (London: Macmillan, 1985), p. 342.

20   Atiyah, *The Arabs*, p. 178; *The Palestine Question*, p. 10. *What was Promised in Palestine?* (London: The Arab Office, 1946) beyond updating and summarizing the significance from the Arab point of view of the key dates and events in the Allies' dealings with the Arabs, says little that is new. Atiyah's arguments on the semantics of the national home for the Jews, and Britain's mandated responsibilities to the Arab inhabitants of Palestine, largely revisit those already made by Ameen Rihani, in *The Fate of Palestine*, and George Antonius, in *The Arab Awakening*.

21   *The Palestine Question*, pp. 15–16; *The Arabs*, pp. 179–80, p. 185.

22   *The Arabs*, p. 235, p. 238.

23   Ibid., pp. 194–5.

24   W. M. Roger Louis, "The Anglo-Egyptian Settlement of 1954," in *Suez 1956*, p. 51.

25   *The Arabs*, pp. 211–14, pp. 240–1.

26   "Suez destroyed any slim possibility that Britain and France would remain major powers in the Arab world. As damaging in Arab eyes as the perceived sin of attacking Egypt and Arab nationalism [. . .] was the fact that the two powers had collaborated with Israel. This collusion confirmed the most extreme Arab nationalist theses, which argued that the great powers' support for the creation of a Jewish state in Palestine had always been motivated by their desire to use it as a pawn against the Arabs." Rashid Khalidi, "Consequences of the Suez Crisis in the Arab World," in *Suez 1956*, p. 380.

27   *The Arabs*, p. 245.

28   Joseph J. Malone, preface, Atiyah, *The Arabs*, 1968, pp. 5–6.

29   Britain's aggression against Egypt shocked and dismayed erstwhile postcolonial admirers like Nehru, who "had great faith in British common sense and could not believe that any British Prime Minister, let alone Eden, would use force on such an issue," and "did not conceal the strength of his feelings and his deep regret that Britain, with her record of liberal policies, should now have become again the symbol of colonialism." S. Gopal, "India, the Crisis, and the Non-Aligned Nations," *Suez 1956*, p. 182, p. 185.

30   Edward W. Said, *Orientalism, Western Conceptions of the Orient* (London: Routledge, Kegan Paul, 1978), p. 224. On Philby's mistaken belief that Ibn Sa'ud could be induced to accept partition of Palestine in return for a $20m Jewish subsidy, see Elizabeth Monroe, *Philby of Arabia* (London: Faber, 1973), pp. 221–5; on the so-called Philby scheme, see Porath, *Arab Unity*, pp. 80–106. (Roosevelt told the British War secretary "that the Arabs were purchasable and that the whole Palestine question was merely a matter of a little bribe." ibid., pp. 88–9.) For Lawrence to Faisal on the advantages of an Anglo-Jewish Palestine, see Monroe, *Britain's Moment in the Middle East, 1914–1971* (London: Chatto & Windus, 1981), p. 65.

31   Albert Hourani, obituary of Edward Atiyah, *The London Times*, 26 October 1964. Atiyah died on October 23 after collapsing during a debate on Arab-

Israeli relations in which he was taking part at the Oxford Union.

32   Anouar Abdel-Malek, *Nation and Revolution*, vol. 2 of *Social Dialectics* (Basingstoke: Macmillan, 1981), p. 75.

33   Edward W. Said, *Culture and Imperialism* (London: Chatto & Windus), p. 318.

Chapter 8: The Politics of Anglo-Arab Discourse

1   Kahlil Gibran, *A Tear and A Smile*, translated by H. M. Nahmad (London: Heinemann,1950), p. 78; Edward W. Said, *Culture and Imperialism* (London: Chatto & Windus, 1993), p. 253.

2   Rashid Khalidi, "Consequences of the Suez Crisis in the Arab World," in *Suez 1956: The Crisis and its Consequences*, ed. W. M. Roger Louis and Roger Owen (Oxford: Clarendon Press, 1989), p. 382.

3   Edward Atiyah, *An Arab Tells His Story, A Study in Loyalties* (London: John Murray, 1946), p. 187; Albert Hourani, *Syria and Lebanon, A Political Essay* (London: Oxford University Press, 1946), p. 2.

4   "According to *As-Sayeh*, an Arabic newspaper of New York, [*The Prophet*] is considered by some to be second only to the books of revelation in its spiritualistic mystical and ethical teachings." "Gibran's Prophet a Religious Service," *Syrian World* (March 1928): pp. 49–50.

5   See Norman Daniel, *Islam and the West, The Making of an Image* (Edinburgh: Edinburgh University Press, 1963).

6   Suheil Bushrui, introduction to, Kahlil Gibran, *The Prophet* (Oxford: Oneworld, 1995), pp. 26– 33, and *Kahil Gibran of Lebanon, a re-evaluation of the life and works of the author of The Prophet* (Gerrards Cross: Colin Smythe, 1987), p. 56. "One or two critics, like the Irish poet AE and the American poet Robert Hillyer, have suggested the adoption of a new critical mechanism for assessing this type of literature deriving from two separate cultural traditions and bound by the prejudices and restrictions of neither." Ibid., p. 81.

7   Khalil Hawi, *Kahlil Gibran, His Background, Character and Works* (Beirut: Arab Institute for Publishing and Research, 1972), p. 156.

8   Bill Ashcroft, Gareth Griffith and Helen Tiffin, *The Empire Writes Back, Theory and Practice in Post-Colonial Literatures* (London: Routledge, 1989), p. 167. The quotation from Foucault is from "The political function of the intellectual," *Radical Philosophy* 17, pp. 12–14.

9   See Hawi, *Gibran*, pp. 67–81.

10   Ameen Rihani, *The Path of Vision, Essays of East and West*, ed. S. B. Bushrui and J. M. Monro (Beirut: The Rihani House, 1970), p. 115.

11   Hisham Sharabi, *Arab Intellectuals and the West: The Formative Years, 1875–1914* (Baltimore: Johns Hopkins University Press, 1970), p. 118, pp. 120–1.

12   Quoted in Bassam Tibi, *Arab Nationalism, A Critical Inquiry* (London: Macmillan, 1981), p. 85.

13   Quoted in Sylvia Haim, *Arab Nationalism: An Anthology* (Berkeley, CA:

University of California Press, 1976), p. 36. Rihani's notion of Christian-
Muslim unity was a variant of that reiterated by al-Husri in his
foregrounding of "the unity of language and history" as the most important elements in the foundation of a nation. On al-Husri's statement, A. L.
Tibawi ("From Islam to Arab Nationalism," in *Arabic and Islamic Themes,
Historical, Educational and Literary Studies* [London: Luzac, 1976], p. 153)
concluded: "Like many concessions made by Muslims it cannot fail to
make a completely secularized Arab nationalism more acceptable to all
shades of Christian opinion."

14   "Who are the Syrians?" *Syrian World*, December 6, 1934. On the racial
make-up of the Syrians, see Philip Hitti, *The Syrians in America* (George H.
Doran, 1924), pp. 19–21.

15   "Rihani Stirs a Hornet's Nest." *Syrian World*, August 11, 1933. One pro-
Rihani writer (ibid.) agreed that "this spirit of defeatism is quite prevalent
in Syria, [. . .] Rihani could have just as well quoted from the popular folk-
songs of Hunein or from the 'Buddhistic and mystical philosophies with
which Naimy comes to us.' This [. . .] [was] a sign of national weakness,
a 'sickly propaganda to recoil before the struggle of life [. . .]'"

16   "Shi'ites protest Rihani criticism." *Syrian World* (September 1931): pp. 25–8.
Rihani's article was "A Passion Play of the East," published in *Travel*
(December 1930): pp. 7–11, pp. 48–9, and *Syrian World* (March 1931): pp.
5–16.

17   "Iraq, Palestine and Syria." Report on Rihani lecture to Chautauqua
Institute, *Chautauquan Daily*, 24 July 1930.

18   Hourani, *Syria and Lebanon*, p. 103.

19   George Antonius, *The Arab Awakening, The Story of the Arab National
Movement* (Beirut: Librairie du Liban, 1969) ; C. Ernest Dawn, "The Origins
of Arab Nationalism," in *The Origins of Arab Nationalism*, ed. Rashid Khalidi
et al. (New York: Columbia University Press, 1991), p. 3.

20   A. L. Tibawi, "From Islam," p. 117.

21   Kamal Salibi, *A House of Many Mansions, The History of Lebanon Reconsidered*
(London: I.B. Tauris, 1988), p. 215.

22   Susan Silsby, "Antonius: Palestine, Zionism and British Imperialism,
1929–1939," (Ann Arbor: University Microfilms, 1986), p. 118. The phrase
"an honest interpreter of events" is Silsby's.

23   Kamal Salibi, *Many Mansions*, pp. 38–9.

24   Antonius, "Memorandum on Arab Affairs," FO 371/27043, E 53/53/65.
According to Ben-Gurion, Antonius told him in 1936 that Arab unity was
only feasible in "Greater Syria from the Taurus Mountains to the Sinai
Desert [. . .] This land constituted one unit and should be reunited."
Yehoshua Porath, *In Search of Arab Unity, 1930–1945* (London: Frank Cass,
1986), p. 62. According to Silsby ("Antonius," p. 295), Antonius saw
Palestine wanting its independence as part of the family of Arab states in
a gradual move to Arab federation that would include the Arab-speaking
states of North Africa.

25   "Islam itself, it must not be forgotten, came from the Arabs and was prop-
agated by Arab arms." Atiyah, *The Arabs* (3rd edn Beirut: Librairie du

Liban, 1968), p. 41.

26 Atiyah, *An Arab Tells His Story*, pp. 190–5.

27 See *Many Mansions*, chap. 10, pp. 182–99.

28 Gibran, *The Garden of the Prophet* (London: Heinemann, 1934). The British journalist, Robert Fisk, uses the expanded passage to preface his acclaimed account, *Pity the Nation, Lebanon at War* (Oxford: Oxford University Press, 1990).

29 Report of Ameen Rihani's lecture in the *London Times*, 8 November, 1928. The lecture is entitled, "Arabia: an Unbiased Survey," *Journal of the Central Asian Society* 16 (1929): pp. 35–55. His lectures at the Chautauqua Institute were reported in *The Chautauquan Daily*, 22–26 July, 1930. For an account of Rihani's nationalist activities by a member of the American Foreign Policy Association, see Elizabeth P. MacCallum, "Rihani – The Man and His Work," *Syrian World* (November 1929): pp. 20–7. The same issue announced that Rihani would be engaged in a "wide circuit of lecture engagements" under the auspices of the American Foreign Policy Association. ("Rihani's December Speaking Program," p. 50.) The December issue reported Rihani as having taken part in a debate on Zionism and Palestine at the Foreign Policy Association, on January 18, 1929. ("Rihani in Debate on Zionist Question," p. 55.)

30 *Documents on the History of Saudi Arabia*, vol. 2, *The Consolidation of Power in Central Arabia Under Ibn Saud, 1925–1928*, ed. Ibrahim al-Rashid (Salisbury, NC: Documentary Publications, 1976), p. 117. The United States had afforded Saudi Arabia diplomatic recognition in 1931. "Mr Twitchell believed that the presence there of an American diplomatic or consular officer would assist him in his efforts to bring American enterprise to Saudi Arabia and he hoped that the flag in this case might precede trade." "Memorandum of Conversation with Mr Kenneth Twitchell Regarding The Kingdom of Saudi Arabia," November 1, 1932, in *Origins of the Saudi Arabian Oil Empire, Secret U.S. Documents, 1923–1944*, ed. Nelson Robertson (Salisbury, NC: Documentary Publications, 1979), p. 53.

31 For comments on Antonius's "Memorandum on Arab Affairs," including remarks about his contacts with the Mufti of Jerusalem, see FO 371/27043, E 53/53/65. J. G. Ward in London thought Atiyah's reports "tendentious" for taking in Syria (they were supposed to be from the Sudan Agency), but L. G. Baggellay was not alone in finding them "illuminating." FO 371/20786, E 5360/351/65.

32 Concerning the Palestinian delegation that came to London in 1921 to present the Arab case, Musa Alami said: "they were a pathetic body. Apart from their secretary, who was a tourist agent and spoke some English, none of them had had any contact with the West, or spoke a word of any language other than Arabic and Turkish; they were living in another world." In London "they were treated like backward children," and were refused an interview with Ministers, being told instead "the Colonial Secretary had already seen Dr. Weizmann [. . .] they should discuss their problems with the Jews." Geoffrey Furlonge, *Palestine is My Country, The Story of Musa Alami* (London: John Murray, 1969), 80–1. See also below, pp.

85–6, for Alami's farcical account of imaginary Arab "influence" in London at that time.

33 Ibid., p. 138.

34 Walid Khalidi, ed., *From Haven to Conquest, Readings in Zionism and the Palestine Problem until 1948* (Beirut: Institute for Palestine Studies, 1971), p. xl. Two examples of effective Zionist pressure in Britain were: in 1930, in the East End of London, Zionists were able threaten the British Government over its White Paper on Palestine by mobilizing local Jewish voters against the government candidate in an election (see ibid., pp. 182–99). And Musa Alami was removed from his private secretaryship to the British High Commissioner for Palestine, Sir Arthur Wauchope, with the aid of Zionist-minded MPs at Westminster (Furlonge, *Palestine My Country*, pp. 101–2).

35 "The Arab people, now struggling for union and solidarity are all agreed on their cardinal objectives, and are on the way to their supreme goal. How can Zionism, in view of this state of things, long survive?" Rihani, *The Fate of Palestine* (Beirut: The Rihani House, 1967), p. 68. Elsewhere ("Palestine and the Proposed Arab Federation," p. 66, *Annals of The American Academy of Political and Social Science* 164 [November 1932]: pp. 62–7) Rihani positions Palestine within the larger Arab whole as "a section of a country that is one in language, in race, in culture in custom and traditions, in religion (except for a few non-Moslem minorities who are equally loyal to the Arab cause), and in national aspirations."

36 This revision of Gellner and Anderson on nationalism was argued by Glen Bowman at a conference at Warwick University entitled "Dreams of Nationhood," 10 September 1996; his paper was entitled "A Comparative Study of nationalist movements: Palestine, Yugoslavia."

37 Atiyah ("Note on Near Eastern Affairs," FO 371/19980, E 8028/381/65) argued:

> In order [. . .] that the Moslem peoples of the Near East should give their support to England in any conflict that might break out between her and the Fascist powers, one imperative condition must be fulfilled – namely, the solution (if a solution can be found at this stage) of the Palestine problem in a manner acceptable to the Arabs.

He went on to propose Anglo-French co-sponsorship of "the creation of some sort of Arab State Federation."

38 "That year was crucial for me, in that Beirut allowed me to reeducate myself in Arabic language and literature; for twenty years I had exclusively studied the literatures of the West, whereas now I could experience the riches of my own tradition." Edward W. Said, *After the Last Sky, Palestinian Lives* (London: Faber, 1986), p. 172. On Said's special position within the Palestine national movement, and his affiliation to Arab culture, see Nubar Horsepian, "Connections in Palestine," pp. 5–18, and Ferial J. Ghazoul, "The Resonance of the Arab-Islamic Heritage in the work of Edward Said," pp. 157–72, *Edward Said, A Critical Reader*, ed. Michael Sprinker (Oxford: Blackwell, 1992).

39 Roger Owen, "Arab Nationalism, Unity and Solidarity," pp. 15–22, in

Sociology of "Developing Societies," The Middle East, ed. Talal Assad and Roger Owen (London: Macmillan, 1983), p. 21.

40 The racism suffered by Syro-Lebanese immigrants to the United States was discussed at length in the pages of *Syrian World* in the late 1920s and early 1930s; see *Crossing the Waters, Arabic-Speaking Immigrants to the United States before 1940*, ed. Eric Hooglund (Washington D.C.: Smithsonian Institution Press, 1987), pp. 37–68.

41 Albert Hourani, *The Emergence of the Modern Middle East* (London: Macmillan, 1981), p. 214; Said, *Culture and Imperialism*, p. 308. I am aware of the arguments directed against Said's schema for colonial and postcolonial writing by Aijaz Ahmad (*In Theory, Classes, Nations, Literatures* [London: Verso, 1992]) and agree that the writers Said chooses to confirm his division do not include authors from the colonial period who adopted stridently anti-colonial positions. In the case of Anglo-Arab discourse, however, Said's distinctions appear to hold up.

42 Anouar Abdel-Malek, *Nation and Revolution*, vol. 2 of *Social Dialectics* (London: Macmillan, 1981), p. 22.

43 Said, "The politics of memory," *Al-Ahram Weekly*, 26 September–2 October, 1996.

44 Malek, *Nation and Revolution*, p. 200.

45 *Culture and Imperialism*, p. 277. Italics in text.

Select Bibliography

Adonis (Ali Ahmed Said). *An Introduction to Arab Poetics*. Translated by Catherine Cobban. London: Saqi Books, 1990.

Amin, Samir. *The Arab Nation*. London: Zed Press, 1978.

Anderson, Benedict. *Imagined Communities, Reflections on The Origin and Spread of Nationalism*. London: Verso, 1983.

Antonius, George. *The Arab Awakening, The Story of The Arab National Movement*. London: Hamish Hamilton, reprinted Beirut: Librairie du Liban, 1969.

——. "The Machinery of Government in Palestine." *Annals of The American Academy of Political and Social Science* 164 (November 1932): pp. 55–61.

——. "Memorandum on Arab Affairs." Public Record Office, London. FO 371/27043, E 53/53/65.

——. "Syria and The French Mandate." *International Affairs* 8 (1934): pp. 523–39.

Ashcroft, Bill, Gareth Griffiths, and Helen Tiffin. The Empire Writes Back: *Theory and Practice in Post-Colonial Literatures*. London: Routledge, 1989.

Atiyah, Edward. *An Arab Tells His Story, A Study in Loyalties*. London: John Murray, 1946.

——. "The Arab League." *World Affairs* I (1947): pp. 34–47.

——. *The Arabs*, 3rd edn. Beirut: Librairie du Liban. 1968.

——. *Black Vanguard*. London: Peter Davies, 1952.

——. "A Further note on Near Eastern Affairs." Public Record Office, London. FO 371/20786, E 5360/351/65.

——. *Lebanon Paradise*. London: Peter Davies, 1953.

——. "Note on Near Eastern Affairs." Public Record Office, London. FO 371/19980, E 8028/381/65.

——. *The Palestine Question*. London: Diplomatic Press and Publishing Company, 1948.

——. "Prospects of The Arab Renaissance." *Quarterly Review* 285, 573 (1947): pp. 471–83.

——. "Report on the Pan-Islamic Arab Movement." London. Public Record Office. FO 371/19980, E 1326/381/65.

——. *What is Imperialism?* London: The Batchworth Press, 1954.

——. *What was Promised in Palestine?* London: The Arab Office, 1946.

Badawi, M. M. *A Critical Introduction to Modern Arabic Poetry*. Cambridge: Cambridge University Press, 1975.

——. "Perenial Themes in Arabic Literature." *British Journal of Middle East*

Studies 20 (1993): pp. 3–19.

Bakhtin, Mikhail. *The Dialogic Imagination, Four Essays by M. M. Bakhtin.* Edited by Michael Holoquist and translated from the Russian by Caryl Emerson and Michael Holoquist. Austin: University of Texas Press, 1981.

Bell, Gertrude. *Gertrude Bell: From Her Personal Papers 1914–1926.* London: Ernest Benn, 1961.

Belsey, Catherine. *Critical Practice.* London, Methuen, 1980.

Berque, Jacques. *Cultural Expression in Arab Society Today* (Langages arabes du present). Translated from the French by Robert W. Stookey. Austen: University of Texas Press, 1978.

Bhabha, Homi K. *The Location of Culture.* London: Routledge, 1994.

——. ed. *Nation and Narration.* London: Routledge, 1990.

Birch, David. *Language, Literature, and Critical Practice.* London: Routledge, 1989.

Bowman, Glen. "A Comparative Study of National Movements: Palestine, Yugoslavia." Lecture delivered at Warwick University, September 10, 1996.

Bullard, Reader. *Two Kings in Arabia, Letters from Jeddah 1923–5 and 1936–9.* Edited by E. C. Hodgkin. Reading: Ithaca, 1993.

Bushrui, Suheil. "Arab American Cultural Relations in the Twentieth Century: The Thought and Works of Ameen Rihani with Reference to His English Works." University of Maryland, Fifth Annual Phillips Lecture, 12 December 1990 (unpublished typescript).

——. *Kahlil Gibran of Lebanon, a re-evaluatation of the life and works of the author of The Prophet.* Gerrards Cross: Colin Smyhte, 1987.

Bushrui, Suheil B., and John M. Munro, eds. *Kahlil Gibran: Essays and Introductions.* Beirut: The Rihani House, 1970.

Cleveland, William L. *The Making of an Arab Nationalist, Ottomanism and Arabism in The Life and Thought of Sati' al-Husri.* Princeton, NJ: Princeton University Press, 1971.

Colla, Elliott. "Between Nation and National Subject: Speculations on National Allegory." *Proceedings, Third International Symposium on Comparative Literature, History in Literature,* pp. 263–70. Cairo: Department of English Language and Literature, Faculty of Arts, University of Cairo, 1995.

D'haen, Theo. "Shades of Empire in Colonial and Post-Colonial Literatures." In *Shades of Empire in Colonial and Post-Colonial Literatures.* Edited by Theo D'haen and C. C. Barfoot, pp. 9–16. Amsterdam/Atlanta: Rodopi, 1993.

Dunnavent, Walter Edward. "Ameen Rihani: Transcendentalism in an Arab-American Writer." Doctoral dissertation, Indiana University, 1991.

Eagleton, Terry. *Literary Theory, An Introduction.* Oxford: Blackwell, 1983.

Fanon, Franz. *The Wretched of the Earth.* Translated by Constance Farrington. Harmondsworth: Penguin Books, 1967.

Furlonge, Geoffrey. *Palestine is My Country: The Story of Musa Alami.* London: John Murray, 1969.

Gellner, Ernest. *Nations and Nationalism.* Oxford: Blackwell, 1983.

Gibran, Kahlil (Jibran Khalil Jibran). *The Forerunner.* London: Heinemann, 1963.

——. *The Garden of The Prophet.* London: Heinemann, 1954.

——. *Lazarus and His Beloved, A One-Act Play.* Edited and with an introduction by Kahlil and Jean Gibran. London: Heinemann, 1972.

——. *The Madman*. London: Heinemann, 1948.

——. *Nymphs of the Valley*. Translated by N.H. Nahmad. London: Heinemann, 1948.

——. *The Prophet*. Edited with annotations by Suheil Bushrui. Oxford: One World, 1995.

——. *Spirits Rebellious*. Translated by N. H. Nahmad. London: Heinemann, 1972.

Hafez, Sabry. *The Genesis of Arabic Narrative Discourse, A Study in the Sociology of Modern Arabic Literature*. London: Saqi Books, 1993.

Haim, Sylvia. *Arab Nationalism: An Anthology*. Berkeley, CA: University of California Press, 1976.

Halliday, Fred. *Islam and the Myth of Confrontation, Religion and Politics in the Middle East*. London: I.B.Tauris, 1996.

Hawi, Khalil S. *Kahlil Gibran, His Background, Character and Works*. Beirut: Arab Institute for Research and Publishing, 1972.

Hitti, Philip K. *The Syrians in America*. New York: George H. Doran, 1924.

Hobsbawm, Eric. *Nations and Nationalism Since 1780: Programme, Myth, Reality*. Cambridge: Cambridge University Press, 1990.

Hodgkin, Thomas. *Letters from Palestine, 1932–1936*. Edited by E. C. Hodgkin. London: Quartet , 1986.

Hoogland, Eric. J. ed. *Crossing The Waters: Arabic-Speaking Immigrants to the United States Before 1940*. Washington, D.C.: Smithsonian Institution Press, 1987.

Hourani, Albert. *Arabic Thought in the Liberal Age 1789–1939*. London: Oxford University Press, 1970.

——. *The Emergence of the Modern Middle East*. London: Macmillan, 1981.

——. *A History of The Arab Peoples*. London: Faber, 1991.

——. *Syria and Lebanon, A Political Essay*. London: Oxford University Press, 1946.

Hourani, Albert, and Nadim Shehadi, eds. *The Lebanese in The World, A Century of Emigration*. London: Centre for Lebanese Studies with I.B. Tauris, 1992.

John, Joseph. "A Dialogue with Mr Tayeb Salih on Season of Migration to the North," *Islamic Quarterly* 36 (1992): pp. 207–17.

Kanafani, Ghassan. *Men in the Sun, and Other Palestinian Stories*. Translated by Hilary Kilpatrick. London: Heinemann, 1978.

Kedourie, Elie. *The Chatham House Version and Other Middle Eastern Studies*. Hanover, NH: Brandeis University Press, 1984.

——. *In the Anglo-Arab Labyrinth, The McMahon-Husayn Correspondence and its Interpretations 1914–1939*. Cambridge: Cambridge University Press, 1976.

——. *Nationalism*. London: Hutchinson, 1966.

Kilpatrick, Hilary. "Arab Fiction in English: A Case of Dual Nationality." *New Comparison* 13 (1992): pp. 46–55.

Khadduri, Majid. *Arab Contemporaries, The Role of Personalities in Politics*. Baltimore: Johns Hopkins University Press, 1973.

Khalidi, Rashid, Lisa Anderson, Muhammad Muslih and Reeva S. Simon, eds. *The Origins of Arab Nationalism*. New York: Columbia University Press, 1991.

Khalidi, Walid, ed. *From Haven to Conquest, Readings in Zionism and the Palestinian Problem until 1948*. Beirut: Institute for Palestine Studies, 1971.

Khouri, Mounah A. "Adonis as Advocate of a New Arab Civilization." In *Arab*

Civilization, Challenges and Responses, Studies in Honor of Constantine K. Zurayk. Edited by George N. Atiyeh, and Ibrahim M. Oweiss, pp. 183–204. Albany, NY: State University of New York Press, 1988.

Khouri, Mona, and Hamid Algar, eds. *An Anthology of Modern Arabic Poetry.* Translated and selected by the editors. Berkeley, CA: University of California Press, 1974.

Louis, W M. Roger, and Roger Owen, eds. *Suez 1956, The Crisis and its Consequences.* Oxford: Clarendon Press, 1989.

Lyotard, Jean-François. *The Postmodern Condition: A Report on Knowledge.* Translated by Geoff Bennington and Brian Massumi. Manchester: Manchester University Press, 1984.

Malek, Anouar Abdel. *Nation and Revolution.* vol. 2 of *Social Dialectics.* London: Macmillan, 1981.

Memmi, Albert. *The Colonizer and the Colonized.* Translated by Howard Greenfeld. London: Earthscan Publications, 1990.

Mehdi, Beverlee T. *The Arabs in America.* Dobbs Ferry, NY: Oceana Publications, 1978.

Monroe, Elizabeth. *Britain's Moment in the Middle East 1914–1971*, 2nd edn. London: Chatto & Windus, 1981.

——. *Philby of Arabia.* London: Faber, 1973.

Naimy, Nadeem. *The Lebanese Prophets of New York.* Beirut: The American University of Beirut, 1985.

Nash, Geoffrey P. "Amin Rihani's *The Book of Khalid* and the voice of Thomas Carlyle." *New Comparison* 17 (1994): pp. 35–49.

Owen, Roger. "Arab Nationalism, Unity and Solidarity." In *The Middle East: Sociology of "Developing Societies."* Edited by Talal Assad and Roger Owen, pp. 15–22. London: Macmillan, 1983.

Porath, Yehoshua. *In Search of Arab Unity 1930–1945.* London: Frank Cass, 1986.

Pratt, Mary Louise. "Linguistic Utopias." In *The linguistics of writing, Arguments between language and literature.* Edited by Nigel Fabb, Derek Attridge, Alan Durant and ColinMacCabe, pp. 48–66. Manchester: Manchester University Press, 1987.

——. *Towards a Speech Act Theory of Literary Discourse.* Bloomington: Indiana University Press, 1977.

Rihani, Ameen. "Arabia: An Unbiased Survey." *Journal of Central Asian Society* 16 (1929): pp. 35–55.

——. *Arabian Peak and Desert: Travels in Al-Yaman.* London: Constable, 1930.

——. *Around the Coasts of Arabia.* London: Constable, 1930.

——. *The Book of Khalid.* New York: Dodd Mead and Company, 1911.

——. *A Chant of Mystics and Other Poems.* Edited by S. B. Bushrui and J. M. Munro. Beirut: The Rihani House, 1970.

——. "The Coming of the Arabian Nights." *Bookman* (June, July 1912): pp. 366–70, pp. 503–8.

——. "Coup D'etat in Baghdad." *Asia* (1937): pp. 436–8.

——. "Dr. I. G. Kheiralla Dies in Syria." *Syrian World* (May 1929): pp. 48–9.

——. *The Descent of Bolshevism.* Boston: The Stratford Company, 1920.

——. "Deserts of Fact and Fantasy." *Syrian World* (December 1929): pp. 5–10.

------. *The Fate of Palestine.* Beirut: The Rihani House, 1967.

------. "From Concord to Syria." *Atlantic Monthly* (February 1913): pp. 284–6.

------. "The Holy Land: Whose to Have and to Hold?" *Bookman* (September 1917): pp. 7–14.

------. *Ibn Sa'oud of Arabia: His People and His Land.* London: Constable, 1928.

------. "Iraq During the Days of Faisal I." Jaffet Library, American University of Beirut, Beirut. MS: 956.704. R572i.

------. Preface and Notes. *The Luzumiyat of Abu'l-Ala.* Beirut: Albert Rihani, 1978.

------. "More Deserts than Are Dreamt Of." *Asia* (1933): pp. 554–61, pp. 578–9.

------. "My Peace Mission in Al-Hijaz." In vol. 2 of *Documents on the History of Saudi Arabia, The Consolidation of Power in Central Arabia Under Ibn Saud.* Edited by Ibrahim al-Rashid, pp. 24–43. Salisbury, NC: Documentary Publications, 1976.

------. "The New Syrian Republic." *Asia* (1938): pp. 51–4.

------. "A Night in Cairo." *Papyrus* (February 1905): pp. 24–8.

------. "Palestine Arabs Claim to Be Fighting for National Existence." *Current History* (November 1929): pp. 272–8.

------. "Palestine and the Proposed Arab Federation." *The Annals of the American Academy of Political and Social Science* 164 (1932): pp. 62–71.

------. "The Pan-Arab Dream." *Asia* (1938): pp. 44–7.

------. "The Pan-Arab Movement." Jaffet Library, American University of Beirut, Beirut. MS: 320.54. R572p.

------. "Pan-Arab Nationalism: Is It a Myth?" *Asia* (1939): pp. 452–5.

------. *The Path of Vision: Essays of East and West.* Edited by S. B. Bushrui and J. M. Munro. Beirut: The Rihani House, 1970.

------. Preface and Notes. *The Quatrains of Abu'l-Ala.* New York: Doubleday, Page and Company, 1903.

------. "Turkey and Islam in the War." Jaffet Library, American University of Beirut, Beirut. MS: 956 R572t.

------. "The Renans in Syria: The Story of the Writing of 'The Life of Jesus.'" *Bookman* (February 1912): pp. 599–611.

------. "A Report on Arabia." In vol.1 of *Documents on the History of Saudi Arabia, The Unification of Central Arabia Under Ibn Saud, 1909–1925.* Edited by Ibrahim al-Rashid, pp. 113– Salisbury, NC: Documentary Publications, 1976.

------. "The White Way of the Desert." Jaffet Library, American University of Beirut, Beirut. MS: 892.78 R572w.

------. "The Young Nation on the Tigris." *Asia* (1932): pp. 602–7, pp. 655–6.

Rihani, Ameen Albert. *Faylsuf al-Freike* [The Philosopher of Freike]. Beirut: Dar al-Jeel, 1987.

Rihani, Albert. *Where to Find Ameen Rihani: Bibliography.* Beirut: Arab Institute for Research and Publishing, 1979.

el-Sadat, Anwar. *In Search of Identity, An Autobiography.* New York: Harper & Row, 1978.

Said, Edward W. *After the Last Sky, Palestinian Lives.* Photographs by Jean Mohr. London: Faber, 1986.

------. *Culture and Imperialism.* London: Chatto & Windus, 1993.

------. *Orientalism, Western Conceptions of the Orient.* London: Routledge, Kegan

Paul, 1978.
———. *The Question of Palestine.* New York: Random House, 1980.
———. *The World, The Text, and The Critic.* Cambridge, MA: Harvard University Press, 1983.
Salibi, Kamal. *A House of Many Mansions, The History of Lebanon Reconsidered.* London: I.B. Tauris, 1988.
Salih, Tayeb. *Season of Migration to the North.* Translated by Denys Johnson-Davies. London: Heinemann, 1980.
Sayegh, Rosemary. *Palestinians: From Peasants to Revolutionaries.* London: Zed Press, 1979.
Shahid, Irfan. "Amin al-Rihani and King 'Abdul-'Aziz Ibn Sa'ud." In *Arab Civilization, Challenges and Responses*. Edited by George N. Atiyeh and Ibrahim M. Oweiss, pp. 231–40. Albany, NY: State University of New York Press, 1988.
Sharabi, Hisham. *Arab Intellectuals and the West, The Formative Years 1875–1914.* Baltimore: Johns Hopkins University Press, 1970.
Silsby, Susan. "Antonius: Palestine, Zionism and British Imperialism, 1929–1939." Doctoral dissertation, Georgetown University. Ann Arbor: University Microfilms, 1986.
Smith, Tony. *The Pattern of Imperialism, The United States, Great Britain, and the late-industrializing world since 1815.* Cambridge: Cambridge University Press, 1981.
Sollors, Werner. *Beyond Ethnicity, Consent and Descent in American Culture.* New York: Oxford University Press, 1986.
Sprinker, Michael, ed. *Edward Said, A Critical Reader.* Oxford: Blackwell, 1992.
Storrs, Ronald. *Orientations.* London: Ivor Nicholson and Watson, 1939.
Thornton, A. P. *The Imperial Idea and its Enemies.* London: Macmillan, 1985.
Tibawi, A. L. *Arabic and Islamic Themes, History, Education and Literary Studies.* London: Luzac, 1976.
Tibi, Bassam. *Arab Nationalism: A Critical Inquiry.* Edited and translated by Marion Farouk Slugettt and Peter Slugett. London: Macmillan, 1981.
Van Der Meulen, D. *Don't You Hear The Thunder? A Dutchman's Life Story.* Leiden: E.J. Brill, 1981.
Williams, Patrick, and Laura Chrisman, eds. *Colonial Discourse and Post-colonial Theory, A Reader.* New York: Harvester Wheatsheaf, 1993.
Yared, Nazik Saba. *Arab Travellers and Western Civilization.* London: Saqi Books, 1996.
Young, Barbara. *This Man from Lebanon: A Study of Kahlil Gibran.* New York: Alfred Knopf, 1956.

Index

Made in the USA
Coppell, TX
09 February 2021

49993283R10108